BIOGRAPHICAL STORY OF THE CONSTITUTION

A STUDY OF THE GROWTH OF THE AMERICAN UNION

BY

EDWARD ELLIOTT

PROFESSOR OF POLITICS IN PRINCETON UNIVERSITY

G. P. PUTNAM'S SONS
NEW YORK AND LONDON
The Knickerbocker Press
1910

COPYRIGHT, 1910
BY
G. P. PUTNAM'S SONS

The Knickerbocker Press, New York

To
MY MOTHER

Preface

MR. BRYCE has remarked that "the Constitution of the United States (including the amendments) may be read aloud in twenty-three minutes." Its brevity required that it should be general and only the framework of government could be outlined. The powers of the Federal Government were enumerated, but their extent was left for future determination through interpretation.

This fact has made it possible for the Constitution to be adapted to the ordinary needs of the national life. At times of crises, as in the Purchase of Louisiana and the Civil War, the bounds of interpretation have been passed and the Constitution has been stretched to fit the occasion; recently we have heard of the need of "finding" constructions that will enable the Federal Government to meet the exigencies of new conditions.

The history of the Constitution is chiefly concerned with the processes of interpretation and adaptation. The life of the nation does not stand still; new ideas, feelings, conditions, and forces are constantly driving it forward, and no immutable instrument of government will suffice; the Constitution, too, must grow, and as the formal process of amendment is too difficult for ordinary purposes, principles of interpretation have, in large measure, taken its place.

The present work does not seek to deal with the finely elaborated doctrines of the courts, but rather with the larger questions of constitutional interpretation, many of which lay beyond the jurisdiction of any court. These questions have been fought out between men and this *Biographical Story of the Constitution* attempts to picture, through the lives of some of the more conspicuous of these contestants, the struggle and its result.

The difficulties of this method of treatment are considerable; there is danger of over-emphasizing the part played by particular individuals, of neglecting that taken by others, and of slighting the economic and social forces that have been at work; yet the increased interest which, it is hoped, will come from the introduction of the personal element may offset these disadvantages. The book will have served a useful purpose if it awakens a further interest in the subject of our constitutional history, or throws light upon the general features of our national life at a time when there is great need for a proper understanding of the relationship of a written and rigid constitution to the forces of that life.

An appendix has been added, composed of documents illustrative of the principal points around which the conflict of opinion has been hottest. A study of these documents, it is believed, will give a truer insight into the thought of the times which produced them than can be had in any other way.

I wish to express my thanks to my colleagues, Professors W. M. Daniels and E. S. Corwin, for their kindness in reading parts of the manuscript, and to Professor Edgar Dawson for reading the whole of it. They are not responsible for the opinions expressed, but I am indebted to them for many helpful suggestions.

E. E.

PRINCETON, N. J., June, 1909.

Contents

CHAPTER		PAGE
I.	The "Fathers"; Inception through Compromise	1
II.	Alexander Hamilton: Growth through Administrative Organization	27
III.	James Wilson: Growth through Speculative Forecast	53
IV.	Thomas Jefferson: Growth through Acquiescence	77
V.	James Madison: Growth through Formulation	101
VI.	John Marshall: Growth through Legal Interpretation	125
VII.	Andrew Jackson: Growth through Democratization	147
VIII.	Daniel Webster: Growth through Rising National Sentiment	167
IX.	John C. Calhoun: Retardation through Sectional Influence	189
X.	Abraham Lincoln: Growth through Civil War	209

Contents

CHAPTER		PAGE
XI.	THADDEUS STEVENS: GROWTH THROUGH RECONSTRUCTION	229
XII.	THEODORE ROOSEVELT: GROWTH THROUGH EXPANSION	251
	APPENDIX	271
	The Declaration of Independence, 1776	273
	Articles of Confederation, 1781	279
	Constitution of the United States, 1789	292
	Jefferson's Opinion on a National Bank, 1791	315
	Hamilton's Opinion on a National Bank, 1791	318
	Kentucky Resolutions of 1798	326
	Virginia Resolutions of 1798	332
	Abstract of Decision in Case of Marbury v. Madison, 1803	335
	Amendments Proposed by Hartford Convention, 1814	337
	South Carolina Ordinance of Nullification, 1832	340
	Jackson's Nullification Proclamation, 1832	345
	Abstract of Dred Scott Decision, 1857	362
	South Carolina Ordinance of Secession, 1860	368

Appendix—*Continued*

   South Carolina Declaration of Independence, 1860 369

   Proclamation of Emancipation, 1863 . 374

Bibliography 377

Index 385

I

"The Fathers." Inception through Compromise

CHRONOLOGY OF CONSTITUTIONAL CONVENTION

1787. May 14. Appointed time of meeting.
      May 25. Quorum first present.
      May 29. Randolph resolutions—Virginia plan proposed.
      May 29. Charles Pinckney submitted draft.
      May 30–June 13. Convention, in committee of the whole, considered Virginia plan and reported favorably.
      June 15. Paterson or New Jersey plan proposed.
      June 18. Hamilton's plan proposed.
      June 19. Paterson plan rejected and Virginia plan adhered to.
      July 5. Committee reports "Connecticut Compromise." Yates and Lansing left.
      July 16. Amended report accepted.
      July 24. Committee of detail appointed.
      Aug. 6. Committee reported draft of Constitution in 23 articles.
      Sept. 12. Committee of revision of style appointed.
      Sept. 17. Adjourned.

I

"The Fathers." Inception through Compromise

IN every generation of our national life there have been men who typified the thought and feeling of the time. Some of them have been creators of the ideas associated with their names; others have been merely the embodiment of general doctrines which seemed to be floating in the air, while still others have given expression to the reactionary tendencies of their day; but in all of them and through all of them we may trace the progress of the Constitution. They typify the views of successive generations upon the great constitutional questions, and by their lives we can measure the stages of advance, now slow, now fast, as the forces at play are halting or quick; as peace or war, economic welfare or crisis, social rest or unrest, holds the reins of the car of progress.

The story of the Constitution and its growth has been told in many fashions and in many forms; but the tale that is told has no ending, for the growth of the Constitution is co-extensive with the growth of the national life. Beginning even as the nation began, weak and diffident, uncertain of its strength and powers, the Constitution has grown with the nation's growth and strengthened with its strength.

The Constitution is not solely the written instrument which is contained within the compass of the few brief pages which the "Fathers" elaborated in their days and weeks of discussion in the convention hall at Philadelphia in 1787; that document was but the skeleton of the colossal constitutional figure of to-day. The story of how the skeleton was clothed with the living tissue of constitutional practice is one of absorbing interest. Constitutions do not grow of their own accord; they are not organisms in which life finds lodgment. They are dead forms till human action transforms them in accordance with the will of those who put them into execution. So the Constitution of the United States, as it came from the hands of the "Fathers," was dead parchment until men transmuted the written word by the alchemy of human action.

That the Constitution is the result of compromise is familiar to all, but there is no better way of bringing to our minds a vivid realization of the great achievements of the "Fathers" than by reviewing the conflicting opinions and tendencies of the time, particularly as they found concrete expression in the men of the Convention and the questions which confronted them.

The ten years immediately preceding the outbreak of the Revolution were filled with scarcely less heated conflict than the years of actual war, but the conflict was waged in a different spirit. Argument and discussion were the forerunners of battles and sieges; questions of government were fought out first in the law courts and the public prints. James Otis, Samuel and John Adams in Massachusetts; Dickinson in Pennsylvania; Dulaney in Maryland; and Patrick Henry in Virginia were only the leaders in whose train there followed a host of able and learned disputants who discussed with unrivalled skill the rights of the colonists and their relations to the mother country.[1] Political discussion was not, however, limited to the question of the relation of the King and Parliament to the colonies.[2] The colonists felt that their liberty was at stake, and not only from the law of England but also from the nature of man and of government they sought to establish their right to life, liberty, and the pursuit of happiness. The great degree of self-government that had been enjoyed in all the colonies, and the character of the social and political relations that had perforce been developed in the settling of a new country, had united to give a democratic complexion to their lives and thoughts of which they themselves had been little aware. Samuel Adams, Patrick Henry, and, a little later, Thomas Paine stood forth as the champions of this new spirit of democracy.

The period of discussion had enabled men to understand more clearly the great questions of government and liberty. The typical eighteenth-century view of the state of nature as man's primitive condition, of the origin of society and of government in contract and the consent of the governed, of the

[1] *Cf.* M. C. Tyler, *The Literary History of the American Revolution.*
[2] *Cf.* C. E. Merriam, *American Political Theories,* p. 41 *ff.*

limitation of the powers of government by the objects for which it was established, formed the essential elements of their theory of government. It was in the main the theory of Locke that the colonists followed; they were little influenced by French ideas save in the single case of Montesquieu. A new phase of their rights was, however, developed by the colonists themselves; they claimed not only the rights of Englishmen, as derived from the law of nature and the great charters of liberty, but also the rights that belonged to them as men—those inherent and inalienable rights of man which they incorporated in the Declaration of Independence and the Bills of Rights.[1]

The years of the war added nothing to the ideas already developed; men could not fight and theorize too; their energies were consumed in the trials and sacrifices of the Revolution; it was a time when the written word was less potent than bayonets and the orator than bullets. Yet these same years gave a practical experience in constitution making and state building such as no other people had ever enjoyed. Every State hastened to establish a constitution in which the effort was made to guarantee the rights so hotly advocated, and the Union that was no stronger than "a rope of sand" owed its fatal weakness to the zealous ardor in behalf of these same rights. The Articles of Confederation came into existence in the course of a struggle against what the colonists regarded as unlawful oppression

[1] *Cf.* Merriam, *op. cit.*, p. 48. Georg Jellinek, *The Declaration of the Rights of Man and of Citizens*, p. 78 *ff.* Translated by Max Farrand.

on the part of a superior power. Union was sought to throw off this yoke of oppression, and the memory of King and Parliament was still too vivid for them to run the risk of losing any of their hard-won liberty and freedom by establishing a strong central authority. Time had not yet forced upon them the unwilling conclusion that strength in government was necessary to liberty, and a strong union to independence; that, in the words of Washington, "influence is not government."[1]

The years immediately following the conclusion of peace are rightly called the "Critical Period of American History." With the successful termination of the Revolution, the spirit of patriotism flagged; the zeal that had animated the earlier part of the struggle gave place to a spirit of indifference to national welfare. Particularism and State pride waxed strong. The Congress of the Confederation might command requisitions to its heart's content, but not a penny could it compel any State to pay into the treasury; the powers conferred upon it were large, but the means for their enforcement were utterly inadequate. The pressure of a foreign foe once removed, the centrifugal forces of disunion were let loose. The Confederation was regarded as having served its purpose. By it the States had attained their independence, but independence once secured, there was no longer any reason why their freedom should be lessened by demands made upon them from a source so little connected with their every-day lives, and the failure of every State to live up to the

[1] F. S. Oliver, *Alexander Hamilton: An Essay on American Union*, p. 100.

obligations imposed upon it by Congress became notorious.[1]

Such a course on the part of the States soon brought the representatives of the enfeebled central government into disrepute at home and abroad. Foreign nations looked for the speedy dissolution of so unstable a union, and were unwilling to engage themselves with a government which gave such slight assurance of permanency, while at home men talked of withdrawal and the establishment of separate confederacies. A pressing source of weakness in the Confederation sprang from the lack of power on the part of Congress to regulate commerce either between the States or with foreign nations; in the absence of this power, the natural jealousies and animosities of the individual States soon found expression in vexatious restrictions and deterrent imposts.

The need of mutual understandings and common regulations was early apparent to men like Washington and Madison in Virginia, and Hamilton in New York. First Maryland and Virginia, then the five States represented at the Annapolis Convention, deliberated upon the perplexing and ruinous conditions of commercial relations but in vain, for these were conditions that could be settled only by common action since they involved common interests. The prospect was gloomy indeed. The craze of paper money had swept over the States and credit had been ruined; Shays's rebellion was in full swing and Congress seemed powerless to crush it. The dispute with Spain over the free navigation of the Missis-

[1] *Cf.* John Fiske, *The Critical Period of American History,* p. 90 *ff.*

sippi had become critical; the Southern States threatened secession and a return to British allegiance if the Mississippi were given up, while the Northern States were of a mind to secede if the river were not closed for twenty-five years in return for a commercial treaty with Spain.[1] In the face of these difficulties and the impotence of Congress to cope with them, the need of action far beyond the powers of the commissioners gathered at Annapolis was clearly evident. Hamilton drafted an address which set forth the need of a general convention of all the States to consider other than commercial questions, and which recommended to the States that they should appoint delegates to a convention to be held in Philadelphia on the second Monday of the following May, "to take into consideration the situation of the United States," and "to devise such further provisions as shall appear to them necessary to render the Constitution of the Federal Government adequate to the exigencies of the Union."[2] The new convention was not merely to regulate commerce but was to undertake a revision of the whole government of the Union. The Congress of the Confederation could not disregard the call of the Annapolis Convention. A failure to sanction it would only forfeit public confidence still further, while the alarm of Shays's rebellion and the desperate condition of the Confederation were urgent factors in inducing the

---

[1] *Cf.* Fiske, *op. cit.*, pp. 208–211; A. C. McLaughlin, *The Confederation and the Constitution*, pp. 91–100; Oliver, *op. cit.*, p. 140.
[2] *Documentary History of the Constitution of the United States of America*, i., 5.

Congress to issue a call for a convention to meet at the same time and place "for the sole and express purpose of revising the Articles of Confederation."[1]

The impression rapidly gained ground that this was the last chance for a permanent union. Should the Convention fail to achieve its purpose, those bonds of union, established however insecurely since Bunker Hill and the Declaration of Independence, seemed destined to be dissolved. With the dissolution of the Union in prospect, the States chose men of the highest character and achievements to represent them, and it is not an idle boast to proclaim this assembly one of the most distinguished bodies that has ever met for political purposes. A review of the names of the members shows that scarce a State was without its representative of national fame, and for the most part they were the men of the revolutionary epoch, gathered together to reap the final fruits of that memorable contest.

Massachusetts found fit representatives of her virtues and her learning in Rufus King, a lawyer who might "with propriety be ranked among the Luminaries" of that age[2]; in Elbridge Gerry, the successful merchant who cherished "as his first virtue, a love for his Country." Roger Sherman, man of the people, shoemaker, almanac-maker, and judge, whose heart was as good as his head, and Oliver Ellsworth, Chief Justice of the Supreme Court of the State, have made the part of Connecticut in the Convention

[1] *Doc. Hist.*, i., 8.
[2] *The American Historical Review*, iii., 310–334, contains the notes of William Pierce, a member of the Convention from Georgia. The quotations and most of the characterizations of members are taken from them.

"The Fathers"

justly famous, while Hamilton from New York was recognized as the most brilliant man of the Convention and of the country. William Paterson of New Jersey, "a Classic, a Lawyer, and an Orator," was the kind of man "whose powers break in upon you, and create wonder and astonishment"; he is best known as the proposer of the "New Jersey plan" and the defender of the equality of the States. Pennsylvania sent more delegates than any other State and among them were not less than four men of lasting fame. Benjamin Franklin, diplomat, man-of-letters, scientist, whom "the very heavens obey," was, next to Washington, America's most conspicuous figure; the Morrises, Robert, the financier of the Revolution, and Gouverneur, the master of style, to whom we owe the literary finish of the Constitution, were little less conspicuous. For the fourth, James Wilson, the rugged Scot, who drew attention "not by the charm of his eloquence, but by the force of his reasoning," ranked "among the foremost in legal and political knowledge." Little Delaware sent John Dickinson, "famed through all America, for his Farmer's Letters"; while Maryland's Attorney General, Luther Martin, was the Convention's most persistent and prolix supporter of the rights of the small States.

Virginia could rival Pennsylvania in the number of her famous delegates. Washington, whose presence in the Convention was the unqualified prerequisite of its success, was unanimously chosen presiding officer; George Wythe, "confessedly one of the most learned legal characters of the present age"; Mason, able, experienced, convincing, and "undoubtedly one of the best politicians in America"; Randolph, young, handsome, and talented; and finally Madison, small and unprepossessing, with no pretence of oratory, but "the affairs of the United States, he perhaps, has the most correct knowledge of, of any man in the Union"; "he blends together the profound politician with the scholar"; thoughtful and earnest, his labors in the Convention in behalf of the Constitution surpass those of any one man. South Carolina was the only one of the remaining States whose representatives have achieved a lasting place in our history; John Rutledge and the two Pinckneys may well close the roster of the famous names of the Convention.

Some distinguished names, however, are missing, and we wonder what might have been the result had Jefferson, instead of courting Republican France by his republican sympathies, been present to champion the cause of the States against the nation; or Patrick Henry, with his fiery eloquence in favor of State sovereignty. What influence might not the aristocratic John Adams, with his leanings toward monarchy and his distrust of the people, have exerted, had he been in the Convention perchance to second and support the strongly centralized plan of Hamilton?

The success of the Revolution had placed beyond the possibility of cavil the right to life, liberty, and the pursuit of happiness. The question now at issue was under what form of government these rights could be best secured; it was yet to be determined how the advantages to be derived from a union of all the States could be combined with the security of life and property enjoyed under the government of each. The first question which confronted the members of the Convention when once assembled was that raised by the resolution of Congress under which they had gathered. Should they adhere to the limitation set by that resolution and restrict themselves to an amendment of the Articles of Confederation, or should they strike out boldly and do what seemed to them best for the general welfare? Should they disregard the Congress and its resolution and, acting as the representatives of the people, produce an instrument of government suited to the country's needs? The question was crucial, was revolutionary, but they were undaunted; believing that no amendment of the Articles of Confederation would suffice, they adopted a resolution declaring "that a national government ought to be established consisting of a supreme Legislative, Judiciary, and Executive."[1] In the discussion of this resolution the difference between a federal and a national government was clearly stated by Gouverneur Morris, who declared that the former was "a mere compact resting on the good faith of the parties"; the latter had "a complete and *compulsive* operation."[2]

At a later stage of the proceedings when the authority of the Convention to take this radical action had again been raised, Randolph asserted baldly that "when the salvation of the Republic was at stake, it would be treason to our trust, not to propose what we found necessary."[3] To this Hamilton

---

[1] *Doc. Hist.*, iii., 162.
[2] *Ibid.*, iii., 22. Notice the difference in meaning in the word "federal" between then and now.
[3] *Ibid.*, iii., 136.

agreed. "The States," he said, "sent us here to provide for the exigencies of the Union. To rely on any plan not adequate to these exigencies, merely because it was not clearly within our powers, would be to sacrifice the means to the end."[1]

To justify the revolutionary character of this action there was inserted in the Constitution the clause providing that "the ratification of the conventions of nine States shall be sufficient for the establishment of this Constitution between the States so ratifying the same,"[2] and furthermore the ratification was to be by conventions in each State, especially elected for the purpose, and not by the State legislatures. The Constitution should rest upon the people, not upon the States.

The decision that a national government ought to be established, consisting of a supreme legislative, executive, and judiciary, did not, however, settle the question as to the nature of the new Union. From the outset there were two well-defined and conflicting opinions on the subject. The small States clung tenaciously to the principle of the Articles of Confederation by which each State had an equal voice with every other State; the large States were equally determined to put an end to a condition of affairs in which their wealth, size, and importance told for nothing. From this struggle of the small and the large States there resulted the first of the great compromises of the Constitution.[3] The contest centred

[1] *Doc. Hist.*, iii., 139.
[2] Constitution, Art. VII.
[3] For a detailed account of the compromises, *cf.* Fiske *op. cit.*, pp. 250–267; McLaughlin, *op. cit.*, pp. 221 *ff*; Max Farrand,

around the "Virginia" and the "New Jersey" plans.[1] The former, elaborated by the delegates from that State and presented by Randolph, provided for a union in which the equality of the States as sovereign political bodies should give way to an inequality based upon wealth and population, in which powers as well as rights should be conferred upon the central authority; the latter, proposed by Paterson of New Jersey, sought to maintain the authority of the States as it had existed under the Articles of Confederation. Large powers, to be sure, were to be lodged in the new government, but the fundamental weakness would still remain; the government would still lack the power of acting directly upon individuals and could proceed only against the States. Any attempt, as Madison had showed, to coerce a State, "would look more like a declaration of war, than an infliction of punishment."[2] The issue was squarely presented. Lansing of New York declared that the plan of Mr. Paterson "sustains the sovereignty of the respective States, that of Mr. Randolph destroys it."[3] Paterson himself asserted that the Convention had "no power to vary the idea of equal sovereignty,"[4] and that he "had rather submit to a monarch, to a despot, than to such a fate."[5] Wilson, on the other hand, contrasted the two plans

---

The Compromises of the Constitution, in the *American Historical Review*, April, 1904; and Alexander Johnston, *American Political History*, ii., 101 *ff.*

[1] *Doc. Hist.*, iii., 17–20 and 125–128.
[2] Gaillard Hunt, *The Writings of Madison*, iii., 56.
[3] *Doc. Hist.*, iii., 128–129.
[4] *Ibid.*, iii., 131.
[5] *Ibid.*, iii., 99.

point by point and always in favor of the Virginia plan,[1] and Randolph saw that "the true question is whether we shall adhere to the federal plan, or introduce the national plan," which would be a resort "to a *national legislation over individuals.*"[2] Hamilton took advantage of the opportunity to express his disapproval of both plans and to "point out such changes as might render a *national one* efficacious,"[3] and Madison argued at length against the evils of the New Jersey plan.[4]

The smaller the State, the more violent, apparently, was the opposition to a national government and a loss of equality. Luther Martin of Maryland protested that he "would rather confederate with any single State, than submit to the Virginia plan,"[5] and Bedford of Delaware did not hesitate to go to the extreme of proclaiming that the small States, rather than submit to the compulsion of the large States, would "find some foreign ally of more honor and good faith," who would "take them by the hand and do them justice."[6]

The compromise by which such widely divergent views were reconciled is generally known as the "Connecticut compromise." Connecticut had from its earliest history made use of the dual system of representation in its legislature, one house representing the towns as equal units, and the other the

[1] *Doc. Hist.*, iii., 132 *ff.*
[2] *Ibid.*, iii., 137.
[3] *Ibid.*, iii., 138 *ff.*
[4] *Ibid.*, iii., 151 *ff.*
[5] Yates, *Secret Proceedings and Debates of the Federal Convention*, p. 194.
[6] *Doc. Hist.*, iii., 261.

people,[1] and when the debate arose in the Convention early in June, on the principle of representation to be followed in the two houses, Sherman of Connecticut proposed that "the proportion of suffrage in the first branch should be according to the respective numbers of free inhabitants; and that in the second branch, or Senate, each State should have one vote and no more."[2] More than two weeks later, after the New Jersey plan had been rejected and the next day after the discussion had grown so violent that Franklin had proposed that henceforth the Convention should open with prayer, Dr. Johnson, another of Connecticut's representatives, expressed the opinion that "as in some respects the States are to be considered in their political capacity, and in others as districts of individual citizens, the two ideas embraced on different sides, instead of being opposed to each other, ought to be combined; that in *one* branch the *people* ought to be represented; in the *other*, the *States*."[3] On the same day, Oliver Ellsworth gave expression to similar views. "We were partly national; partly federal. The proportional representation in the first branch was conformable to the national principle and would secure the large States against the small. An equality of voices was conformable to the federal principle and was necessary to secure the small States against the large."[4]

---

[1] Farrand, *Compromises of the Constitution* in *Am. Hist. Rev.*, note 1, p. 480, rejects this explanation of the origin of the designation of the compromise.
[2] *Doc. Hist.*, iii., 101.
[3] *Ibid.*, iii., 237.
[4] *Ibid.*, iii., 245–246.

On this middle ground he trusted a compromise would take place. Whether or not Connecticut's example and representatives are responsible for the compromise, at least their proposals contained the principle upon which agreement was finally reached. Proportional representation in the lower house met in part the demand of the large States for adequate recognition of their size; equality of representation in the Senate soothed the wounded pride of State sovereignty and gave to the small States reasonable ground of security. Such in substance was the report of the Committee that had been appointed when the Convention reached a deadlock on this question; such to-day is the principle of representation in the two houses of our national legislature.

The first great conflict of the Convention then was a struggle between the large States and the small, between a growing spirit of nationalism and a tenacious desire for local independence, and after long and bitter contests victory rested entirely with neither party, but had been won by those men in the Convention who desired a strong central government resting upon a different foundation from the Articles of Confederation, but who were nevertheless unwilling to leave the small States without effectual means for the protection of the rights to be enjoyed under the new form of union.

The very terms of the compromise by which a disruption of the Convention had been prevented carried with them the seeds of further controversy. Equal representation in the Senate seemed a sufficient guarantee of the rights of the small States, but their sense of security was measurably lessened when the Convention agreed that the members of the Senate should vote per capita and not by States. The question, moreover, of the proportion of representation in the lower house presented difficulties scarcely less acute than the fundamental problems which had already been settled.

The necessity of expansion toward the West was evident, and the probability of the formation of new States caused no little anxiety to some members of the Convention. Gouverneur Morris desired the Atlantic States to "keep a majority of votes in their own hands"[1] in order that they might not be controlled by the West. "If the Western people get the power into their hands they will ruin the Atlantic interests. The back members are always the most averse to the best measures."[2] Gerry and King proposed "to secure the liberties of the States already confederated" by prohibiting the number of representatives in the lower house from the new States ever exceeding that of the old States.[3] Mason and Madison, however, represented the better attitude in their vigorous defence of the right of the future States to be admitted to the Union on terms of equality with the older States,[4] and in this the Convention supported them. Wilson spoke after the manner of the true democrat when he declared that "the majority of people wherever found ought in all questions to govern the minority."[5]

[1] *Doc. Hist.*, iii., 305.
[2] *Ibid.*, iii., 312.
[3] *Ibid.*, iii., 332.
[4] *Ibid.*, iii., 307 and 314.
[5] *Ibid.*, iii., 330.

While the origin of the first fundamental difference of opinion among the members of the Convention grew out of political considerations, the second ground of divergence was social in its nature. In the discussion of the question of representation in the two houses, Madison had already expressed it as his opinion that the antithesis of the States was due not to their difference of size, but to climate and to their having or not having slaves.[1] Charles Pinckney, too, had based the real distinction between the States upon the divergent economic interests of North and South.[2] A sharp line of distinction began to be drawn between these two sections, the interests of which Butler declared "to be as different as the interests of Russia and Turkey."[3]

In determining the number in accordance with which representation in the lower house should be apportioned, the question at once arose whether the slaves should be counted as a part of the population. The fundamental notion of the end and aim of all government was the preservation of property; the wealth, therefore, of the respective States should be taken into account in any scheme of representation. In the South the problem was complicated by the existence of a peculiar kind of wealth, for slaves were both property and human beings. Butler and General C. C. Pinckney insisted that the blacks should be included equally with the whites in the rule of representation, and not at a three-fifths ratio as proposed. "An equal representation ought to be al-

---

[1] *Doc. Hist.*, iii., 254.
[2] *Ibid.*, iii., 263.
[3] *Ibid.*, iii., 639.

lowed for them," said Butler, " in a government which was instituted principally for the protection of property, and was itself to be supported by property."[1] Wilson, on the other hand, could see no reason why the blacks should be admitted at a three-fifths ratio. "Are they admitted as citizens? Then why are they not admitted on an equality with white citizens? Are they admitted as property? Then why is not other property admitted into the computation? These were difficulties however which he thought must be overruled by the necessity of compromise."[2]

The terms of the compromise resulted from a suggestion of Gouverneur Morris who " moved to add to the clause empowering the Legislature to vary the Representation according to the principle of wealth and number of inhabitants, a proviso that taxation shall be in proportion to Representation."[3] This was amended to apply only to direct taxes.[4] Such a provision was a two-edged sword, but no logical objection to it could be made. If the slaves were to be counted in determining representation, the slave-holding States must pay the bill in direct taxes, and the same would be true of the new, but poor, States of the West. The South was willing to run the risk, and it was determined that " representatives and direct taxes shall be apportioned among the several States . . . according to their respective numbers, which shall be determined by adding to the whole number of free persons, including those

[1] *Doc. Hist.*, iii., 309.
[2] *Ibid.*, iii., 317.
[3] *Ibid.*, iii., 319.
[4] *Ibid.*, iii., 320.

bound to service for a term of years, and excluding Indians not taxed, three-fifths of all other persons."[1]

The antagonism of the Eastern and Southern States was not allayed by the compromise on representation, but continued until it was settled, so far as the work of the Convention was concerned, by a compromise, the effects of which are just beginning fully to be comprehended. The Eastern States had become convinced of the necessity of the regulation of commerce by the general government, and their conviction was shared to a limited degree by the Middle States and Virginia. The passage of a Navigation Act by Congress appeared to them highly desirable. Georgia and South Carolina on the other hand, by reason of their rice and indigo culture, deemed it absolutely essential to their welfare that the importation of slaves should not be prohibited. C. C. Pinckney accordingly declared that a vote to abolish the slave trade would be received by South Carolina as "a polite way of telling her that she was not wanted in the Union."[2] It was necessary to retain the support of these two States if the Constitution was to have the slightest hope of adoption. Fortunately, the belief was prevalent that not only the importation of slaves, but slavery itself, would soon die out. It had practically disappeared from the Northern States, and Whitney's invention had not yet raised cotton to the position of king, had not yet made it the great "staple product" which demanded slavery as an economic necessity. Accordingly Congress was given the power " to regulate

[1] Constitution, Art. I., sec. 2.
[2] Fiske, *cp. cit.*, p. 263.

commerce with foreign nations, and among the several States, and with the Indian tribes," [1] but "the migration or importation of such persons as any of the States now existing shall think proper to admit, shall not be prohibited by the Congress prior to the year one thousand eight hundred and eight, but a tax or duty may be imposed on such importation, not exceeding ten dollars for each person." [2]

Marshall first seized on the possibilities of the so-called "commerce clause" of the Constitution, and successive courts have not been slow to make it keep pace with our modern commercial and industrial evolution. In more recent times both Congress and the Executive have been seeking new worlds for the Federal Government to conquer; no provision of the Constitution is being more zealously scrutinized than this in the search for means to cope with the great industrial problems of the day. Upon the slender thread of commerce "among the several States," judicial decisions and legislative enactments have suspended a weight of federal powers that must have snapped any less elastic provision, and the end is not yet.

No subject before the Convention drew forth more differences of opinion than the character of the Executive [3]; whether it should be single or plural, what powers should be conferred upon it, and how it should be chosen were all objects of the liveliest

[1] Constitution, Art. I., sec. 8.
[2] Const., Art. I., sec. 9.
[3] Farrand, *Compromises*, in *Am. Hist. Rev.*, p. 485 *ff*, treats of the compromise respecting the Executive at some length and to him I owe much that is here said.

concern and the greatest diversity of opinion. No less than thirty votes were taken concerning various phases of the method of election alone. The differences of opinion manifested over this question divided the members along new lines. We have seen large States and small striving for supremacy, we have witnessed North and South diverge along lines destined continually to divide them till the significance of Mason and Dixon's line was wiped out by blood. Now, however, in the character and choice of the Executive the more fundamental distinction between aristocracy and democracy makes itself felt. A direct election of the Executive by the people found no favor in the eyes of men whose faith in the mass of mankind had been so sorely tried by the events of recent years, whose inherent regard for birth and breeding had been greatly strengthened by the license and excesses of the democratic mob, and whose conservative instincts and traditional respect for rights of property had been greatly alarmed by fiat money and by Shays's rebellion. Some indirect form of election seemed to them necessary to preserve the whole government from ultimate destruction from too much democracy. It was felt, however, that an election by the people would give an advantage to the large States; even under the electoral system in which each State was to have a number of electors equal to the number of its Senators and Representatives, the advantage would still remain with the large States; the terms of the compromise only become evident when we know that it was supposed that in a majority of cases no election would result because of the failure of any one candidate to secure a majority; in that case it was first proposed that the election should fall to the Senate in which the States were equally represented. Here the advantage would be with the small States. Because of the many objections that arose to giving additional powers to the Senate, it was finally decided to bestow this power upon the House of Representatives, but with the provision that each State should have only a single vote. Thus was the principle of the compromise retained and the one conspicuous failure of the Convention's work completed.

The main features of the form of government elaborated in the Convention are familiar. Throughout the whole structure ran the principle of the separation of the powers of government and the system of checks and balances. The principle was adopted that all matters which were of common interest should be entrusted to the Federal Government, while the far larger field of purely local interests should be reserved by the States. "The task," said Madison, "was to draw a line of demarcation which would give the General Government every power requisite for general purposes, and leave to the States every power which might be most beneficially administered by them."

The power of the Federal Government has grown steadily; more and more the National Government has been brought into contact with the ordinary affairs of daily life. The principal means through which this growth of power has taken place has not been the constitutional method of amendment, which, since the infancy of the nation, has been possible only under the stress of civil war, but has been the power of "interpretation." The faculty of interpreting the law has achieved a peculiar prominence in our system through the existence of a written constitution which is the supreme law of the land; it is the duty of the courts to test all laws by the standard of the Constitution, and in doing so they must determine what, under all the circumstances, the Constitution means. Interpretation must in the long run reflect the life of the people and give expression to their lasting convictions or law will become the oppressor instead of the protector of rights; back of the legal formulas lie the forces of society which infuse into them the breath of life.

That such has been the case in our own national life can scarcely be questioned when we reflect upon the transformations wrought by steam and electricity; railroads and telegraphs have often been slender bonds, but without them we may easily picture a land of many unions instead of one. Not only has a single union of the whole country been made possible by these material forces, but also the life of the people has been brought closer together; common interests have multiplied as rapidly as have the means of communication. It is, therefore, a natural result of such growth that we have witnessed a like growth in that part of the Constitution dealing with the regulation of common interests. Interpretation is but the synonym of growth and expansion under conditions which have multiplied the common elements of our national life.

II

Alexander Hamilton. Growth through Administrative Organization

ALEXANDER HAMILTON

1757.	Jan. 11.	Born on the island of Nevis, West Indies.
1769.		Clerk in office of Nicholas Cruger. Wrote description of a hurricane.
1772.	October.	Arrived in Boston.
1773.		Entered King's College, now Columbia University.
		Visited Boston.
	July 6.	First public speech, made at the "Meeting in the Fields."
1774–5		Wrote *A Full Vindication* and *The Farmer Refuted*, which were attributed to Jay and Livingston; also other pamphlets.
1776.		Given command of New York artillery company.
1777.		Appointed staff officer and Military Secretary to Washington.
1780.		Letter to James Duane on national bank.
1781.	Feb. 16.	Break with Washington.
		Brevetted Colonel at Yorktown.
1782.		Delegate to Continental Congress.
		Admitted to the bar.
1786.		Attended Annapolis Convention. Drew up address. Elected to State Assembly.
1787.		Delegate to Philadelphia Convention.
	June 29.	Withdrew temporarily from Convention.
	Sept. 17.	Affixed name to Constitution.
1787–88.		Delegate to last Continental Congress.
1787–88.		*Federalist* written.
1788.		Member of the New York State Convention.
1789.	Sept.	Appointed first Secretary of the Treasury.
1790.		Reports on the Public Credit.
		Financial policy accepted.
1791.		National Bank established.
1794.		Quelled Whiskey Rebellion.
1795.	Jan. 31.	Resigned from Secretaryship.
1798.		Friendship with Adams broken.
		Made Inspector-General with rank of Major-General.
1799.		Promoted to Commander-in-Chief.
1800.		Favored Jefferson's election over Burr.
1803.		Charged with Burr's defeat for Governor of New York.
1804.	July 11.	Duel with Burr at Weehawken.
	July 12.	Died.

II

Alexander Hamilton. Growth Through Administrative Organization

THE life of Alexander Hamilton illustrates as does no other in American history the truth that the essence of government lies in the spirit of the governors, that its real character is determined by that of the men who administer it, and that its form and direction reflect the will and desire of those entrusted with the guidance of its destinies. Autocratic governments are confessedly the image of the autocrat, and the likeness is striking or faint in proportion as his will dominates those who serve him. The same is true of governments that are constitutional in form; the opportunity for the free play of a strong personality upon the most fundamental relations of government still exists. Where there is a written and rigid constitution, where the form of government is carefully elaborated and committed with due solemnity to a written document, and where this is done with the settled determination to fix the nature and character of the State to be organized, it may be thought that the influence of the individual will be all but eliminated, that only within the narrow limits of the written specifications can he pursue his circumscribed course, with here and there a slight adjustment of the parts of the governmental machine, to mark his share in the work. Such at least has been the attitude taken towards our own Constitution by the multitudes who have made of it a political fetish, and who have refused to see that an institution is dependent for its character upon the men who give it reality in the world of events.

The framers of the Constitution were well aware that the true nature of the government to be instituted and of the Union to be created by the Constituition was yet to be determined. The compromises of the Convention had produced a government "partly national and partly federal," and there were grave fears that it could not be made to work at all. No man felt sure what the result would be. Hamilton, however, foresaw the possibilities of growth that stretched out before the national government.[1] Above all others he felt the need of a strong central government and more than all others he contributed to make the new Union a nation.[2] Hamilton's part in fashioning the mere outward form of government was small; his great services lay in the influence he exerted upon its adoption through the masterly exposition in the papers of the *Federalist* and in the determining influence he exercised over the years of its infancy, when, as Secretary of the Treasury, his ruling spirit dominated every branch of the government and for the time being set at naught the care-

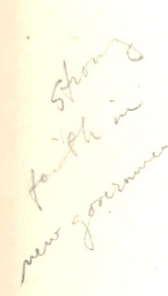

---

[1] *Cf. Works*, ed. by H. C. Lodge, i., 423.
[2] *Cf.* F. S. Oliver, *Alexander Hamilton*, p. 186–187.

fully devised system of the separation of the powers of government.[1] His mastery of the legislative branch of the government was little less complete than his ascendancy over Washington,[2] and from his administrative direction there sprang up a tradition of strength in the government which all the fervor of the Jeffersonian triumph could not overcome.

The great passion of Hamilton's life was love of an orderly direction in human affairs; mankind in the mass he regarded as weak, and this weakness demanded the strength of government if the human race was to enjoy the blessings of liberty. A strong government was necessary to restrain the natural disorders of society, whatever the character of its organization. Order and strength were inseparable in all his thought of government; his practical experience had demonstrated that social disorder and governmental weakness were correlative terms,[3] and the verdict of history has confirmed his experience.

Hamilton was born on the little island of Nevis, in the West Indies, on January 11, 1757.[4] His father was James Hamilton of the Scotch Hamiltons, honest, but unsuccessful, and his mother was a French Huguenot. In his character we find the elements of both races[5]; there is all the strength of will, keenness of logic, and depth of penetration that

[1] *Cf.* H. J. Ford, *Rise and Growth of American Politics*, p. 81.
[2] *Cf.* Oliver, *op. cit.*, pp. 73 and 262.
[3] *Cf. Works*, v., 343.
[4] For the facts of Hamilton's life see the biographies by his son, J. C. Hamilton, by H. C. Lodge, J. T. Morse, Jr., and W. T. Sumner.
[5] *Cf.* Morse, *Life of Alexander Hamilton*, i., 2.

may be accorded to the most typical of Scotch intellects; side by side with these sterner qualities there was an ease and grace of manner, a fluency of speech, a gaiety and brightness of temperament, and a lucidity of statement truly Gallic in its nature.

The early death of his mother and the incapacity of his father soon compelled the lad to shift for himself. At the age of thirteen we find him acting as clerk for a certain Nicholas Cruger, of St. Christopher, and despising the grovelling condition of a clerk; so precocious was he that within a year he was left in charge of the entire business while the master made an extended trip to the Northern colonies. His business career, however, was destined to be of short duration. A hurricane that devastated the island made such a deep impression upon the sensitive youth that he wrote a description of it for a local paper; the wonder and admiration of the islanders were excited by the beauty of his language and the vividness of his portrayal, and some of his more prosperous relatives, doubtless at the instigation of the Rev. Hugh Knox, who had been his tutor, determined that such unusual gifts should have an opportunity for unhindered development, and in consequence they decided to send him to the colonies of the mainland to be educated.

Hamilton arrived in Boston in October of the year 1772, and after a short time spent at Elizabeth, N. J., he matriculated at the early age of seventeen at King's College, now Columbia University. It is an interesting story which tells of the desire of young Hamilton to enter the College of New Jersey at

Princeton, and of his lack of success because of the uncompromising attitude taken by the trustees toward his desire to enter " upon the condition that he might be permitted to advance from class to class with as much rapidity as his exertions would enable him to do."

The lad's work at King's College was pursued with great success for the next two years, unhindered by the growing spirit of political unrest. The repressive measures enacted against the rebellious colony of Massachusetts elicited the sympathy and active co-operation of all the colonies. The spirit of united action found its first expression in the Continental Congress of 1774, and in the actual assistance rendered Massachusetts in that trying year. The air was alive with the breath of political arguments, and that of King's College not least of all; its distinguished President, Dr. Miles Cooper, was loyal to his King and Church and for his pains was almost made to suffer the fate of many a less distinguished Tory. His escape was due to the quickness of Hamilton in aiding him to flee by a rear gate while the mob was already clamoring at the front.[1] It was no doubt due to the influence of Dr. Cooper, as much as to his own strong love of order and reverence for tradition, that Hamilton at first inclined to the side of established government; but a visit to Boston in 1774 and contact with the Patriots, whose zeal was at fever heat, served to dispel all doubt from his mind and to commit him unalterably to the Patriot cause.

[1] Morse, *Life of Alexander Hamilton*, i., 18.

It was almost immediately upon his return that the chance came to display his new-born enthusiasm; being present on July 6th at a public meeting " in the fields," he listened with disgust to the speakers, not so much at what they said as at what they left unsaid, and when they had finished, this lad of seventeen, slight of frame and delicate of feature, the very picture of youth, forgetful of self and mindful only of the cause at stake, mounted the platform.[1] The crowd, too, apparently was dissatisfied with what it had heard, for it greeted the stripling with the half-mocking, half-favoring cry of " The Collegian! Hear the Collegian!" Almost at the first sound of his voice the throng was silenced; their hearts were filled with the great emotion that stirred his own bosom, and they forgot the childlike face and figure; gazing with rapt attention at his eager countenance, they seemed to feel in him the incarnation of those new thoughts and feelings which the past ten years had begotten.

The years from 1775 to 1785 were big with events both in the country's history and in Hamilton's life. His first public speech was soon followed by two anonymous pamphlets. So able were they that the authorship was commonly attributed to Jay and Livingston. When it became known that Hamilton was the author, he was immediately accepted as a leader of the Patriot cause and in 1776 was placed in command of a New York artillery company which became in six months the model of the army for discipline and efficiency. Because of ability dis-

---

[1] *Cf.* Oliver, *op. cit.*, pp. 27–28.

played at the battles of Long Island and White Plains and in the retreat across New Jersey, Washington appointed him a member of the general staff, with the commission of lieutenant-colonel in the Continental army. From the first he acted as secretary, and for five years he was indispensable to Washington. A warm personal friendship sprang up between the two men which suffered but a single break, that of 1781, when Hamilton, incensed at a rebuke administered by Washington, resigned.[1] Desire for military glory doubtless played its part in the resignation, for he soon took the field as a lieutenant-colonel of the New York State troops, and was fortunate enough to be present at the siege of Yorktown, where he headed a storming party and was brevetted colonel for bravery in battle. As the war was practically at an end, Hamilton resigned his commission and began the study of law in New York, where his admission to the bar was soon signalled by a rapid rise to the head of the profession.

By his marriage to Miss Elizabeth Schuyler in 1780 Hamilton had allied himself with the distinguished Schuyler family, and this alliance brought him friends and connections on a large scale. In November, 1782, he took his seat in the Continental Congress, then sitting at Philadelphia, that same Congress which, after its hasty flight from Philadelphia, sought refuge in Nassau Hall at Princeton in June, 1783. Finding himself in a hopeless minority and realizing that his efforts were futile, he resigned,

[1] *Cf. Works*, ix., 232, for Hamilton's account in a letter to his father-in-law.

convinced above all things that the Congress and the Articles of Confederation must be swept away before the country could be rescued from the anarchy into which it was fast drifting.[1] Freed by his foreign birth from the local attachments which made it so difficult for most men to transfer any part of their allegiance to a national government, he could perceive the need of a strong central power. His sympathies were ever national, not local; not New York but America was the land of his adoption. "The great idea, of which he was the embodiment, was that of nationality."[2]

As early as 1780, in the midst of his arduous duties as aide-de-camp to Washington, he had discovered and disclosed in a letter to James Duane the deficiencies of the Confederation and the way in which these defects might be remedied.[3] "The fundamental defect," he wrote, "is a want of power in Congress." "But the Confederation itself is defective, and requires to be altered. It is neither fit for war nor peace." The complete inefficiency of the Confederation in its conduct of the war was a matter of which he could judge from practical experience; the ill-fed and ill-clothed troops bore convincing testimony to his mind of the inability of an assemblage of diplomats to carry on the struggle to a successful conclusion. The heart of the difficulty lay in the disordered finances; the remedy could only be found if the Confederation "should give Congress complete sovereignty, except as to that part of internal police

---

[1] *Cf.* Oliver, *op. cit.*, pp. 125–126.
[2] Lodge, *Life of Alexander Hamilton*, p. 282.
[3] *Cf. Works*, i., 213.

which relates to the rights of individuals," if the direction of affairs should be placed in the hands of competent individuals, and if a national bank should be established. He outlined the plan of such a bank and urged it as indispensable in securing the certain revenues without which "government can have no power."

It was in this same letter that he gave expression to a view that may be taken as typical of all his later attitude toward constitutional interpretation. After reproaching Congress for not having made better use of its powers, he declared that "undefined powers are discretionary powers, limited only by the object for which they are given—in the present case the independence and freedom of America."

During the three years following his withdrawal from Congress, Hamilton devoted himself to his profession and to the creation of a stronger national sentiment among the people. When the opportunity came to set in motion the train of events that he hoped would lead to the consummation he so devoutly desired, he was not slow to avail himself of it. He was the one to seize upon the Annapolis Convention as the psychological moment to appeal for concerted action to revise the moribund Articles of Confederation in order to make them equal to the exigencies of the Union.[1]

The particularist spirit of independent statehood was nowhere stronger than in the controlling faction in Hamilton's own State. Governor Clinton and his party dreamed of a great State of New York, inde-

---

[1] *Cf.* Oliver, *op. cit.*, p. 142.

pendent, free, and mighty by reason of its favorable geographical position, and in this great State Clinton, its governor, would be greater than ever he might hope to be in a New York that was merely one of a Confederation of thirteen. So in the Assembly of 1786, which chose the delegates to the Constitutional Convention called to meet in Philadelphia in the following spring, all that Hamilton could secure was his own appointment among the delegates. The two other delegates chosen by the Legislature were followers of Clinton, men given over completely to the spirit of separatism, ready and willing, even determined, to sacrifice the Union to the selfish interests of individual statehood.[1] Yates and Lansing were men of unblemished personal character, but the narrowness and selfishness of their political views has condemned them forever. Yet there is a crumb of comfort to be extracted from their action, for their withdrawal from the Convention stands as an everlasting proof of their belief that the Convention had started upon a revolutionary and wholly unjustifiable course; that it had abandoned its sole function of revising the Articles of Confederation. To attempt to formulate a constitution upon any other basis than that of the Articles, said Lansing, was to do something to which the State of New York would never consent, and had she realized that such would be the action of the Convention, would never have sent delegates.[2]

Almost immediately after the opening of the Con-

[1] Fiske, *Critical Period*, p. 225, characterizes them as "extreme and obstinate Antifederalists."
[2] *Cf. Documentary History of the Constitution*, iii., 129.

vention, there was presented to it for its determination the question as to the kind of union that should be contemplated in the new Constitution. The struggle over this question centred round the "Virginia" and "New Jersey" plans. There could be no question which one of these Hamilton would prefer if compelled to make choice. Among the many who at this time showed distrust of the spirit of democracy, none stands out more prominently than he. Though Sherman of Connecticut might say that "the people should have as little to do as may be about the Government,"[1] and Gerry that "the evils we experience flow from the excess of democracy,"[2] it was Hamilton who had the courage to propose to the Convention a scheme of government which left little or no place for popular power, in which the President and Senate should hold office during good behavior and the governors of the States should be appointed by the general government.[3] For five hours Hamilton held the Convention under the sway of his eloquence while he set forth his ideas on government. A brilliant speech, which, says Fiske, "while applauded by many, was supported by none." Up to this time Hamilton had taken very little part in the proceedings of the Convention. The reason for this we do not know; perhaps it was that he was sceptical of the result, and believed the Convention incapable of agreement upon any plan that

---

[1] *Doc. Hist.*, iii., 26.
[2] *Ibid.*, iii., 26.
[3] *Ibid.*, iii., 149 *ff.*, and *Works*, i., 350 *ff.* Later in the proceedings of the Convention Hamilton proposed a three years' term for the President.

would be strong enough to save the Union; perhaps it was because he was constantly outvoted by his colleagues from New York and was embarrassed thereby. Whatever the reason may have been, we are always surprised and disappointed that he did not play a larger part in determining the form of the Constitution.

But there was little hope of recognition from that assembly of such views as Hamilton proclaimed. It may have been quite true, as he said, that "the British government was the best in the world," but it would have been folly to suppose that the Convention would accept or act in accordance with such doctrine. Nor are we led to believe that Hamilton was so devoid of political sagacity as to suppose it would. Much more probable does it seem that he wanted to go on record as the advocate of a strongly centralized government, if thereby he might convince any of the importance of strength as an element of government. The Articles of Confederation were cursed beyond all else by weakness; he saw it clearly; he despaired of accomplishing what he desired; what better could he do than to set a high standard of what he believed to be best? Too high a standard to be realized, perhaps, but in the reaction, would the members of the Convention go quite so far on the road toward a loose confederacy? Might they not be emboldened to give a fair measure of power to the central government? Finding himself unable to contribute to the deliberations, and knowing full well that any action he might take would be regarded as purely personal, and in no sense as the action of his State, Hamilton withdrew from the

Convention, not to return again until near the close of its sessions, in time to affix his signature to the final document.

Though Hamilton found the "New Jersey" plan "utterly untenable," and though "he saw great difficulty in establishing a good national government on the Virginia plan," yet when he perceived that the Constitution was the best that could be had under the circumstances, that it offered a chance of escape from the anarchical condition into which the country had fallen, there was none so zealous as he in the advocacy of its adoption. Associating with himself Madison and, for a short period, Jay, he began the publication of that now famous series of papers called the *Federalist*. Here was set forth, in a manner since unrivalled, the very essence of the new government that was to be established.[1] With the clearest of logic there was demonstrated the evils of the Confederation and the fashion in which these evils were to be cured by the new federal arrangement; brilliant in style and persuasive in manner, these papers went forth carrying conviction with them. To them more than to any other one agency was due the final adoption of the Constitution, for though written for the people of New York State, their influence was felt in all the States which had not yet acted.[2] To this day they remain an authoritative exposition of our fundamental instrument of government and a testimony to the insight and learning

---

[1] Fiske, *op. cit.*, p. 225, is led by his enthusiasm to describe it as "the greatest treatise on government that has ever been written."

[2] There is a great divergence of opinion as to the actual in-

of their authors. To Hamilton is due the credit of originating the idea and of contributing by far the larger number of the papers.

With the conclusion of the *Federalist,* Hamilton's labors in behalf of the adoption of the Constitution were by no means over. The Legislature of New York was hostile to the Constitution and was under the control of Governor Clinton. When Hamilton began his contest with the majority, defeat seemed inevitable; that he won in the end and thereby saved New York for the Union and mayhap the Union itself, may well be accounted one of his greatest triumphs. It was indomitable will, the tact of a diplomat, the skill of a parliamentary tactician, the eloquence of a persuasive personality, and the justness of the cause that triumphed over a bigoted and selfish opposition.[1] It was no more than fitting that in the celebration of the victory in New York City, the ship of state should be inscribed HAMILTON.

It would be impossible to bring within our view all of Hamilton's conclusions regarding the nature of the new Union. It may be worth while, however, to consider such as have been and still are the battle-ground of party strife.

In the first place, Hamilton accepted as indisputable

---

fluence exerted by the *Federalist.* In support of the view presented in the text, the following may be noted: Curtis, *Constitutional History,* i., 280; Fiske, *Critical Period,* p. 342; Oliver, *op. cit.,* p. 168; Morse, *op. cit.,* i., 266; Lodge, *op. cit.,* p. 67. For the contrary view, J. B. McMaster, *History,* i., 484, and A. C. McLaughlin, *The Confederation and the Constitution,* p. 308.

[1] *Cf.* Oliver, *op. cit.,* pp. 176–179.

the view that the Constitution was not an amended form of the Articles of Confederation, but that it was a "confederated republic," "an assemblage of societies, or an association of two or more states into one state." It was more than a confederacy, inasmuch as the power of the central government could be exerted upon individuals and not merely upon States; it was less than a consolidated State, because the existence of the several States had been most carefully preserved.[1] The Convention had aimed only at a partial consolidation of the States in a union in which they retained all rights previously enjoyed and which had not been expressly delegated to the Federal Government. The delegation of powers was not only to the Federal Government but to the State governments as well. This conception of a delegation of power rests upon the view which sees in the people the sovereign, the possessor of supreme powers; a part of these powers the people had delegated to the State governments, a part they would delegate to the Federal Government by the adoption of the Constitution, and still another part they would retain.[2] It is the old idea of Locke and the people's power of revolution viewed from a different angle and wearing a slightly altered dress. Hamilton, however, regarded the Federal Government as the judge of its own powers; if it overstepped its bounds, the people were to judge of the fact and to institute the correction. The Constitution to Hamilton was not a treaty, but "the supreme law of the land, a

[1] *Cf. The Federalist,* Ford's edition, Nos. 9, 15, and 16, and *Works,* ii., 9.
[2] *Ibid.,* No. 23.

government, which is only another word for POLITICAL POWER AND SUPREMACY." [1]

The States, moreover, were in no danger; in proportion as they stand nearer to the people will they demand a greater share of their affection; " we love our families more than our neighbors; we love our neighbors more than our countrymen in general. On these principles, the attachment of the individual will be first and forever secured by the State governments." [2] The very existence of the Federal Union rests upon the States, and the balance between the national and State governments is of the utmost importance. " It forms a double security to the people. If one encroaches on their rights they will find a powerful protection in the other." [3] On the other hand, speaking of those who stood for a complete freedom of the States within the Union, we find Hamilton using these significant words: " They seem to aim at things repugnant and irreconcilable; at an augmentation of federal authority, without a diminution of state authority; at a sovereignty in the Union and complete independence in the members. They still in fine seem to cherish with blind devotion the political monster of an *imperium in imperio*." [4]

On the question of the separation of the powers of government, that doctrine of Montesquieu's which was itself based upon a misconception, we do not find the doctrinaire opinion which has so often made

[1] *Federalist*, No. 33.
[2] *Works*, ii., 70. *Cf. Federalist*, Nos. 17 and 30.
[3] *Ibid.*, ii., 28.
[4] *Federalist*, No. 15.

itself felt to the detriment of the country in the relations of the various branches of government. A separation of legislative, executive, and judicial functions was regarded, to be sure, as a cardinal principle of political philosophy, at least in those governments in which the citizens enjoy the blessings of liberty and freedom. In Hamilton's eyes the separation could not and must not be complete. The Judiciary, having "neither force nor will but merely judgment," should be independent; the Legislative and Executive were mutually dependent and should act merely as checks upon each other, not as blocks to bring the action of government to a standstill.[1]

That Hamilton had fathomed the true nature of the new government is clearly manifested in his reply to the objection made to the Constitution on the ground that it did not contain a Bill of Rights. Such a Bill of Rights, he thought, would furnish no security to liberty. In origin these bills were stipulations between kings and their subjects by which the latter secured the abridgment of the royal prerogative; consequently there was no place for them in a constitution founded upon the power of the people. "We, the people of the United States . . . do ordain and establish this Constitution for the United States of America." Here, he said, was "a better recognition of popular rights than volumes of those aphorisms which make the principal figure in several of our State bills of rights."[2]

---

[1] *Federalist*, No. 78, and Ford, *op. cit.*, p. 81.
[2] *Federalist*, No. 84.

Important as was Hamilton's part in securing the adoption of the Constitution and in giving us a theoretical exposition of its nature, it was insignificant when compared with the tremendous influence he exerted upon the living form this lifeless document should take.[1] The pressing need of the government under the Articles of Confederation had been money. The failure of the States to furnish the requisitions made upon them had resulted in the bankruptcy of the general government, with a consequent loss of respect at home and abroad. The immediate cause of the Constitutional Convention lay in the financial necessities of the government as illustrated by its lack of power to impose taxes and to regulate commerce. So it became the first and most important duty of the new Federal Government to establish itself upon a firm financial footing. The one man suited for the task was Hamilton and to him Washington turned. Appointed Secretary of the Treasury in 1789, he carried through the first Congress that great series of acts providing for the assumption of the foreign and domestic obligations, both of the Confederation and of the States; for levying an excise and for the establishing of a National Bank. In the words of Webster, he " smote the rock of the national resources, and abundant streams of revenue gushed forth; he touched the dead corpse of Public Credit, and it sprang upon its feet."

The failure of the Confederation had been due to financial weakness; the safety of the new government lay in financial strength; Hamilton felt that he must

[1] *Cf.* Oliver, *op. cit.*, pp. 183–248.

bind men to it by hoops stronger than steel; that he must replace affection by interest and offset lack of patriotism by financial obligation. Money was to him "the vital principle of the body politic."[1] Hence it was that he took the first step toward enlisting the men of wealth in the cause of the new government. With the assumption of the domestic debt by the Federal Government, a host of individuals were made to feel that its success was their prosperity, its failure their ruin, and by the very fact of the assumption of the State debts the Federal Government took its stand ahead of the States as something bigger and better than they. The men of the States looked beyond them, in this one respect at least, to a higher power. The assumption of the State and national debts was, however, but one step in the process of allying wealth and central governmental authority. Preceding it was the passage of an act of lasting consequence providing for the regulation of commerce by the imposition of important duties, a tariff which was to furnish both revenue and protection. Following the assumption bills came an act levying an excise tax and providing for an internal-revenue service. As the crowning stroke in Hamilton's policy of centralization, an act was passed providing for the establishment of a National Bank.

Here for the first time there arose the question of

---

[1] *Federalist*, No. 30. As early as 1780 in a letter to Morris in which he advocated the establishment of a National Bank, Hamilton had realized the value of uniting "the interest and credit of rich individuals with those of the State."—*Works*, iii., 332.

the extent of the powers of Congress. The financial needs of the government were so urgent that little thought had been given to the title of the act to levy import duties; it was no time for questioning the purposes of the bill beyond that of raising revenue and so the power of Congress to protect infant industries passed unchallenged. The funding and assumption bills might well be opposed on the grounds of expediency, or the resulting position of inferiority of the States, but there could be no serious claim presented that Congress had no right to do these things. Far otherwise was it, however, with the proposal to establish a National Bank. It was vigorously objected that nowhere does the Constitution give Congress the right to charter such a bank; but on the other hand the tenth amendment had been added especially providing that "the powers not delegated to the United States by the Constitution, nor prohibited by it to the States, are reserved to the States respectively or to the people." To this objection Hamilton made ready answer with another provision of the Constitution, the so-called "Elastic Clause," the fertile source of the "implied powers," which provides that Congress shall have the right "to make all laws which shall be necessary and proper for carrying into execution the foregoing powers, and all other powers vested by this Constitution in the Government of the United States."[1] Hamilton, in an opinion which Judge Story pronounced "one of the most masterly disquisitions that ever proceeded from the mind of man,"

[1] Art. I., Sec. 8, clause 18.

claimed that the establishment of a National Bank was a proper measure and one needed to set the national government on its feet. His opponents, led by Jefferson, contended that the bank was not necessary and if not necessary, it could not be established from motives of mere convenience.[1]

The possibilities of the strength of the Federal Government from these measures of Hamilton rapidly began to excite alarm, but the moneyed and manufacturing classes were already allied with the Federal Government and the bank was established. With the establishment of the National Bank, Hamilton's constructive efforts in shaping the future of the Constitution were finished; he had left the impress of his genius upon the instrument of government, and had marked out the path that national development has ever since pursued. He sought to establish a government in which wealth should stand at the helm, guiding and steadying the ship of state. He distrusted the turbulence of democracy and believed in the rich and the well-born; he feared the multitude and trusted the chosen few. For the Republic he sought strength in wealth, and desired the national government to reach out, under the doctrine of loose construction, for all those powers that might be proper for the existence of a nation.

Upon the issue presented by these questions, the natural divergence between Hamilton and Jefferson widened until they stood at the head of opposing

[1] *Works*, i., 445 *ff*. Opinion as to the Constitutionality of the Bank of the United States. Jefferson's opinion may be found in his *Works*, Memorial edition, iii., 145–153. For extracts from both opinions see the Appendix.

factions, the beginnings of the two great parties which, despite changes of name, have in essence remained the same. To-day, as in the presidency of Washington, the people are arrayed under the banners of "loose" and "strict" construction, though our speech may be in slightly altered terms. The rivalry and jealousy between Hamilton and Jefferson became so keen that in 1794 Jefferson retired from the Cabinet; in the next year Hamilton resigned to give attention to his personal affairs.

The remaining years of Hamilton's life were not purposeless, though they added nothing to his already great achievements; they were spent in the effort to continue the government in the course upon which he had started it, and his must have been a strange nature that would not have been saddened by seeing the country slowly but surely drifting away from his ideal and beyond his control. The Virginia Resolutions of 1798, with their claim of the right of the States to judge of the constitutionality of laws, and the Kentucky Resolutions of the next year, with that insidious doctrine of the right of nullification which had as its logical successor the yet more dangerous right of secession, filled his mind with anxious forebodings. He loved with a passionate ardor the nation he had done so much to create. "If this Union were to be broken," he cried, "it would break my heart."

In the election of Jefferson, Hamilton witnessed the triumph of the most implacable foe to all his ideas—a triumph to which his own sacrifice of self to patriotism contributed—and the dark shadow of failure fell for the first time across his path, but the bitterness of his last years must have been tempered by that great national act to which he saw his opponent driven—the purchase of Louisiana. We must ever sincerely lament his tragic death on the fields of Weehawken, which robbed our country of its greatest intellect while still in its prime; for his own sake we can but wish he might have been spared another decade to witness the survival and ultimate triumph of the principles he cherished so passionately.

III

James Wilson. Growth through Speculative Forecast.

JAMES WILSON

1742.	Sept. 14.	Born near St. Andrews, Scotland.
1757.		At Universities of Glasgow, Edinburgh, and St. Andrews.
1765.		Came to America.
1765–66.		In New York.
1768.		Admitted to Philadelphia bar.
1769.		Moved to Carlisle.
1778.		Settled in Philadelphia.
1775–78. 1782–83. 1785–87.		Continental Congress. Signer of Declaration of Independence.
1787.		Member of Constitutional Convention.
1788.		Member of Pennsylvania Convention.
1789–90.		Member of State Constitutional Convention.
1789–98.		Associate Justice of U. S. Supreme Court.
1790–92.		Professor of Law in the College of Philadelphia, which in 1792 became the University of Pennsylvania.
1798.	Aug. 28.	Died at Edenton, N. C.

III

James Wilson. Growth through Speculative Forecast.

FOR depth of legal learning and soundness of judgment in political affairs, James Wilson of Pennsylvania was unsurpassed by any member of the Constitutional Convention. Hamilton may have been more brilliant or Madison a deeper student of the art of government, but neither could rival Wilson in insight and originality. With all the logical precision of his Scotch intellect, he surveyed the conditions around him, analyzed, classified, and arranged the facts of political life in their proper categories, and deduced from them his conclusions with respect to the kind of government needed. There were not lacking others who did the same thing, but they failed to equal Wilson in penetration and the ability to follow principles to their logical conclusions. No member of the Convention had a firmer grasp than did Wilson of the one great question to be settled—that of union with independence.

The creation of a new state, national in the extent of its jurisdiction and supreme in matters of common interest, with the preservation of State freedom in purely local matters, was a novelty in the realm of political speculation. Confederations there had been a plenty; we ourselves had made trial of one and because of its failure the Convention had been called. Many desired to adhere to the old form of government, deeming it sufficient if its powers should be enlarged; others desired a consolidation of the States into one wherein the individual States should be only administrative districts. Between these two views stands the one finally adopted by the Convention. The idea of a Federal State, embracing all the people of the component States but not dependent upon the States themselves, within which the individual States continue an independent existence, was both new and complex. Other men perceived certain phases and aspects of this new conception, but none possessed so comprehensive a view, as did Wilson, of this Federal Republic, which was to be a state above States, a state embracing States, and yet not composed of those States so much as of the people within them who were regarded as forming a single nation.

As we look back upon the men of the Convention, Wilson seems to have had the clearest conception of the future course of government in the United States; his ideas were those toward which we have ever since been working.[1] Like Hamilton, he not only took part in the work of the Convention, but also in the far more important work of infusing into the dead body of the written document the living

---

[1] *Cf.* B. A. Konkle, *James Wilson and the Constitution;* and L. H. Alexander, *James Wilson, Patriot,* and *The Wilson Doctrine,* p. 14, for a quotation from President Roosevelt's speech at Philadelphia, October 4, 1906.

power of practice. Hamilton's great service lay in organizing the administrative department of the government along the lines of its financial life. Wilson played a less obtrusive but a scarcely less important part in setting in motion the judicial functions outlined in the Constitution and more fully determined by the first Congress, in establishing the Supreme Court upon the lofty plane it has since preserved and in making it the national organ of a truly national state.[1]

Until within recent years Wilson and his work were known and appreciated only by the few who delved into the dusty records of his time; even now there are many who do not associate his name with any great idea, and the number who rank him as he so justly deserves, along with the great men of the revolutionary era, is extremely small; but thanks to the many students of this epoch of American history, the justification of James Wilson as one of the great thinkers of our country advances steadily. It is not altogether clear, when we review his long and important services, why he should have been lost sight of so completely after his death. Doubtless the heat of party passions had somewhat to do with belittling his services and obscuring his name. Men who in 1788 had burned in effigy "James Wilson, the Caledonian," for his "aristocratic tendencies," for his love of a strong government and his advocacy of the Federal Constitution within the State of Pennsylvania, would not soon lay aside their hatred; moreover, with the triumph of the Democratic-

---

[1] *Cf.* H. L. Carson, *The Supreme Court of the United States.*

Republicans within two years after his death, his views could have found acceptance with only a small minority of the people. Doubtless, too, the fact that his large fortune was swept away just before his death cast a shadow upon the fame of his services to his country as in the similar case of his friend Robert Morris. Wilson was cordially disliked by that very considerable element of Pennsylvanians who opposed the adoption of the Constitution on the ground that it deprived the State of its sovereign rights and the people of their guarantees of liberty and safety. These men ridiculed the Federalists for their hostility to democracy and their distrust of the people, but in reality they preferred to be first in Pennsylvania than second in the Union. They dreaded the strong hand of law and order and saw in its establishment a lessening of the license they called liberty.

James Wilson was born near St. Andrews, Scotland, in 1742.[1] After several years at the Universities of Glasgow, Edinburgh, and St. Andrews, he came to America in 1765 and settled in Philadelphia; for two years he studied law under John Dickinson, and in 1768 at the age of twenty-six was admitted to the bar. He began the practice of law at Carlisle, but the growth of his interests led him in a few years to settle in Philadelphia. The natural inclination of his mind was congenial to the character of political topics then under discussion and it is not

---

[1] For the facts of Wilson's life see Konkle, *op. cit.*, and *Biography of the Signers of the Declaration of Independence*, ed. by Sanderson, iii., pp. 259–301. Where there is a divergence of view respecting dates I have followed Konkle.

surprising to find him entering at once into the public discussion being carried on. In 1775 he was chosen a member of the Second Continental Congress and in the following year was one of that immortal number of signers of the Declaration of Independence. From this time forth he was engaged almost constantly in the public service. From 1775 to 1777, from 1782 to 1783, and from 1785 to 1787, he was a member of the Continental Congress. His services in that body are coincident with the three great periods in its history: the first is that of the Declaration of Independence and the proposal of the Articles of Confederation; the second is that of the final adoption of the Articles after the wise and statesmanlike efforts of Maryland had resulted in securing the cession by the various States of their Western lands and the creation of a lasting tie and common interests; the third and final period is that of the summoning of the Constitutional Convention and the acceptance of its work.

In the Constitutional Convention Wilson labored indefatigably to fashion the instrument in symmetry and power, and in the Pennsylvania State Convention he strove no less zealously to secure its adoption. In 1789 Washington appointed him an Associate Justice of the Supreme Court, a position which he continued to fill with distinction till his early death while on circuit at Edenton, North Carolina, in 1798.

The field of Wilson's activity is left incomplete without some notice of the fact that from 1790 to 1792 he was professor of law in the College of Philadelphia, now the University of Pennsylvania.

In his law lectures we find a systematic presentation of his views on the nature of the Federal Government, for they were concerned far more with the philosophy of law, the nature of the state, and the character of the Federal Government than with any particular branch of private law.[1] That Wilson was a thinker of originality is evident from his boldness in rejecting the time-honored definition of law as consecrated by the name of Blackstone. He rejects the conception of law as a rule of action laid down by a superior, and regards it as receiving its binding force from "the consent of those whose obedience the law requires."[2]

In the Convention, "none with the exception of Gouverneur Morris," says McMaster, "was so often on his feet during the debates or spoke more to the purpose."[3] From the record of these speeches we can gather a fairly accurate conception of Wilson's services in the making of the Constitution and of his ideas respecting the kind of government he desired to see established. It would be absurd to imagine that all the members of the Convention had an appreciation of the great changes that were being made, or that they would have approved if they had known, nor is it to be supposed that any of them foresaw the full force of what they did. They were neither seers nor prophets, but practical men for the most part, intent on making a new application of their political wisdom and experience to the new conditions that had arisen. They were not

[1] *Works*, ed. by J. DeW. Andrews, 2 vols., Chicago, 1896.
[2] *Ibid.*, i., 88.
[3] *History of the People of the United States*, i., 421.

doctrinaires with a theory of government to put into execution, but earnest seekers for some remedy for the anarchical condition into which the political relations of the States had fallen, for some sort of governmental arrangement that would replace the anarchy that was imminent. If here and there among the members there was to be found a man whose gaze penetrated even a short way into the future, who saw with some clearness the form and nature of the new Union, he is a distinct exception. That there were such men cannot be denied, and foremost among them stands Wilson.

First of all it should be noted that Wilson, far from being an " aristocrat " as his enemies charged, was a firm believer in democracy. " He was for raising the Federal pyramid to a considerable altitude," he declared, yet " for that reason wished to give it as broad a basis as possible. No government could long subsist without the confidence of the people." [1] As an indication of his trust in the people there may be cited his zealous advocacy of the election by the people of the Executive [2] and the members of both branches of the legislative body.[3] " He wished for vigor in the government, but he wished that vigorous authority to flow immediately from the legitimate source of all authority," and again, " the legislature ought to be the most exact transcript of the whole society. Representation is made necessary only because it is impossible for the

[1] *Documentary History of the Constitution*, iii., 28.
[2] *Ibid.*, iii., 39–49.
[3] *Ibid.*, iii., 31 and 40.

people to act collectively." [1] Speaking again on the subject of representation, Madison reports him as saying, " if we are to establish a national government, that government ought to flow from the people at large." [2] Finally there could be no clearer confession of his allegiance to the principle of democracy than we find in the course of the discussion of the equal representation of the States in the Senate—a proposal which Wilson vigorously opposed —when he declared that " the majority of the people wherever found ought in all questions to govern the minority." [3] " He was a believer in democracy and in nationalism—the first man," it has been said, " in all our history who united the two opinions."

The debates on the rule of suffrage in the national legislature were numerous and protracted, for in this question was contained the struggle between the large and the small States. It was in the course of the discussion of this part of the Randolph or " Virginia plan," on June 9th, in the Committee of the Whole, that Brearly of New Jersey proposed " that a map of the United States be spread out, that all the existing boundaries be erased, and that a new partition of the whole be made into thirteen equal parts." [4] Paterson of New Jersey followed in a lengthy speech on the powers of the Convention under the resolution of Congress; on the idea of a national as distinguished from a federal government, or a confederacy, which presupposed sovereignty in its members. Wilson replied:

---

[1] *Documentary History of the Constitution*, iii., **70**.
[2] *Ibid.*, iii., **81**.
[3] *Ibid.*, iii., **330**.
[4] *Ibid.*, iii., **96**.

James Wilson 63

We have been told that each State being sovereign, all are equal. So each man is naturally a sovereign over himself, and all men are therefore naturally equal. Can he retain this equality when he becomes a member of civil government? He can not. As little can a sovereign State, when it becomes a member of a federal government. If New Jersey will not part with her sovereignty it is vain to talk of government. A new partition of the States is desirable, but evidently and totally impracticable.[1]

The Committee of the Whole reported Randolph's plan as amended on June 13th, and the next day Paterson asked time to present a " purely federal " plan and " contradistinguished from the reported plan." On the 15th Paterson submitted the so-called " New Jersey plan," and Randolph's plan was recommitted that there might be a full and free discussion of both. On the following day the two plans were discussed at length by Lansing of New York and by Paterson himself, both of whom stated very clearly the difference in the character of the plans submitted; both advocated the New Jersey plan, which did not contemplate any change in the nature of the new Union from that under the Articles of Confederation. Wilson likewise contrasted the two plans, point by point, but always in favor of the Virginia plan, which contemplated the establishment of a national government, consisting of a supreme Legislative, Executive, and Judiciary.[2] On June 19th the Committee of the Whole rejected Paterson's plan and reported Randolph's plan unchanged, upon

[1] *Documentary History of the Constitution*, iii., 100.
[2] *Ibid.*, iii., 132 *ff.*

which " Mr. Wilson observed that by a national government he did not mean one that would swallow up the State governments, as seemed to be wished by some gentlemen. He was tenacious of the idea of preserving the latter. He thought, contrary to the opinion of (Colonel Hamilton) that they might not only subsist but subsist on friendly terms with the former. They were absolutely necessary for certain purposes which the former could not reach."[1] The danger was rather that the national government would be devoured by the State governments, though " he saw no incompatibility between the national and State governments provided the latter were restrained to certain local purposes; nor any probability of their being devoured by the former."[2]

But it was the clearness with which Wilson perceived the true nature of the Federal State to which I wish to call special attention. His views on this subject are best seen in his discussion of the question whether the members of the second branch of the legislative body should be chosen by the Legislatures of the States.

He was opposed to an election by the State legislatures. In explaining his reasons it was necessary to observe the twofold relation in which the people would stand: 1, as citizens of the general government; 2, as citizens of their particular State. The general government was meant for them in the first capacity; the State governments in the second. Both governments were derived from the people—both meant for the people—both therefore ought to

[1] *Documentary History of the Constitution*, iii., 162–163.
[2] *Ibid.*, iii., 76.

James Wilson

be regulated on the same principles. . . . With respect to the province and objects of the general government they [the State governments] should be considered as having no existence. The election of the second branch by the Legislatures, will introduce and cherish local interests and local prejudices. The general government is not an assemblage of States, but of individuals for certain political purposes—it is not meant for the States, but for the individuals composing them; the *individuals*, therefore, not the *States*, ought to be represented in it.[1]

Again in the debate on this same question he asks, "Can we forget for whom we are forming a government? Is it for *men*, or for the imaginary beings called *States?*"[2]

As in this question of representation, so throughout the course of the debates Wilson stood for the creation of a strong national power to which the States should be subordinate, though independent within their own spheres. That this is the result Wilson believed had been accomplished by the Constitution is conclusively shown in his lectures on law at the College of Philadelphia in the winter of 1791–92 and in his decisions after his appointment to the Supreme Court of the United States.

Wilson was one of the earliest professors of American constitutional law, and his exposition of the nature of the Federal Union was one of the first attempts to set forth a systematic analysis of the powers and relationships of the States and the nation. His lectures constitute the first authoritative

---

[1] *Documentary History of the Constitution*, iii., 208–209.
[2] *Ibid.*, iii., 250.

discussion of the Constitution from any other standpoint than that of political advocacy or opposition. The *Federalist,* to be sure, had preceded Wilson's lectures by a couple of years, but magnificent as are those essays, fundamental as they are to our constitutional history, they must always suffer from the fact that they were written with a persuasive purpose; their object was to secure the adoption of the Constitution by the people of New York. Their purpose marred their symmetry and completeness. Wilson, on the other hand, wrote after the Constitution had been adopted and put into operation for more than a year. There was no need for advocacy or apology but only for a calm and unprejudiced exposition; and one who reads these lectures must of necessity be impressed with a sense of the importance attaching to their delivery in the mind both of the lecturer and of his audience.

Philadelphia was at this time the chief city of the country in wealth and culture, and the seat of the new national government had just been transferred to it from New York. The brilliant society which centred in the city has been styled " The American Court." The opening lecture was of sufficient interest and importance to attract the presence of Washington and a distinguished company of ladies and gentlemen from this " court."

Wilson was a political philosopher as well as a jurist, and in his thought concerning the nature and origin of civil society he had arrived at conclusions differing radically from the accepted views of the times. Society, to be sure, he regarded as based upon compact or the consent of the individuals, but society is not, therefore, artificial[1]; it is natural and necessary; the state of nature is not a state of war of all against all since in it men are ruled by good and not by evil desires, yet without society man can not accomplish for himself or for others the things desired. Wilson is, therefore, in accord with the Aristotelian conception of man as a social and political animal. The social contract unites men into a body politic or corporation[2] which he regarded as a moral person.[3] In the state of nature all men are free and equal in rights and obligations[4] and this freedom and equality are not lost in civil society. Natural liberty is not abridged but increased by the establishment of society, for a man "will gain more by the limitation of other men's freedom, than he can lose by the diminution of his own."[5]

The powers of individuals, enjoyed before the contract, remain as an aggregate in society.[6] The supreme or sovereign power of the society, therefore, resides in the citizens at large. In this moral person, this corporation, thus created by contract, the voice of the majority must pass for the voice of the whole, for the minority is bound by its consent originally given to the establishment of society.[7] There is thus laid the broad foundation for that democracy we have already noted as an integral part of his political views.

[1] *Cf. Works*, i., 253 *ff.*
[2] *Ibid.*, i., 271–272.
[3] *Ibid.*, i., 304–305.
[4] *Ibid.*, i., 275.
[5] *Ibid.*, ii., 300.
[6] *Ibid.*, i., 169.
[7] *Ibid.*, i., 227.

Wilson carefully distinguished between society or the state, and government; society preceded government which is merely the agent of society for the performance of certain functions which society is unable to perform for itself.[1] Now this moral person, which is society or the state, may constitute its government in any fashion it chooses, and with us it has chosen a written constitution as the instrumentality; this constitution it may change whenever it chooses.[2]

Furthermore in all states there must be a power from which there is no appeal, a power absolute, supreme, and uncontrollable. Where is this power lodged? Certainly not in constitutions, for we have just seen that they may be changed at will by the people. This supreme power, sovereignty, resides in the people, in the citizens at large, and is paramount to all constitutions. Moreover it is inalienable in its nature and indefinite in extent, being the powers of the individuals which, after the contract, remain as an aggregate in society, and "all the other powers and rights, which result from the social union."

"All these powers and rights, indeed, cannot, in a numerous and extended society, be exercised personally; but they may be exercised by representation." The delegation of sovereign powers, however, is not alienation and carries with it always the power and right of resumption. There can, moreover, be no subordinate sovereignty; the people have not parted with it; they have only dispensed such

[1] *Cf. Works,* i., 343.
[2] *Ibid.,* i., 14–15 and 375.

portions of power as were conceived necessary for the public welfare.[1]

The application that Wilson made of these principles to the Federal Union leaves little to be desired in completing his conception of its nature. The Federal Union he regarded as a Federal Republic, the vital principle of which he sees set forth in Montesquieu's definition as a form of government " by which several states consent to become citizens of a larger state, which they wish to form. It is a society formed by other societies, which make a new one." [2]

This Federal Republic is not a consolidated government if thereby the destruction of the States is meant—nor a confederacy, a mere alliance of sovereign States, but a union of States so that the individual State governments are retained and a general government is established. " Its own existence, as a government of this description, depends on theirs." [3] " The people of the United States must be considered attentively in two very different views —as forming one nation, great and united; and as forming, at the same time, a number of separate States, to that nation subordinate, but independent as to their own interior government." [4]

That the whole people of the United States was conceived of by Wilson as forming " one nation, great and united," is nowhere more clearly shown than in his discussion of the purely democratic prin-

[1] *Cf. Works*, i., 169.
[2] *Ibid.*, i., 312.
[3] *Ibid.*, ii., 17.
[4] *Ibid.*, ii., 7.

ciples at the basis of the Federal Constitution. The source of all power he saw in the people, a source totally unknown under the Articles of Confederation. The preamble to the Constitution, "We, the people of the United States, do ordain and establish this Constitution," was to Wilson a practical declaration of that principle; we can easily imagine we are listening to Webster when he declares that this preamble was not for show but meant what it said; that the Constitution is not a compact but an ordinance and establishment of the people. "He could not answer for what every member thought, but believed it could not be said they believed they were making a compact; he could discover no trace of compact in the system. Compact requires more parties than one. The Constitution was not founded upon compact but upon the power of the people."

The general principle upon which a dividing line was to be drawn between the State and the national government was clear, though the practical application presented difficulties. Whatever in its nature and operation extended beyond the individual State ought to be comprehended within the Federal jurisdiction. The people of the United States formed one great community, the people of the different States formed communities on a lesser scale. Hence Wilson believed that different proportions of legislative powers should be given to the governments according to the nature, number, and magnitude of their objects. But the "truth is, that, in our governments, the supreme, absolute, and uncontrollable power remains in the people."[1]

[1] *Works*, i., 543.

James Wilson

The further development of these ideas was carried on by Wilson in his service upon the bench of the Supreme Court during a period just short of ten years in length. These were, moreover, the first years of the Court's history—years of doubt and uncertainty regarding the rights and powers of the Court, of struggle to establish the Court on a plane of equality with the Legislative and Executive branches of the government,—but Wilson never faltered in his application of his theories to the actual conditions of government as they arose. Had he lived a few years longer he would without doubt have ranged himself on the side of Marshall in the famous case of Marbury v. Madison, for in his discussion of the relation of the various departments of the government, that portion of his lectures dealing with the power of the court to declare a law unconstitutional is so strikingly like the decision that we are constrained to believe that Marshall had read and was familiar with Wilson's argument.[1]

Not alone in the power of the court to declare a law unconstitutional does Wilson anticipate Marshall. His "argument upon the Bank of North America stands as a constitutional exposition second to no constitutional argument or opinion delivered before or since. Indeed, it not only embraces every ground of argument which Marshall was called upon to tread, but it assumed and defended precisely the position which was necessarily taken in the legal-tender decisions."[2] A single sentence from this remarkable argument, made, to be sure, before the

[1] *Works*, i., 416.
[2] *Ibid.*, i., xv. (Memoir).

adoption of the present Constitution, but even more applicable to it than to the Articles of Confederation, will reveal the clear insight that Wilson possessed into the ultimate nature of the central government and will astonish us by its twentieth-century tone. It is easy to imagine that we are listening to a passage from the judgments in the "insular cases," in which the doctrine of inherent powers has found a recent recognition and expression.

"Whenever," said Wilson, "an object occurs, to the direction of which no particular State is competent, the management of it must, of necessity, belong to the United States in Congress assembled."[1] The Federal state, then, possesses inherent as well as enumerated powers. Where the object involved is beyond the power of the States, and where that power is one ordinarily possessed by sovereign nations, there the United States as a sovereign nation must be supposed to enjoy this power.

Finally it fell to Wilson to participate in the decision of the first great constitutional case to be presented to the Supreme Court, the case of Chisholm v. Georgia.[2] A citizen of another State had sued the State of Georgia in the Supreme Court and the State had refused to recognize the jurisdiction of the Court. Georgia protested vigorously against the indignity of being haled into court like a common debtor. Though the Constitution declared that the jurisdiction of the Supreme Court extended to cases between a State and the citizens of another State, it was contended that the intention of the

[1] *Works*, i., 558.
[2] *United States Supreme Court Reports*, 2 Dallas, 419.

framers of the Constitution was to give jurisdiction in such cases only when the State voluntarily submitted to or invoked the jurisdiction. The States, it was said, were sovereign and to compel a State to submit to the jurisdiction of the Court was to rob it of its sovereignty, to reduce it to a position of inferiority to the Federal Government.

At the outset of his opinion Wilson formulated the question presented to the Court in these terms: " Do the people of the *United States* form a *nation?* " He then considers the question from the three standpoints of general jurisprudence, the law of nations, and the Constitution of the United States, and as a result of each he arrives at an affirmative answer. Though the word sovereign may be unknown to the Constitution, it was because the people, serenely conscious of the fact that they were sovereign, " avoided the ostentatious declaration." " The people of the United States, among them Georgia, ordained and established the present Constitution." " The people of the United States intended to form themselves into a *nation* for *national purposes* "— " *as to the purposes of the Union, therefore, Georgia is not a sovereign State.*" As Judge Cooley has said:

Justice Wilson, the ablest and most learned of the associates, took the national view, and was supported by two others. The Chief Justice was thus enabled to declare the opinion of the court that, under the Constitution of the United States, sovereignty belonged to the people of the United States. . . . It must logically follow that a nation as a sovereignty is possessed of all those powers of independent action and self-protection which the successors of Jay subsequently demonstrated were by implication conferred upon it.[1]

Wilson, like Hamilton, was freed to a great extent by the fact of his foreign birth from local prejudices and State pride. America was the country of his adoption and his patriotism embraced the whole of it; not merely one of the thirteen States but all together claimed his allegiance. From the signing of the Declaration of Independence to his untimely death in 1798, Wilson was an ardent supporter of the idea of a national state. In the Constitutional Convention, in the Pennsylvania State Convention, in his lectures, and upon the bench he labored for its realization. The compromises of the Constitution left that instrument such a compound of conflicting views and opposing tendencies that its real nature became apparent only as it was put into operation. First, the Executive and Legislative branches, under the guidance of Hamilton, rushed forward toward the goal of nationalism but with too great haste; the inevitable reaction brought the triumph of the forces of decentralization in these departments, while the Judiciary, following the lead of Wilson, continued to interpret the Constitution in the broadest national sense.

The kind of a national union desired by Wilson could not be achieved in the face of the opposition of the individual States. He was more national than his generation. The supremacy of the Union was not finally settled till the Civil War. Since then the doctrine of James Wilson has held the field; the

[1] *Constitutional History as Seen in American Law*, pp. 48–49.

sovereignty of the nation and the ultimate powers of the Federal state are ideas that are daily being used to extend the sphere of Federal activity, while ex-President Roosevelt has proclaimed that he could find no better guide for his own political actions than the theories of James Wilson of Pennsylvania.[1]

[1] *Cf.* Alexander, *op. cit.*, p. 1.

IV
Thomas Jefferson. Growth through Acquiescence

THOMAS JEFFERSON

1743.	April 13.	Born at Shadwell, Albemarle Co., Va.
1767.		Admitted to bar.
1769.		Member of House of Burgesses.
1775.		Delegate to Continental Congress at Philadelphia.
1776.	June 11.	Committee to draft Declaration of Independence.
		Resigned.
1779.		Elected Governor.
1780.		Re-elected.
1783–84.		Member of Continental Congress.
1784.		Commissioner to France.
1785–90.		Minister to France.
1790–94.		Secretary of State.
1798.		Wrote Kentucky Resolutions.
1797–1801.		Vice-President.
1801–09.		President.
1803.		Louisiana Purchase.
1806.		Embargo.
1819.		Founded University of Virginia.
1826.	July 4.	Died.

IV

Thomas Jefferson. Growth through Acquiescence

NONE of the statesmen of the Revolutionary period has exerted a greater influence upon the succeeding generations of his countrymen than Jefferson, but his influence has differed from that of all the rest for it has been upon the spirit of the people and their attitude toward their institutions rather than upon the formation of the institutions themselves. As the embodiment of the spirit of democracy, his name is still a potent rallying cry for a multitude of men. It is illustrative of the peculiar character of his influence that men claim him as their political guide whose views bear little or no resemblance to his.

Jefferson's cardinal political principles were trust in the people and an antipathy to government—principles in themselves contradictory. Modern democracy has been more logical, for its trust in the capacity and soundness of the masses has led it to claim for them an ever increasing control over, and a constant enlargement of, the sphere of governmental activities. Jefferson's fear of the tyranny of government has been converted into a demand that government by the people should be government for the people; his anxiety lest it should prove an instrument to deprive them of their liberty has been replaced by the determination to make it serve their interests. As a result we see two processes of political development going hand in hand; the one looking to a steady enlargement of the direct participation of the people in the constitution of governmental agencies, and the other stretching out eagerly for new ways in which the government may serve the general interest. There is no longer the dread that government may prove an engine for the destruction of popular liberties, and herein democracy shows itself more consistent than did Jefferson.

Hamilton, Wilson, and Jefferson present an interesting contrast in their ideas of government and their attitude toward the participation of the people in it. Hamilton believed in a strong government in the hands of the few, because he had no faith in the great mass of mankind [1]; Wilson believed in a strong government because he had this faith and, while agreeing with Hamilton in the value and efficacy of government as an agent in the progress of civilization, insisted that the foundation of all government should rest upon the broad basis of popular consent; thus established it should be invested with a considerable degree of authority that

[1] Hamilton recognized, however, that in a republic, at least, all power must come from the people. "The fabric of American empire ought to rest on the solid basis of the consent of the people. The streams of national power ought to flow immediately from that pure, original fountain of all legitimate authority."—*Federalist*, No. 22.

order and security might result.[1] Jefferson desired as little of government as might be, since to him all government was a limitation upon the freedom of the individuals under it[2]; since he distrusted government as a means of progress, the essence of his belief was *laissez faire*.

Jefferson was a well-to-do country gentleman of Virginia, of a family long established in the State but not numbered among the aristocratic inner circle.[3] Born in 1743, he was graduated from William and Mary College in 1762, studied law under the great master, George Wythe, and was elected a member of the House of Burgesses in 1769. The temper of the colonists toward the Crown showed itself immediately upon the assembling of the Burgesses to which Jefferson had been elected; within three days the Governor dissolved them for passing a set of resolutions "odiously like a Bill of Rights," and eighty-eight of the delegates, among them Jefferson, met the next day in the long room of the Raleigh tavern and framed a non-importation agreement against Great Britain.

At the next meeting of the Burgesses in 1773,

---

[1] *Documentary History of the Constitution*, iii., 28. "He was for raising the federal pyramid to a considerable altitude, and for that reason wished to give it as broad a basis as possible. No government could long subsist without the confidence of the people."

[2] "I am convinced that those societies (as the Indians) which live without government enjoy in their general mass an infinitely greater degree of happiness than those who live under European governments." Quoted in Morse, *Thomas Jefferson*, p. 83.

[3] The more important biographies of Jefferson have been written by Morse, Parton, Randall, Schouler, and Tucker.

Jefferson with some half a dozen bold spirits met privately and determined to establish a committee of correspondence to facilitate the interchange of news among the colonies. The result was that the Burgesses were again dissolved, but nevertheless the committee met on the following day and issued an invitation to the other colonies to appoint similar committees. Again the following year Jefferson was a leader in the House of Burgesses which proclaimed a day of prayer and fasting in behalf of Massachusetts, then suffering on account of the Boston Port Bill; again the Governor dissolved them; again they met in the tavern and passed disloyal resolutions, among them a resolution suggesting an annual general congress of all the colonies, and another calling for a Virginia convention to meet on the first of the following August. Jefferson, though elected a representative from Albemarle, was prevented by illness from attending the State convention. The draft of instructions he hoped would be given by the convention to the delegates elected by it to the general conference proved too radical. They were, however, printed in pamphlet form under the title of *A Summary View of the Rights of British America*, and received wide circulation both in England and America.

Soon afterward Jefferson was appointed a delegate to the Second Continental Congress, in which he took his seat on June 21, 1775, having delayed in Virginia long enough to draw up a reply to the "olive-branch" of Lord North. In the Congress his talents, those of a writer, not a speaker, won recognition, and his draft was the reply accepted and promulgated by Congress to Lord North's "conciliatory proposition." Jefferson unquestionably thought that separation from the mother country was daily approaching, yet "he was too thoughtful not to be a reluctant revolutionist, but for the same reason he was sure to be a determined one." [1]

Events moved rapidly in the years of 1775–6. Paine's *Common Sense* had gone broadcast over the country with its bold plea for independence. Lexington and Concord had been fought, Washington had been appointed commander-in-chief, and Boston had been besieged, when Virginia instructed her delegates to move that Congress should declare "The United Colonies free and independent States." [2] On June 11th, Congress appointed a committee, of which Jefferson was a member, to prepare a Declaration of Independence. The actual task of drawing the document was entrusted by the committee to Jefferson. Such skill did he show in formulating the thoughts in all men's minds, that, save for a few slight changes proposed by Franklin and Adams in the committee, the Declaration stands to-day as Jefferson composed it.[3] That it was in no sense new, Jefferson himself fully recognized. Its object was "not to find out new principles, or arguments, never before thought of, not merely to say things which had never been said before," but "it was intended to be an expression of the American mind." [4]

[1] Morse, p. 26.
[2] On June 7th, Richard Henry Lee of Virginia offered resolutions in Congress declaring the colonies free and independent States.
[3] *Works*, i., 26 *ff*.
[4] *Ibid.*, xvi., 118.

This declaration, the political creed of that and succeeding generations, is too familiar to require extensive notice.[1] Human equality, the natural and inalienable rights of life, liberty, and the pursuit of happiness, the protection of these rights as the function of government, the consent of the governed as the foundation of all just governments, and the ultimate right of revolution when government fails to perform its functions, are the fundamental principles embraced in it. They are also the basic principles of all Jefferson's subsequent political thinking.

Though re-elected to Congress on June 20, 1776, Jefferson declined to serve, believing, as he later said, that he could be of more use in forwarding the work of remodelling the social and political fabric of his native State, for with the sundering of the ties of allegiance to the mother country, it became necessary "to lay aside the monarchical, and take up the republican, government," which, in a letter to Franklin in 1777, he declared the State of Virginia had done "with as much ease as would have attended their throwing off an old and putting on a new suit of clothes."

It was a period of revolution, of destruction and re-creation, and the people were ripe for social and political changes. There was little need of change in most of the New England States; how little, is evidenced by the continuation of the old colonial charters of Connecticut and Rhode Island as their State constitutions until well into the nineteenth century. In Virginia there was need of more radical change before the life of the State and its

[1] *Cf.* the Appendix for the text.

political and legal institutions could rest upon a democratic basis. Within her borders had been developed the nearest approach to an aristocracy to be found anywhere upon this side of the Atlantic. Her great estates, descending by entail and primogeniture and supported by slavery, had tended to develop a landed gentry, an aristocracy of birth and wealth, which had been also in large measure a political aristocracy, for the political power of the colony had been to a great extent in their hands. Jefferson was not by birth a member of the inner circle of this class; he was, furthermore, by nature a radical and a reformer, and he was not slow to take advantage of the disturbed political conditions to put into execution his democratic beliefs.

Elected a member of the House of Delegates, he began at once the work of reform, and just a week after he took his seat on October 11, 1776, he brought in a bill abolishing the whole system of entail, and almost without a struggle the basis of the pseudo-aristocracy was swept away. Primogeniture soon met with a like fate. "At least," implored Pendleton, "if the eldest son may no longer inherit all the lands and slaves of his father, let him take a double share." "No," said Jefferson, the leveller, "not till he can eat a double allowance of food and do a double allowance of work."

His next attack was upon the established church. He desired complete religious freedom, but the most he could accomplish was to induce the legislature, the majority of whom were churchmen, to take the first steps in that direction. But his efforts were not in vain, for the spirit that he typified grew in strength till in 1786 his original "bill for establishing religious freedom" was passed with only slight amendments. His elaborate plan for a school system met with too decided an opposition from the rich planters ever to be wholly adopted, but education was one of his cardinal principles, and to his untiring interest in its promotion, the University of Virginia ever stands as a noble witness.

Jefferson was also appointed a member of a commission to effect a general revision of all the laws of Virginia. A civil and a criminal code were soon drawn up, the latter noted for its abolition of the severe penalties of the previous law. Much of this work was too democratic to meet with immediate approval and adoption, but the next ten years saw the realization of practically all of his measures. His proposals formed a sort of reservoir from which succeeding legislatures drew.

Only in the matter of slavery did Jefferson meet with entire defeat. He was always an opponent of slavery, but the commission could only report a "mere digest of the existing laws," hoping by amendment, when the bill should be proposed, to secure freedom to those born after a certain day. He felt that the negro was by nature inferior to the white in mental capacity, and that "the two races, equally free, cannot live in the same government," and that the attempt could only result in the extinction of one race or the other. Such a view led him to prepare a scheme of colonization, visionary and costly beyond the possibility of fulfilment.[1]

---

[1] For a detailed account of Jefferson's services in the House of Burgesses at this time, see Morse, pp. 36–50.

The reforms, both actual and potential, during his two years of membership in the Legislature, must always be reckoned among Jefferson's most lasting and brilliant achievements. He did not accomplish them alone and single-handed. He was the leader around whom was gathered a group of brilliant young men, among them Madison, for so large a part of his life Jefferson's devoted follower. Jefferson caught up the spirit of the people and gave it expression almost before they became conscious of their own desires. His abiding faith in the multitude, in the great mass of the people, in the correctness of their judgment and the justness of their cause, was the secret of his success as the greatest political leader this country has produced. But it was a leadership with, not against, a rising tide of popular desire. One cannot well imagine Jefferson standing alone in the maintenance of convictions opposed to the popular will.[1]

In 1779 Jefferson was elected Governor of Virginia to succeed Patrick Henry, and for two years filled the office with little credit to his reputation. They were years of sore trial for the State, which suffered from repeated inroads and invasions by the British. Jefferson was pre-eminently a lover of peace, and as war-governor he found himself in a situation with which his inclinations and abilities did not fit him to cope, and at the close of his second term he retired with a heart filled with bitterness and resentment and with the express intention of withdrawing forever from public life. For three

[1] Oliver, 267. Book iv., chap. i., pp. 251–270, contains an extremely clever analysis of Jefferson's character.

years he devoted himself to his private interests. At the end of this time he was recalled from his retirement by an election to Congress in 1783, where he had the pleasure of signing the treaty with Great Britain which recognized the Independence he had been instrumental in proclaiming seven years before. It fell to his lot, also, to hand over to Congress Virginia's deed to the Northwest Territory and to prepare for it a plan of government in which slavery was to be forever prohibited after the year 1800.

In 1784 Jefferson retired from Congress and almost immediately was appointed to aid Franklin and Adams in the negotiation of commercial treaties, and in the following year was made sole Minister to France where he remained until 1790.

These years of foreign residence were years of tremendous importance for France and for America. In France they witnessed the brewing and breaking of the storm of revolution which was destined to sweep away all remnants of the old order of despotism, to run through the mad follies of the Reign of Terror, to degenerate into brutal and unbridled license, and to give way finally to a military despotism.

In America they beheld what seemed to be a fruitless effort to reap the rewards of a revolution already successfully accomplished; beheld a jealousy and distrust of government that boded ill for the success of liberty; then saw a reaction set in against what, to sober minds, seemed not far removed from anarchy, and heard no little talk of the failure of republican institutions and the need of the strength and order of a monarchy. Truly Liberty seemed in a perilous plight! That it was saved both from monarchy and disintegration was due to the wise counsels and patriotic efforts of the men of the Convention, who were willing to sacrifice personal preferences to the general good, and who were not afraid of the spirit of compromise.

No Frenchman could have been more interested in the success of the Revolution in France than was Jefferson, and no one had better opportunities of observing its progress than he. The French found in him a kindred spirit, and took him into their counsels. He had been a leader in the revolutionary movement in his own country, and had proclaimed the equality of mankind in the Declaration of Independence. Little wonder, then, that he sympathized with the French people in their efforts against government, or that "they recognized him as one of themselves, a speculative thinker concerning the rights of mankind, a preacher of extreme doctrines of political freedom, a deviser of theories of government, a propounder of vague but imposing generalizations, a condemner of the fetters of practicability—in a word, by the slang of that day, a 'philosopher'; and they liked him accordingly."[1]

It did not take such experiences to make of Jefferson a radical in matters of government; they only served to strengthen and confirm opinions already existing, for a radical he was by nature. So it is not to be wondered at that a man, who, almost while the Convention was in session at Philadelphia, could say that rebellion "is a medicine necessary for the sound health of government," and "God forbid we should

[1] Morse, p. 77.

ever be twenty years without such a rebellion" (as Shays's),[1] should, when the Constitution was published, have said that there were in it "things which stagger all my dispositions to subscribe to what such an Assembly has proposed."[2]

Cut off for five years by his mission to France from anything like close association with America, he knew it only as it was during the fervor of the revolutionary struggle, when mutual interests and the common need of defence held the colonists together; he lacked personal experience of the slackening of the bonds of union, of the dangers and distress resulting to the government of the Confederation, of its utter inadequacy and failure. Missing the full significance of the years of the "Critical Period," untouched by the keen struggle within the Convention itself, with an antipathy to all strong governments, his first criticisms of the Constitution were indeed severe, but upon further consideration and under the influence of the arguments of men like Madison and Monroe, he came to view it as did many others, as the best that could be secured under the circumstances and as worthy of adoption for the good it brought, hoping that a favorable moment would come for correcting what was amiss in it.[3] In the end his chief objections to it lay in the absence of a Bill of Rights and in the re-eligibility of the President. The first was soon removed by the adoption of the first ten amendments which the advocates of the Constitution did not

[1] *Works*, vi., 372.
[2] *Ibid.*, vi., 370.
[3] *Ibid.*, vi., 392.

oppose so much in theory as on the ground that they were unnecessary, now that a republican form of government was to be set up in which the rights of the people could only be encroached upon by their own representatives. Jefferson's zeal for such a declaration would seem to be but another manifestation of that visionary element in his nature which delighted in vague generalizations and high-sounding phrases, the futility of which was never apparent to him.[1]

The second objection has been practically removed by the custom, inaugurated by Washington and followed by succeeding Presidents, of limiting the holding of the office to two terms.

Immediately upon his return from France, Jefferson was appointed by Washington the Secretary of State. The new government had been established nearly a year when he arrived in New York on March 21, 1790. Hamilton had already secured the passage of the bills for the assumption of the public debt, both foreign and domestic, but his third measure providing for the assumption by the new government of the debts contracted in the war by the individual States had met with defeat by a narrow margin in the House of Representatives. Then was enacted that first bit of "log-rolling" by which Hamilton agreed to turn over enough Northern votes to secure the location of the national capital upon the Potomac and Jefferson enough Southern votes to ensure the passage of the third assumption bill. It was a transaction that Jefferson soon came bitterly to regret, and for his part in it could offer no better

[1] Oliver, *op. cit.*, p. 258.

excuse than to impugn his own political wisdom by declaring he had been duped by Hamilton. The truth would seem to be that Jefferson did not appreciate at the time the full significance of Hamilton's financial measures in strengthening the powers of the Federal Government. Such a view seems all the more credible when we reflect that Jefferson was hopelessly unable to understand the financial policy of Hamilton and as late as 1818 spoke of it as a "puzzle."

The opposition between the two men was not slow in developing. It could not have been otherwise. They were essentially different in every characteristic of mind and taste. Hamilton, young, daring, and impetuous, ready of tongue and pen, matchless as debater and controversialist, an ardent advocate of order and strength in government, credited with a strong taste for monarchy and an equally strong distrust of republican institutions and the judgments of the people; an aristocrat in temper and bearing, with an aristocrat's fine imperiousness and hardly concealed contempt for the common herd: Jefferson, middle-aged, slow, and cautious, a compound of dreamer and political seer, skilled likewise in writing but lacking in the art of speech, with a natural bent toward peace and a dislike of open combat so strong that his enemies called him sly; a hater of all governments, with an earnest desire to have as little of the evil as possible; a radical, a revolutionist, an ultra-democrat, for whom an abiding faith in the masses served almost for a religious creed; an unrivalled organizer and leader, knowing how to guide and direct without seeming to command.

It was inevitable that these two should differ, almost that they should typify the contending forces of all our national life.

Hamilton struck out boldly in the direction in which he had foreseen lay the only hope of safety for the new government. While the machinery of it was new and untried, when none could tell with certainty whether the various parts, not made altogether to anybody's liking, would work in harmony when once the motive power was applied, and while many doubted if it could be made to go at all, he saw with a statesman's eye that money was the universal solvent of most, if not all, the difficulties; it would serve as fuel for the engine and lubricant for the creaking joints to render workable the patchwork of the Convention. He set out, therefore, to enlist men's interest until their patriotism could be awakened, and, almost before it was realized, he had started the new government along the road to fame and fortune by that masterly series of financial measures that culminated in the establishment of a National Bank. Jefferson, as we have seen, did not at first appreciate the full significance of these successive steps, but once aroused, his suspicions far outran what the facts would justify; his imagination saw countless dangers in this financial " puzzle " which he could not understand, and his fears so far got the better of his judgment as to lead him to see, in all that Hamilton was doing, the deep-laid plots of a " monarchist "; he professed to believe that Hamilton was bent on subverting republican institutions by the aid of a " corrupt squadron " in the Legislature, bound to him by the financial favors they had secured through his financial measures.[1]

Genuinely alarmed for the safety of all his ideas of government, Jefferson set to work to hinder and thwart Hamilton in every way he could. To stop this mad career of the government on its road to monarchy was his first object; that accomplished, it would then be time to set about undoing what had already been done.

To accomplish these purposes Jefferson bent all his talents of organization and all the resourcefulness of his versatile mind, but it was a task of herculean difficulty that confronted him. As an opponent, he had a man of consummate ability and courage, without a match in an open debate or a written discussion, the head of a party composed of a large part of the wealth and culture of the nation —a party devoted to its leader and his principles, a party upon which it was generally known that Washington looked with sympathy and which enjoyed in consequence the prestige of his great name. But Jefferson was not daunted by the prospect of such an overwhelming opposition; the nucleus of a party was ready to hand, composed of all those elements in any way discontented with the course of the Federalists or with their leader; and these were not a few, for Hamilton made bitter enemies as well as staunch friends, and his policies excited fear in other minds than that of Jefferson. It was not the work of a day or of a year to consolidate these elements and to gather to them the great mass of the people; no one knew this better than Jefferson, and no one with less confidence in the ultimate triumph of the

[1] *Cf.* Morse, *op. cit.*, p. 100 *ff.*

masses of the people would have had the courage to lead the fight. Though it might be long in coming, Jefferson foresaw the final victory of mere numbers if only they could be brought to act in harmony, and trusting to his own ability to furnish the organization necessary to produce harmonious action, he could patiently await the day of victory.

That his triumph came so soon was largely due to the sudden shifting of popular interest from domestic to foreign affairs. The wave of popular enthusiasm for Republican France threatened to become tidal in its force, and destructive of that admirable position of neutrality so heartily desired by Washington. Jefferson was thoroughly in sympathy with the efforts of the French people and was not to be discouraged by the foolhardy conduct of a Genêt on this side, or the wild excesses of the Reign of Terror, or the pusillanimity of the Directory, on the other side of the Atlantic, though he was shrewd enough to abstain from countenancing them, that when the reaction came as a result of offended national dignity, he was able quietly to step aside only to reappear later as all the greater leader because he had foreseen and even predicted these very results.

It was trouble with France which gave rise to the now famous Alien and Sedition Acts, and the no less famous Virginia and Kentucky Resolutions of 1798 and 1799. In their desperation at the malignant assaults made upon President John Adams, and the almost unbridled license of the Republican press in its abuse of their principles, the Federalists were goaded into passing these laws, putting into the hands of the Chief Executive such great powers over individual liberty and containing such unwarranted infringements of the right of free speech that the country over, a loud and angry cry arose against their unconstitutionality. Jefferson and the Democratic-Republican party eagerly seized the opportunity to fasten the odium of it upon the Federalists.

This, however, was not sufficient for Jefferson; even the bounds of "loose" construction had been exceeded and the integrity of the Constitution was at stake. To bring this home to the people of the individual States, to secure their co-operation in putting a check upon the unwarranted exercise of power by the Federal Government, and in doing so to give expression at the same time to his fundamental notion that it was merely a league of States, a "voluntary confederation," in which the States retained their sovereign right of ultimate judgment in all matters affecting their reserved rights, Jefferson chose the medium of the State Legislatures of Virginia and Kentucky. With his own hand he prepared the resolutions he wished presented to, and adopted by, the Kentucky Legislature, while to his devoted friend and follower, Madison, was deputed the like task for the Legislature of Virginia.[1]

Hot-headed Kentucky, however, was not yet ready to go the full length proposed by Jefferson, and in the Resolutions of 1798 contented itself with declaring that the Constitution was a compact to which the States were parties; that by it they had established a government of definite and limited powers, reserving to themselves or to the people all other powers; that every assumption by the general gov-

[1] *Cf.* G. Hunt, *Life of James Madison*, p. 251.

ernment of undelegated powers was null and void, and that each State as a party to the compact had a right "to judge for itself, as well of infractions as of the mode and measure of redress." The Alien and Sedition laws were emphatically declared to be "altogether void and of no force" and the other States were called upon to join her in securing measures of redress.

In his original draft, Jefferson had asserted that "where powers are assumed which have not been delegated, a nullification of the act is the rightful remedy; that every State has a natural right in cases not within the compact, (*casus non foederis*), to nullify of their own authority all assumptions of power by others within their limits," and in a second set of Resolutions, passed in the following November (1799), the Legislature of Kentucky, acting upon this suggestion, made an alarming addition to its previous Resolutions, when it declared "that the principle and construction ... that the general government is the exclusive judge of the extent of the powers delegated to it, stop not short of *despotism,* since the discretion of those who administer the government, and not the *Constitution,* would be the measure of their powers: That the several States who formed that instrument, being sovereign and independent, have the unquestionable right to judge of the infraction; and, *That a nullification, by those sovereignties of all unauthorized acts done under color of that instrument, is the rightful remedy."* [1]

The nullification of an act of the Federal Govern-

[1] *Cf.* Appendix for text of the Virginia and Kentucky Resolutions.

ment by a single State perhaps went further than Jefferson had really intended. Certain it is that late in life he took a different view. " The ultimate arbiter," he said, " is the people of the Union, assembled by their deputies in convention at the call of Congress, or of two thirds of the States." And Madison was at great pains to show that it was not a " constitutional," but a " natural " right,—that of revolution,—which was meant by both the Virginia and Kentucky Resolutions.[1]

The triumph of Jefferson in the election of 1800 did not bring the overthrow of the measures which had given strength to the government. There was, to be sure, some attempt made in the earlier years to lessen the expenses of the central government, and the army and navy underwent what Jefferson himself called a " chaste reformation "; but Hamilton had correctly estimated Jefferson's character and course when he wrote to Bayard that " he [Jefferson] is as likely as any man I know to temporise, to calculate what will be likely to promote his own reputation and advantage; and the probable result of such a temper is the preservation of systems, though originally opposed to them, which, being once established, could not be overthrown without danger to the person who did it." [2] External reforms there were, but not a single limitation of dangerous powers or curtailment of latent strength. In the purchase of Louisiana, moreover, the doctrine of " strict construction " received an irremediable hurt. Jefferson

[1] *Letters and Other Writings of James Madison*, vol. iv., *passim*.
[2] *Works*, x., 413.

acknowledged that "the executive, in seizing the fugitive occurrence which so much advances the good of their country, has done an act beyond the Constitution. The legislature . . . must ratify and pay for it, and throw themselves on their country" for an act of indemnity.[1] He drew up an amendment to the Constitution to cover the case and urged his friends not to make the Constitution a "blank paper by construction"[2]; but his party skipped lightly over the constitutionality of the acquisition, the amendment was not pressed, and Jefferson acquiesced.[3]

Strange conduct this for a man who believed the Constitution was a compact entered into by sovereign States for the attainment of certain specific objects, and that any measure likely to change the fixed relationships thus established must be agreed to by all the parties. Little reverence had he for the security furnished by "the possession of a written constitution," when the provisions of that constitution stood in the way of accomplishing purposes he desired! Not all the Federalist stretches of constitutional provisions in the twelve years of their power could surpass this one in importance, and Jefferson, as the leader of the Democratic-Republican party, must share in the responsibility for it. In the course of his two administrations, the Democratic-Republican party performed successfully the larger part of the feat of swallowing the Federalist party and its principles. His futile efforts

[1] *Works*, x., 411.
[2] *Ibid.*, x., 419.
[3] *Ibid.*, x., 420. "If, however, our friends shall think **differently**, certainly I shall acquiesce with satisfaction."

to maintain our rights against England and France were carried through Congress without question, and the Embargo, with its Enforcing Acts, surpassed the Alien and Sedition Laws in their encroachments upon individual liberty.

Jefferson's later years were spent in the retirement of Monticello, whither the country turned again and again for words of wisdom from the "Sage." He beheld the great triumph of Democracy, but with it the growth of a truly national sentiment, coincident with an ever increasing power in the hands of the national government. His success was in his faith, not in his works. From the standpoint of actual achievement in national affairs, only the Louisiana Purchase saves him from complete failure; from the standpoint of political influence his faith in the people makes him a vital force to-day. His greatest fault was that " he died, as he had lived, in the odour of phrases "[1]; his greatest virtue that he was wise enough to sacrifice phrases to reality, to accept in practice what he rejected in theory.

[1] Oliver, p. 256.

V

James Madison. Growth through Formulation

JAMES MADISON

1751. March 16.	Born in King George County, Va.
1771.	Graduated from College of New Jersey.
1774.	Member of Committee of Safety from Orange County.
1776.	Delegate to State Convention.
1780.	Delegate to Continental Congress.
1784–86.	Representative in State Legislature.
1786.	Represented Virginia at Annapolis Convention.
1786–88.	Delegate to Continental Congress.
1787	Member of Constitutional Convention.
1789–97.	Member of Congress and leader of Republican Party.
1798.	Author of Virginia Resolutions.
1801–09.	Secretary of State.
1809–1817.	President.
1812–14.	War. (June 18, 1812–Dec. 24, 1814.)
1829.	Member of Virginia Constitutional Convention.
1836. June 28.	Died at Montpelier, Va.

V

James Madison. Growth through Formulation

MADISON has often been called the "Father of the Constitution" and the title is well-bestowed, for no man saw more clearly than he the weakness of the Confederation and the need for a stronger Union; no one strove more diligently or successfully to secure the Annapolis, and later the Constitutional, Convention; no one in the Federal Convention was more influential in determining the form the new constitution should take; no one was more valiant in defence of the work of their hands, and no one was more skilful in securing its adoption; not alone in the convention of his native State, but, through the *Federalist,* in those of other States, his influence in favor of ratification was strong.

When the work of formulation and adoption was over, only the first step toward national Union had been taken; in it Madison played a principal part; in the second step of administering the new government that had been formed, in bringing into operation national forces, Madison appears as leader of the opposition in Congress, and there arose a bitter personal and political animosity to Hamilton and to all of his measures that tended toward a strong Federal Government.[1]

In the Constitutional Convention and in the State conventions for adopting the Constitution, parties divided on the question of the kind of government to be instituted, on the question whether it should be a loose confederation of sovereign States or a Federal Government, national in its purposes and extent and supreme within its sphere. After the adoption of the Constitution the question that divides them is not one of kind, but of extent. How far has this national government been entrusted with powers by the Constitution?

On the question of the interpretation of the Constitution, Madison followed the lead of Jefferson rather than that of Hamilton and ranked himself under the banner of "strict construction." To his old friends the change appeared a desertion from motives of political preferment. Though motives of policy and personal friendship for Jefferson had their weight, a deeper motive must be sought. It will be found in the real difference between the States, which Madison repeatedly declared was not between the large and the small States, but between the North and the South, between commerce and agriculture, between free and slave, and Madison followed Virginia and the South.[2]

As President, Madison carried out the policies of Jefferson till forced into an unwelcome party war

[1] S. W. Gay, *James Madison*, p. 144 *ff*.
[2] *Ibid.*, p. 164. "The institution of slavery and its consequences formed the line of discrimination."

James Madison

in violation of his personal feelings and of his political faith. The results of the war did more to strengthen the bond of union and sense of national feeling than any previous event in the country's history, and Madison thereby became the unconscious agent of the centralizing forces to which he was so ardently opposed. The later years of his life were spent in trying to teach his countrymen the true exposition of the Constitution, but his words fell upon the ears of unresponsive, though deferential, hearers.

For more than forty years Madison filled, almost without interruption, some public office, but his talents were not always of the sort that fitted him for the performance of the duties of the position to which he was called. His career falls naturally into the three periods of legislative activity, executive functions, and retirement devoted to exposition. The first closed with his retirement from the Virginia Assembly in 1800, the second with the conclusion of his second term as President in 1817, and the third with his death in 1836.

Born of a well-to-do Virginia family in 1751, graduated from the College of New Jersey at Princeton in 1771, Madison entered upon a career of political life with more than the average social and intellectual equipment.[1] Almost immediately upon his return from college, where he had lingered for an additional year of study, he was made a member of the "Committee of Safety" of his native county of Orange. Two years later he was a delegate to the State convention which instructed its representatives in the Continental Congress to propose a Declaration

[1] Biographies by Rives, Gay, and Hunt.

of the Independence of the colonies. The convention then proceeded to draw up a Bill of Rights and a constitution; Madison was appointed a member of the committee on the constitution and at the age of twenty-three made his first attempt at formulating an instrument of government. To him is to be attributed the authorship of the clause in the Bill of Rights declaring that "all men are equally entitled to the free exercise of religion according to the dictates of conscience." [1]

In 1780 we find him making his entrance into national affairs—if such they could be called—as a delegate to the Continental Congress, where he soon became chairman of the Committee on Foreign Relations; he opposed vigorously the proposed cession of the Mississippi valley to Spain in return for an alliance, and only under protest would he instruct Jay to this effect; when the surrender of Cornwallis made the recall of the instructions possible, he lost no time in doing so. Already he caught some glimpse of the future of the United States; already there was dimly conscious to his mind some vision of the great nation that should go sweeping to the Pacific, and from this time until the Constitution was adopted there was no stauncher advocate than he of the establishment of a union with a strong central government;—a union and a government strong enough to enable the people to enter into the great heritage of the West, as well as of the East.

Like most of the thoughtful men of the day, Madison saw that the weakness of the Confederation was rooted in its powerlessness to raise money; the lack

[1] Gay, *op. cit.*, p. 16.

of money in this case was the root of all evil, for, as he said, that lack " is the source of all our public difficulties and misfortunes."[1] He persistently urged upon Congress and the States the adoption of adequate revenue measures. The Articles of Confederation provided that the expenses of the war should be borne by the States in proportion to the value of their lands. Upon a proposal to amend this provision and to substitute population for lands, the question immediately arose whether the slaves should be counted in the enumeration; after much heated discussion and sharp divergence between the Northern and the Southern States, Madison proposed " in order to give a proof of the sincerity of his professions of liberality, that slaves should be rated as five to three."[2] The proposal was adopted and became the precedent for the action of the Federal Convention four years later in the compromise on representation.

Madison was a leading spirit in the movement that led up step by step to the calling of the Constitutional Convention. He first suggested to Jefferson, then a delegate in Congress, the " anomalous condition of things on the Potomac," and proposed a conference with the Maryland delegates upon the subject. They received Jefferson's suggestion for a commission favorably and the Legislature of the State appointed it, but when the commissioners met with those from Virginia they found themselves unable to settle all the questions involved. Pennsylvania and Delaware had interests in any commercial

[1] *Writings*, ed. by Gaillard Hunt, vi., 93.
[2] Gay, *op. cit.*, p. 41.

regulations for the river and it was determined by the Legislature of Maryland, upon consideration of the report of the commissioners, to widen the scope of action and an invitation was issued to all the States to send delegates to a convention at Annapolis. Madison, in the Virginia Legislature, secured the appointment of commissioners from the State. The story of how the Annapolis Convention led to the calling of the Convention at Philadelphia has already been told.[1]

Among the distinguished delegates from Virginia Madison's name ranks next to that of Washington. Feeling the tremendous importance of the issue at stake, he set about to fit himself as fully as possible for the high task by mastering the history of confederacies and federal arrangements, both ancient and modern, and after the Convention had begun its deliberations, with almost incredible assiduity, he made notes of the debates while they were in progress; these he subsequently transcribed at length, thus furnishing us with an invaluable record of the struggle that raged round the forming of the Constitution and leaving a priceless commentary on the character and talents of the members.[2]

Madison, in conference with the other delegates from Virginia, drew up in advance the outline of a government which Randolph submitted to the Convention and which became known as the "Virginia plan."[3] This plan provided for a radical change in the nature of the Union, the change from a mere

[1] Cf. Chap. I.

[2] *Writings*, vols. iii. and iv. "Journal of the Constitutional Convention." Found also in Elliot's *Debates*, vol. v., and in the *Documentary History of the Constitution*, vol. iii.

[3] *Writings*, iii., 17 ff, and *Doc. Hist.*, iii., 17 ff.

league of discordant states to a national state, exercising its authority directly and, within its sphere, supremely over the individuals composing it.

Madison believed it essential, if the Union was to be preserved, that there should be a change from the basis of the old Confederation: its foundation was laid in fundamental error and a return to first principles was necessary; its defects were radical and unalterable so long as the Union remained a mere confederacy.[1] The chief faults of the Confederation were three in number: first, that it attempted to exercise authority over the States in their corporate capacity without reaching the individuals who composed them; second, that each State had an equal voice in the deliberative council of the Union; third, that it lacked the sanction of the authority of the people for its laws. So long as these defects remained, there could be no hope of strength or unity of action in the government; but Madison was far from desiring a consolidation of the States which would destroy their identity and individuality. Like Wilson, he desired a confederated republic, "an association of two or more states into one state," —a "form of government by which several smaller states agreed to become members of a larger one, which they intend to form." Yet Madison never seemed to grasp with the same precision and clearness as Wilson, the idea of a new state thus formed, composed of the individuals of all the States. There is lacking any clear-cut conception of the whole people, united by the Constitution into a single state,

---

[1] *Writings*, iii., 200 *ff*, and *Doc. Hist.*, iii., 151 *ff*.

irrespective of the existence of the State governments, for the purposes for which it was established.

Wilson had said that, " in considering the national government and its purposes, the State governments were to be regarded as non-existent."[1] To such a conception as this Madison never attained. For him the national government is always a compound form, partaking both of a national and a federal character. " In its foundation it is federal, not national; in the sources from which the ordinary powers of the government are drawn, it is partly federal and partly national; in the operation of these powers, it is national, not federal; in the extent of them, again, it is federal, not national; and, finally, in the authoritative mode of introducing amendments, it is neither wholly federal nor wholly national."[2] Though Madison declared the Constitution to be the supreme law of the land, though he denied that it was a treaty, dependent on the good faith of the individual States, and though he maintained that the national government is the judge of its own powers, and that if it oversteps its bounds the people are to judge and to institute correction, yet the States as sovereignties and their governments subtended a far larger angle in his horizon than in that of Wilson or Hamilton.

This became evident in the first Congress, in which Madison was a representative from Virginia. Despite the extent of his labors in the Constitutional Convention to secure strength for the new government; despite the vigor of his advocacy of its adop-

[1] *Writings*, iii., 279, and *Doc. Hist.*, iii., 209.
[2] *Federalist*, Ford's edition, No. 39.

tion, both in the *Federalist* and in the Virginia Convention, when once the Constitution was adopted and the new Federal Government set in motion, Madison found himself immediately in opposition to Hamilton and his financial measures. The great difficulty that had confronted the members of the Constitutional Convention had been to secure even a minimum of strength for the central government; to accomplish this end Madison labored with a zeal and ardor of expression which it is difficult to reconcile with his later and more cautious views. As the new government which had been wrought out with such infinite toil and solicitude, which seemed so new and weak in comparison with the great States of Virginia and Massachusetts, grew in a single night under the magic spell of Hamilton's financial measures and constitutional doctrines, Madison drew back before the work of his own hands and, as a member of Congress, sought to stem the rising tide of federal greatness that seemed to him to threaten with extinction the States, the basis of the Union.[1] He could no longer follow Hamilton and an old political and personal friendship was broken; a new association with Jefferson and the strict constructionists was formed. But Madison could never break away altogether from old traditions and association; he could never become the radical democrat and extremist in regard to the limitation of the powers of all governments, and of the Federal Government in particular, that Jefferson was.

The success of the Federalist party and the intemperate abuse of the Democratic-Republicans com-

[1] Gay, *op. cit.*, p. 144 *ff*.

bined to drive the former party to pass those extreme measures, the Alien and Sedition Acts of 1798. They were the culminating points in the long series of measures by which the power of the central government had been increased since Hamilton had first introduced his financial measures nearly ten years before. They proved to be the final straw that broke the supremacy of the Federalist party. Threatening as they did the rights of individual liberty, as well as conferring undue power upon the Executive, they were far more influential as the end of a series of aggressions than they could ever have been had they stood alone. They went further than the good sense of the people deemed wise, and after their passage nothing could have stayed the doom of the Federalist party.

The opponents of the measures and of the party that had fathered them, everywhere raised the cry that the acts were unconstitutional. No one assailed the measures more vigorously, or more covertly, than Jefferson, whose position as Vice-President made it inexpedient for him to come out openly as the leader of the opposition, and whose disposition always led him to fight through others. Jefferson, however, was the recognized leader of the Democratic-Republican party, and it was well understood that anything done by the party or its more prominent representatives was done either at his instigation or with his acquiescence.

On this occasion action was taken at the instigation of Jefferson in the form of the Kentucky and Virginia Resolutions of 1798; a draft for the former was made by Jefferson with his own hand, but it was somewhat modified before adoption by the Legislature. The Virginia Resolutions were drawn up by Madison after consultation with Jefferson, and are worth a detailed consideration, both from their importance at the time and from the later significance attached to them upon the proposal of the doctrine of Nullification.[1]

It must be borne in mind that at this time the right of the Supreme Court to declare a law unconstitutional had not been determined; it was an open question about which different views were held; the existence of the right in any part of the machinery of the dual form of government, and its location in the event it did exist, were alike unsettled. Though the authors of the *Federalist* had maintained the existence of such a power and had ascribed it to the Supreme Court,[2] yet the Constitution itself said not a word on the subject, and it took the wonderful cogency of Marshall's logic in the famous case of Marbury *v.* Madison in 1803, to present in an irrefutable manner this function as indispensably lodged in the Supreme Court, and, by inference, in the other courts.[3] If such were not the case, then all the labor of constitution-makers in State and nation to raise the instrument of government above the plane of ordinary laws had been in vain; all their efforts to give an added permanence and stability to the fundamental law were futile; the assertion contained in the Constitution itself that it was the supreme law of the land was utterly false, and

---

[1] *Cf.* Appendix for the Resolutions.
[2] *Cf. Federalist,* Nos. 44 and 78.
[3] *U. S. Supreme Court Reports,* 1 Cranch 137.

the new experiment in government made by the United States was doomed to failure.

It was the third of the Virginia Resolutions that the Nullifiers seized upon more than thirty years later, and that caused Madison many weary hours of explanation in seeking to free Jefferson and himself from the charge of being the authors of the new doctrine.[1] After declaring that the powers of the Federal Government were the result of a compact to which the States were parties, that these powers were no further valid than they are authorized by the grants enumerated in that compact, this resolution closed with the assertion

That, in case of a deliberate, palpable, and dangerous exercise of other powers not granted by the said compact, the States, who are the parties thereto, have the right and are in duty bound, to interpose for arresting the progress of the evil, and for maintaining within their respective limits the authorities, rights, and liberties appertaining to them.

At first glance it seems not unreasonable to credit Madison and the Virginia Resolutions of 1798 with propounding a doctrine which approaches perilously near Nullification. Madison's explanation, given in 1829, of what was meant by this third resolution of 1798, may be regarded as his final conception of the nature of the Union, and is best understood in connection with his general views upon the question of government. That civil society, or the state, was the result of contract among the individual members was

[1] *Cf. Letters and other Writings of James Madison,* vol. iv., p. 229.

an idea common to Madison as to all the political philosophers of the age; from the days when he was writing for the *Federalist* to the time of his latest utterance he regarded the social compact as the basis of all political and social life. By it the consent of all was replaced by the consent of the majority and from it came all power in a free government. The Constitution of the United States he held to be of a double character; it is at one and the same time both the original social compact, that admittedly lay at the basis of all civil society, and the compact by which the people in the social state agreed to a government over them.[1] This latter compact it is which is between the individuals as embodied in the States, hence no State can release itself at will from the compact. "The real parties to the constitutional compact of the United States," said Madison, "are the *States*—that is, the people thereof respectively in their sovereign character, and they *alone*."[2] Madison differed radically from the Nullifiers and, later, the Secessionists: he denied that the parties to the compact are the States in their organized capacity, or that the Union is a league or the Constitution is a treaty. "States have no more right to break away than have cities within a State." The Constitution "is a compact among the States in their highest sovereign capacity, and constituting the people thereof one people for certain purposes, it cannot be altered or annulled at the will of the States individually." Madison is careful to point out that in the Virginia Resolutions the plural "States" is used

[1] *Letters*, etc., iv., 63.
[2] *Ibid.*, iv., 18.

and to deny to the individual "State" the right to nullify a law of the Federal Government. "Virginia," he declared, "asserted that the States, as parties to the constitutional compact, had a right and were bound, in extreme cases only, and after a failure of all efforts for redress under the forms of the Constitution, to interpose in their sovereign capacity for the purpose of arresting the evil of usurpation and preserving the Constitution and the Union," while "the doctrine of the present day in South Carolina asserts, that in a case of not greater magnitude than the degree of inequality in the operation of a tariff in favor of manufactures, she may of herself finally decide, by virtue of her sovereignty, that the Constitution has been violated; and that if not yielded to by the Federal Government, though supported by all the other States, she may rightfully resist it and withdraw herself from the Union."[1]

According to the doctrine of 1798, ours is a "*constitutional union*"; "the error," said Madison, in writing to Edward Livingston in 1830, "in the comments on the Virginia proceedings has arisen from a failure to distinguish between what is declaratory of opinion and what is *ipso facto* executory; between the right of *the parties* to the Constitution and of a *single* party; and between resorts within the purview of the Constitution and the *ultima ratio* which appeals from a Constitution, cancelled by its abuses, to original rights paramount to all constitutions."[2]

In short, the Virginia Resolutions, as interpreted by Madison in 1830, recognized the right of revolu-

[1] *Letters*, etc., iv., 44.
[2] *Ibid.*, iv., 80.

tion, which the Nullifiers were attempting to erect into a constitutional right. As he said in his famous letter to Edward Everett, in the same year:

In the event of a failure of every constitutional resort, and an accumulation of usurpations and abuses rendering passive obedience and non-resistance a greater evil than resistance and revolution, there can remain but one resort, the last of all, an appeal from the cancelled obligations of the constitutional compact to original rights and the law of self-preservation. This is the "ultima ratio" under all governments, whether consolidated, confederated, or a compound of both; and it cannot be doubted that a single member of the Union in the extremity supposed, but in that only, would have a right, as an extra and ultra constitutional right, to make the appeal.[1]

The Federal Union, then, was no mere league, no "rope of sand" to be broken by any State at its pleasure, but a strong national government which rested upon the consent of the sovereign people of the States, and which "operated directly on individuals, not on States."

Madison was undoubtedly sincere when he asserted again and again that there was no inconsistency between his views in 1798 and in 1830, but the interpretation placed by him in the latter year upon the Virginia Resolutions was certainly not the interpretation placed upon them in the former year by the vast majority of his fellow countrymen.

When Jefferson was inaugurated President in 1801,

[1] *Letters*, etc., iv., 101.

he appointed Madison his Secretary of State. The second phase of the latter's career, that of an Executive, now begins. Hitherto his political activity had been confined to the making of laws and of constitutions; for the next sixteen years he filled in succession the two highest executive offices in the land. Madison was by natural instinct and training a student and few men of his time equalled him in his knowledge of the history of governments. With his study there was soon mingled, as we have seen, a practical experience in the problems of government which ran the gamut from lowest to highest, from member of a Committee of Safety through the Congress of the Confederation, the Constitutional Conventions of the United States and of Virginia, the Assembly of his State and the House of Representatives to the Secretaryship of State and the Presidency for two terms. Such an active participation in the affairs of practical politics kept him from following the visionary ideals of a student's chamber. Lacking in imagination, he was lacking also in fire and brilliancy; there was no spark of genius as in Hamilton, no homely wit as in Franklin. Instead there was careful consideration that approached hesitancy; solidity that escaped being heavy only by virtue of the lucidity and learning that accompanied it. In addition there was a reasonableness and an evenness of mind that fitted him most admirably for the great part he played in the Constitutional Convention. With too much of calm deliberation and too little of the element of quick determination, he failed of being a successful Executive. The temper of his mind was best suited to the consideration of the principles of government as they were to be read in history and interpreted by experience.

Jefferson and a large majority of the party regarded Madison as the logical successor to the Presidency in 1809 and as the perpetuator of democratic principles. Jefferson's administration had given more than one severe wrench to the principles proclaimed in 1800 and Madison succeeded to a greatly modified form of democratic principles. Jefferson had found it utterly impossible to undo the constructive work of Hamilton; reductions in the army and navy, in government expenses and taxes, left the powers of the Federal Government undiminished; possession of power by the Democratic-Republicans was a far different thing from its exercise by the Federalists who, they thought, were sure to use it for the people's harm.

Early in Jefferson's first administration, the process of absorbing the principles and practice of the Federalists had begun. The two events that contributed most to drive the Jeffersonian Democrats into acting upon the principles of their rivals were the purchase of Louisiana and the second war with England. Madison, as Secretary of State, assisted in the negotiations that culminated in the purchase and he shared Jefferson's conscientious scruples regarding the constitutionality of the acquisition; even more did he doubt the legality of that clause of the treaty providing for the reception of the inhabitants of the ceded territory as citizens, or, in other words, he doubted the advisability of making the Constitution follow the flag by treaty arrangements. That the Constitution does not follow the flag merely as the result of the acquisition of territory, whether by treaty or by conquest, has come to be the settled doctrine of the Supreme Court.

The War of 1812 was forced upon Madison by the new spirit that found entrance into Congress in 1811, and the charge was made that he agreed to war as the price of a second term.[1] Certain it is that a policy of war meant turning his back upon principles that had been regarded as fundamental; it meant an increase of the army and navy, of taxation and public debt; it meant vigorous action on the part of the central government and an exercise of authority by it that a decade before would have been regarded as fatal to liberty.

Had it not been that the war was a party war, carried on in the face of an opposition from the remnant of the Federalist party that came dangerously near disunion, its nationalizing effect might have been vastly greater. It nevertheless succeeded in gathering together and crystallizing into a strong sense of patriotism and national sentiment, the varied elements begotten by national growth and expansion and by the brilliant victories of a national navy. American pride had been enlisted on the side of the national government. However discreditable in its origin and conduct, the war firmly established the government of the United States both at home and abroad. For the first time there was a conscious recognition of its permanency and its supremacy. Around it had gathered the sentiment of a growing national feeling. Madison's part in this development was negative rather than positive; the war was not

[1] Gay, *op. cit.*, p. 296–297.

of his seeking, but was forced on him by the young generation that had come out of the West, whose spirit was embodied in Henry Clay. "We ask for energy," they said, "and we are told of his moderation; we ask for talent, and the reply is his unassuming merit." Whether he realized it or not, whether he desired it or not, Madison upon his retirement from the presidency left behind him a nation, for the first time conscious of its nationality and just beginning to pride itself on its greatness and its unlimited possibilities. After the war it would have been ridiculous for any State to put forward pretensions of comparing in dignity, honor, or respect, to say nothing of power, with the Federal Union. The Union was well launched upon the sea of nationality, upon which it has since sailed, with many a blow and now and again a storm, but always with increasing power and always attended by increasing respect and admiration from the great body of the people.

After his retirement from the Presidency in 1817, Madison spent the remaining years of his life at his home, Montpelier, second only to the "Sage of Monticello" in the people's eyes. He engaged in a voluminous correspondence with his friends in which he gave fresh expression to his views upon many of the disputed questions regarding the character and power of the Federal Government. He still believed the government was compounded of federal and national elements; the Constitution, though a compact, was not one to which the State governments were parties, nor the State governments on the one hand and the Federal Government on the other; "the parties are the States, *i. e.,* the people thereof respectively in their sovereign character and they alone." The Supreme Court was still regarded as the rightful arbiter in controversies between the Federal and the State governments regarding their powers; "if it concur in usurpations, remonstrances, instruction, recurring elections, impeachment, and amendment are the remedies open to the people, and should all these prove of no avail, there is the final right of revolution and rebellion."

His long career in the public service, the important part he had taken in the Constitutional Convention, his age and his learning and the esteem in which he was held contributed to lend importance to his views. Two things tended to minimize their influence: in the South, new and special interests were rapidly forcing men into constructions of the Constitution which were far narrower than the limits of the "strict construction" of the Democratic-Republicans; in the North the spirit of nationality was far outrunning "Madisonian Federalism." There was no middle ground that could be held successfully between the conflicting tendencies, and Madison's views were regarded by both parties as temporizing and they satisfied neither.

The members of the Constitutional Convention were far from unanimous in their opinions regarding their own work, and some points they had purposely left unsettled because of the impossibility of agreement regarding them. They had taken a middle ground through many compromises, but the forces of national development could not be restrained by "parchment barriers." The elements of national discord could be hushed for a time, but they could not be reconciled by any nice adjustment of phrases, and sooner or later they were destined to break forth into warring factions which were the fiercer for their long restraint.

Madison, however, was dimly aware of a change that was taking place in men's thought, though he stood too near it to be able to perceive it with clearness. What we now recognize as a fundamental change in the philosophic basis of thought was to him but a new use of language.[1] The doctrines of Nullification and Secession are to him "errors which have their source in the silent innovations of time on the meaning of words and phrases." His attitude is nowhere more clearly shown than in his view of sovereignty. In the debates of the Constitutional Convention, in the pages of the *Federalist,* and in his letters and writings down to his death, Madison proclaims the doctrine of a divided sovereignty.[2] Sovereignty is identified with supreme power and this power is divided between the States in their united and in their individual capacities. It was inconceivable how a confederated republic could be established if sovereignty could not be divided. In 1830, five years before his death, he gives utterance to a protest against a new idea that was just beginning to make its appearance under the auspices of no less distinguished a name than that of Calhoun, then at the height of his power. This new idea pro-

---

[1] See a very illuminating article *The Social Compact and the Constitution,* by A. C. McLaughlin in the *American Historical Review,* April, 1900.

[2] *Cf. Letters,* etc., iv., 390, Sovereignty.

claimed the indivisibility of sovereignty, an idea that Madison felt was subversive of the whole system of government. "If sovereignty cannot be thus divided," he declared, "the political system of the United States is a chimera, mocking the vain pretensions of human wisdom."[1] We have come to believe that Calhoun was right in his view that sovereignty cannot be divided, but it took the strife of battle through four long years to determine that though Calhoun was right in declaring that sovereignty was indivisible, he was wrong in attempting to locate that undivided sovereignty in the individual States and not in the Federal State.

[1] *Letters,* etc., iv., 61.

VI

John Marshall. Growth through Legal Interpretation

JOHN MARSHALL

1755.	Sept. 24.	Born in Fauquier Co., Va.
1775.		At outbreak of Revolution joined Virginia troops.
1777.	May.	Promoted to Captaincy.
1779.	Aug 19.	Returned to Virginia to take charge of militia. Heard law lectures at William and Mary College.
1780.		Admitted to Bar at Williamsburg.
		Delegate to House of Burgesses.
		Returned to his company.
1781.		Resigned and took up practice in Fauquier Co.
		Removed to Richmond.
1782–88.		Delegate to House of Burgesses.
1788–91.		Delegate to House of Burgesses.
1788.		Member of Virginia Constitutional Convention.
		Declined position of Attorney-General under Washington.
1791–97.		Lawyer at Richmond.
1797.		Marshall, Pinckney, and Gerry appointed special envoys to France.
1798.		Returned to New York.
1799–1800.		Representative in Congress.
1800.		Secretary of State.
1801–1835.		Chief Justice of the Supreme Court.
1807.		Tried Burr.
1835.	July 6.	Died at Philadelphia.

VI

John Marshall. Growth through Legal Interpretation

THE success of the Democratic-Republican party and the election of Jefferson to the Presidency in 1800 did not result in depriving the Federalists of all influence and control over national affairs. Though the wave of triumphant democracy had swept away the Federalist majority in both Houses of Congress and had seated the guiding spirit of the movement in the chair of the Chief Executive, it fell back baffled before the Supreme Court.

The theory of the makers of the Constitution that a separation of the powers of government was essential to liberty, that it was necessary to balance part against part, and to oppose power to power, as a check upon the natural tendency of all governments to strengthen themselves at the expense of the people, now brought unconcealed chagrin to that very party which was loudest in its outcries against the dangers of centralization. Though the Legislative and Executive branches of the government were controlled by the Democratic-Republicans, the Judiciary remained under Federalist prepossessions. The Supreme Court under the leadership of the greatest of its Chief Justices, John Marshall of Virginia, was just entering upon its career as interpreter of the Constitution. Despite the angry protests of the Democratic-Republicans, it continued the development of the national theory of the Union which had been so successfully begun during the twelve years of Federalist supremacy.

The active, planning will of the Federal Government was dominated by that party which stood for lessening the powers of the central government and maintaining the sacredness of local self-government as the safest guarantee of liberty. The Supreme Court, representing "judgment," not "will," as the authors of the *Federalist* had declared, was pervaded with the spirit of the party that desired a strong central government—and judgment triumphed over will.

In the Constitutional Convention much distrust of democracy had been evidenced by the "Fathers" and many ingenious devices had been contrived to stay the hot temper of the masses; the more deliberate Senate was to check the hasty action of a House too close to popular passions to be altogether trusted, and a President's veto afforded still further guarantee of deliberate legislative action. Moreover, every check and balance of one part of the governmental machinery against another furnished a possible opportunity for the minority to prevent or delay the action of the majority, and of one party to balk its rival of complete control of the government for years after the tide of popular favor had swept that rival into the elective offices. The whole question of parties and consequently the possibility of a deadlock between them, seems to have been but dimly perceived by the framers of the Constitution.

For more than thirty-four years Marshall served as Chief Justice and under his fostering care the interpretation of the Constitution in a national sense went on apace. It would, however, be as absurd to ascribe this development solely to the action of the Court as not to recognize the fact, that, without its action, the development would have been impossible. Other and important influences were at work in the same direction; the Democratic-Republican party found itself unable to overthrow the constructive measures of the Federalists and was obliged to accept in practice, though it rejected in theory, the principles of their opponents. As a result of this process of absorption, both parties came to recognize the supremacy of the Constitution and the function of the Supreme Court as its interpreter, to acquiesce in the view that a nation had been created by the Constitution and to take pride in its glory and greatness.

The period of the blind worship of the Constitution as the chief cause of national greatness begins and the struggle of parties over " loose " and " strict " construction proves insufficient to preserve their separate existence. The War of 1812 had been the principal cause of uniting all men under the banner of nationality. For the first time the spirit of the nation triumphed over that of the States; the old view of the Union as a mere league of States was pushed into the background, until another generation, under the strong pressure of economic suffering, should summon Nullification to its defence. Even then only South Carolina felt the burden to be intolerable; another generation of cotton, slavery, and the tariff was required to mould the Southern States into a "solid South," to draw them together into a common purpose and movement; when this took place Nullification had given way to its more logical, as well as more destructive, successor, Secession.

No name could be more typical of the great constitutional development of this period than that of John Marshall, the "expounder of the Constitution." Marshall was born in Fauquier County, Virginia, on September 24, 1755 [1]; he received his early education under a private tutor and at the outbreak of the Revolution had begun the study of the law. His heart was always with the patriot cause and he at once joined the Virginia troops, was soon promoted to a captaincy and took part in the battles of Monmouth, Brandywine, and Germantown, and in the storming of Stony Point. In 1779 he returned to Virginia to take charge of the militia, and occupied his leisure by hearing the law lectures then being delivered at William and Mary College by the distinguished jurist, George Wythe, and in 1780 was admitted to the bar at Williamsburg. Believing that he was again needed in the army, he returned alone and on foot to his company, but resigned the following year after the surrender of Cornwallis, and began

[1] *Cf.* A. B. Magruder, *John Marshall*, in American Statesmen Series; H. Flanders, *Life and Times of John Marshall*, in *Life and Times of the Chief Justices of the United States*, vol. ii., pp. 279–550, and G. Van Santvoord, *Lives of the Chief Justices*, vol. iv., pp. 293–456.

the practice of law in Fauquier County and then at Richmond, where his success was immediate and distinguished.

Marshall, like most young Virginia lawyers, entered politics and in 1780 was elected a delegate to the House of Burgesses, in which he continued to serve almost uninterruptedly for ten years. In 1788 he was a member of the Virginia Constitutional Convention and lent his active support in favor of the adoption of the Federal Constitution. It is a little surprising that Marshall was not a member of that distinguished body of delegates from Virginia to the Convention at Philadelphia; certainly both his talents and his reputation would have justified his selection, for he declined the post of Attorney General in Washington's Cabinet to devote himself to the practice of his profession. Marshall's next public service was in 1797, when, with Pinckney and Gerry, he was sent as a special envoy to France on the mission that gave rise to the famous X Y Z letters. Upon his return to New York he was tendered a public banquet by Congress and in the following year he was elected a member of the House of Representatives. President Adams appointed him Secretary of State in 1800 and Chief Justice of the Supreme Court in the following January. This position Marshall filled with distinguished honor till his death on July 6, 1835, at Philadelphia.

As notable and as varied as were his public services, Marshall's greatest service to his country was rendered as a judge, and it is upon his interpretation of the Constitution as the supreme law of the land, and upon his decisions of the large questions that arose out of the complex relations of the States and the nation, that his fame must rest. To appreciate fully Marshall's influence upon the development of the Constitution, we must remember that he dominated the Court during the years of his Chief Justiceship, that the vast majority of the opinions upon constitutional questions were rendered with his sanction and support, and that most of the important opinions were written by him.[1] Only one question of importance to the interpretation of the Constitution had been decided previous to his becoming a member of the Court. This was the case of Chisholm v. Georgia, in which Justice Wilson had expressed his opinion so emphatically that the Union was a nation, sovereign for the purposes for which it had been created, and, within its sphere, independent of the States.[2]

The first task of Marshall and the Court was to demonstrate what has been called the "efficiency" of the Constitution.[3] The Constitution had nowhere expressly conferred upon the courts the power to declare a law unconstitutional, and at the February term in the year 1800, Mr. Justice Chase had said, in the case of Cooper v. Telfair:

Although it is alleged that all acts of the legislature, in direct opposition to the prohibitions of the Constitu-

---

[1] *Constitutional History as Seen in American Law*, article by Hitchcock, *Constitutional Development in the United States as Influenced by Chief Justice Marshall*, p. 57. This is an excellent work to which I am much indebted.

[2] 2 Dallas, 419.

[3] Hitchcock, *op. cit.*, p. 76.

tion, would be void, yet *it still remains a question, where the power resides, to declare it void.*[1]

Such a declaration is all the more important in view of the Virginia and Kentucky Resolutions of 1798-99, which declared that the power resided in the States, the parties to the compact, in case " of a deliberate, palpable, and dangerous exercise of other powers not granted by the said compact."

It seems self-evident to us that this power should reside in the courts, that it should be their duty to declare void any law repugnant to the Constitution, and, in doing so, to judge of the extent of the powers delegated to the Federal Government; but in the face of the cry that this would make the discretion of the court and not the Constitution the measure of those powers, neither the court nor the country had taken the position that the Supreme Court must be the final arbiter in the event of a conflict between the States and the nation over the extent of the delegated powers. This position, however, Marshall assumed in the case of Marbury *v.* Madison in 1803.[2]

Madison, as Secretary of State under Jefferson, refused to issue to one William Marbury his commission as a Justice of the Peace for the District of Columbia, although the facts showed that Marbury had been nominated to the Senate by President Adams, that the nomination had been confirmed by the Senate, and that the commission had been signed and sealed, but not delivered to Marbury, before the administration of Adams closed.

[1] 4 Dallas, 19.
[2] 1 Cranch, 137.

Marshall delivered the opinion of the Court in this important case. After determining that the appointment was complete with the signing and sealing of the commission, and that in consequence Marbury had a right to the office and a remedy for his exclusion, he took up the question of the right of the Court to grant the remedy prayed for. The Constitution confers upon the Supreme Court original jurisdiction "in all cases affecting ambassadors, other public ministers and consuls, and those in which a State shall be a party."[1] In all other cases to which the judicial power of the United States extends, the Supreme Court shall have appellate jurisdiction. Under the terms of the Judiciary Act, the power had been conferred upon the Court of issuing a mandamus, the remedy sought by Marbury, in cases other than those involving appellate jurisdiction. Such an exercise of original jurisdiction had not been conferred by the Constitution and the question of the supremacy of the Constitution when in conflict with an ordinary law was squarely presented; the "efficiency" of the Constitution was to be tested.

Marshall's opinion is so clear and convincing, goes so directly to the heart of the whole matter, and sets forth so correctly the true and essential nature of a written and "rigid" Constitution that it ought to be familiar to all. The people, said Marshall, have an original right to determine such principles for their government as in their opinion shall most conduce to their own happiness; that the principles thus established are fundamental and designed to be permanent; that the original and supreme will of

[1] Art. iii., Sec. 2.

the people organizes the government, distributes and limits the powers as it sees fit, and commits the limitations to writing. The government of the United States is of this character.

To what purpose are powers limited, and to what purpose is that limitation committed to writing, if those limits may, at any time, be passed by those intended to be restrained? . . . The Constitution is either a superior paramount law, unchangeable by ordinary means, or it is on a level with ordinary legislative Acts, and, like any other Acts, is alterable when the legislature shall please to alter it. If the former part of the alternative be true, then a legislative Act contrary to the Constitution is not law; if the latter part be true, then written constitutions are absurd attempts, on the part of the people, to limit a power in its own nature illimitable. . . . It is emphatically the province and duty of the judicial department to say what the law is. Those who apply the rule to particular cases must of necessity expound and interpret the rule. If two laws conflict with each other, the courts must decide on the operation of each. . . . This is of the very essence of judicial duty. If, then, the courts are to regard the Constitution, and the Constitution is superior to any ordinary Act of the legislature, the Constitution, and not such ordinary Act, must govern the case to which they both apply.

Thus the "efficiency" of the Constitution was demonstrated. The power of the Court to uphold the supremacy of the Constitution and to restrain Congress within the limits set by that instrument was established. The importance of the decision can not be overestimated, for it in reality determined the nature both of the Constitution and of the Union;

it confirmed the doctrine of the limitation of the powers of the Federal Government and the peculiar function of the Supreme Court to maintain the limitations set by the Constitution; it determined where the power lay to declare a law in conflict with the Constitution void. While it denied to the Federal Government the right to extend its powers at will, it nevertheless assumed for it the right, through one of its branches, to judge of the extent of the powers conferred upon it by the Constitution. The Federal Government was one of limited powers, but of the limits of those limits it itself was to judge.

The decision shows, moreover, very clearly that it was not Marshall's desire to exalt the Court above the other departments; he states as explicitly as could be desired the true function of the Court; it cannot out of the fulness of its power, sit in judgment on the acts of Congress and declare such acts unconstitutional, but it must wait till the individual case is brought before it; its decision, then, shall be rendered irrespective of the law in violation of the Constitution. Nor has it any intention "to intermeddle with the prerogatives of the Executive" or to consider questions which involve Executive discretion. "There exists and can exist," says Marshall in this same decision, "no power to control that discretion. The subjects are political. They respect the nation, not individual rights; and being intrusted to the Executive, the decision of the Executive is conclusive." Political policies have never been made the subject of judicial decision by the Court, and in this recognition of the limits to its own sphere, it assured itself of the almost unquestioned support of the nation in that ever widening field of true judicial interpretation that lay before it. Following close upon the establishment of the "efficiency" of the Constitution, came a second problem of importance, that of the "extent" of the judicial power.[1] "The nation, the Constitution, and the laws were in their infancy,"[2] and the great question was whether the system would work. The solution of this question depended in large measure upon the success of the Judiciary in assuming a position of equality to the Executive and Congress within the limits of the delegated powers, and in establishing itself above all State courts.

How the former was attained has been shown in the case of Marbury *v.* Madison. The contest between the Federal and the State Judiciary was keen and prolonged, with frequent touches of bitterness and violence. For a decade Marshall was at war with the Supreme Court of his native State, and the most violent opponent of his efforts to secure the supremacy of the Federal Supreme Court was Judge Roane of the Supreme Court of Virginia.[3] Roane was dangerous because he was the mouthpiece of the Democratic-Republicans of that State. Marshall believed that "the whole attack, if not originating with Mr. Jefferson," was "obviously approved and guided by him." The conflict with the Virginia court extended from 1813 to 1821 and may be traced in three of Mar-

---

[1] Hitchcock, *op. cit.*, p. 82.
[2] *Ibid.*, *op. cit.*, p. 56. Quotation from Chief Justice Waite.
[3] *American Historical Review*, July, 1907: *Chief Justice Marshall and Virginia*, by William E. Dodd.

shall's decisions,—Martin v. Hunter's Lessee (1813),[1] McCulloch v. Maryland (1819),[2] and Cohens v. Virginia (1821).[3] Its heat was due to differences of opinion with respect not only to the legal but also to the political questions involved, and Virginia Republicans did not hesitate to proclaim Marshall a traitor to his State.

In the first case an appeal was taken from a decision of the Virginia court to the United States Supreme Court on the ground that rights granted by the treaty of 1783 had been denied, and the decision of the Virginia court was reversed. Judge Roane and his associates formally announced that the decision of the United States Court would not be obeyed. Public opinion in Virginia fully sustained the local court, while the opinion of Judge Roane was a political manifesto in favor of State sovereignty. The Supreme Court at once took notice of the refusal of the Virginia court; the case was gone over again, the points of the former opinion were reaffirmed, and the United States marshal was ordered to execute the decision of the Supreme Court.

The contest of ideas and the rivalry of men was, however, far from finished with the settlement of this case. In 1819 the conflict was renewed in the case of McCulloch v. Maryland; once again Marshall and Roane were antagonists. In this case the doctrine of the "implied powers" of the Constitution was accepted by the Court, its right to determine the

[1] 1 Wheaton, 304.
[2] 4 Wheaton, 316.
[3] 6 Wheaton, 264.

constitutionality of laws, already affirmed in the case of Marbury *v.* Madison, was reasserted, and the right of Congress to establish a National Bank was settled. To Roane the exercise of such power by the Court was a usurpation. In a series of papers contributed to the Richmond *Enquirer,* he put forward the view of the Virginia and Kentucky Resolutions and declared, that, if Marshall's view prevailed, the "rights and freedom of the people of the States" were lost and that a resort to force might be found necessary.

The attention of the public was soon directed elsewhere by the high-handed proceedings of General Jackson in Florida, and upon this picturesque figure the fire of the Virginia malcontents was directed, to the relief of the Supreme Court.

The third and final conflict between Marshall and the State court came in the case of Cohens *v.* Virginia. Of the opinion it has been said that no other decision "affords a more splendid example of Marshall's intellectual power, his profound political insight, or his unalterable devotion to the Union."[1] The questions presented to the Court, said Marshall, in rendering the decision,

maintain that the nation does not possess a department capable of restraining peaceably, and by authority of law, any attempts which may be made, by a part, against the legitimate powers of the whole; and that the government is reduced to the alternative of submitting to such attempts, or of resisting them by force. They maintain that the Constitution of the United States has provided no tribunal for the final construc-

[1] Hitchcock, *op. cit.,* p. 90.

tion of itself, or of the laws or treaties of the nation; but that this power may be exercised in the last resort by the courts of every State in the Union. That the Constitution, laws, and treaties may receive as many constructions as there are States; and that this is not a mischief, or, if a mischief, is irremedial.

Again, after quoting that part of the Constitution which declares that

this Constitution, and the laws of the United States which shall be made in pursuance thereof, and all treaties made or which shall be made under the authority of the United States, shall be the supreme law of the land, and the judges in every State shall be bound thereby, anything in the Constitution or laws of any State to the contrary notwithstanding,[1]

the Chief Justice continued in words of solemn and convincing import:

This is the authoritative language of the American people; and, if gentlemen please, of the American States. It marks, with lines too strong to be mistaken, the characteristic distinction between the government of the Union and those of the States. The general government, though limited as to its objects, is supreme with respect to those objects. This principle is a part of the Constitution; and if there be any who deny its necessity, none can deny *its authority.*

. . . .

The people made the Constitution, and the people can unmake it. It is the creature of their will, and lives only by their will. But this supreme and irresistible power to make or to unmake resides only in the whole body of

[1] Art. vi.

the people; not in any subdivision of them. The attempt of any of the parts to exercise it *is usurpation, and ought to be repelled by those to whom the people have delegated their power of repelling it.*

Having demonstrated the " efficiency " and the " extent " of the judicial power, having established the right of the Court to disregard a law repugnant to the Constitution, having maintained its supremacy in all matters arising out of the Constitution, and having shown its power to uphold the Federal authority, the Court had yet another important question to settle under the leadership of Marshall. Though the Constitution enumerated, it did not define the powers which it granted and the process of definition, as Marshall said, " is perpetually arising, and will probably continue to arise as long as our system shall exist." [1]

The enumeration of the delegated powers closes with the statement that Congress shall have power " to make all laws which shall be necessary and proper for carrying into execution the foregoing powers, and all other powers vested by this Constitution in the Government of the United States, or in any department or officer thereof." [2] In the case of the United States *v.* Fisher,[3] in 1804, Marshall had laid down the fundamental principle of interpretation when he said:

In construing this clause it would be incorrect, and would produce endless difficulties, if the opinion should

[1] *McCulloch v. Maryland*, 4 Wheaton, 405.
[2] Art. i., Sec. 8.
[3] 2 Cranch, 358.

be maintained that no law was authorized which was not indispensably necessary to give effect to a specific power. . . . *Congress must possess the choice of means,* and must be empowered to use any means which are in fact conducive to the exercise of a power granted by the Constitution.

Following the line of argument developed by Hamilton in his memorial on the constitutionality of a National Bank, Marshall gave the stamp of judicial approval to the principle of "implied powers" as contained in this so-called "elastic clause" of the Constitution.

The same question, as we have seen, was presented to the Court in 1819 in the case of McCulloch *v.* Maryland. The earlier opinion was reaffirmed in still more emphatic language. "Let the end be legitimate," said Marshall, "let it be within the scope of the Constitution, and all means which are appropriate, which are plainly adapted to that end, which are not prohibited, but consist with the letter and spirit of the Constitution, are constitutional." [1]

"That the States have no power, by taxation or otherwise, to impede, burden, or in any manner control any means or measures adopted by the government for the execution of its powers," [2] was established in this as well as in subsequent cases. The Court declared "that the power to tax involves the power to destroy; that the power to destroy may defeat and render useless the power to create." [3] "The question is, in truth, a question of supremacy;

[1] 4 Wheaton, 421.
[2] Hitchcock, *op. cit.,* p. 94.
[3] *McCulloch v. Maryland,* 4 Wheaton, 316, 431.

and if the right of the States to tax the means employed by the general government be conceded, the declaration that the Constitution, and the laws made in pursuance thereof, shall be the supreme law of the land, is an empty and unmeaning declaration." [1]

Among the powers delegated to Congress was that "to regulate commerce with foreign nations and among the several States, and with the Indian tribes." [2] Out of this clause have grown all the attempts, recently so numerous, by legislation and judicial decision, to regulate and control "interstate commerce." Most of the fundamental principles which have governed the action of Congress and the courts were laid down by Marshall. We can only indicate some of the more important. In Gibbons v. Ogden [3] it was determined that commerce was not merely traffic but was commercial intercourse of all kinds; that it included navigation, that the power vested in Congress was complete and exclusive, and that the exercise of this power must extend within the territorial jurisdiction of the States, and " must include every case of commercial intercourse which is not a part of the purely internal commerce of a single State." These principles have found application and enlargement in a host of cases from that day to this, all carrying out the fundamental ideas of Marshall.

Turning to the express limitations put upon the power of the States by the Constitution, we find some of Marshall's most important decisions, par-

[1] *McCulloch v. Maryland*, 433.
[2] Const., Art. i., Sec. 8.
[3] 9 Wheaton, 189.

ticularly those involving the sanctity of contract. Most notable among these stands the Dartmouth College case, in which the old and the young champion of national strength and unity won added fame. Marshall, the judge, and Webster, the advocate, never showed to finer advantage their faith in the Constitution and the Union than in this case.

Finally it remains to notice a decision which has been of the utmost consequence in the history of our growth as a nation and which has found fresh application in the past ten years as a result of our policy of imperialism. Jefferson, it is well known, believed that in the acquisition of Louisiana he "had done an act beyond the Constitution," and he went so far as to draft an amendment to the Constitution which provided for the incorporation of the new territory in the United States. The general approval with which the purchase was received rendered the amendment unnecessary, and Congress appropriated the money necessary to complete the transaction and passed all laws required to carry the treaty into execution. Twenty-five years later, in the case of the American Insurance Co. *v.* Canter,[1] in which the validity and the effect of the treaty providing for the purchase of Florida in 1819 were called in question, Marshall concluded the matter so far as judicial determination was concerned in the following words: "The Constitution confers absolutely on the government of the Union the powers of making war and of making treaties; consequently that government possesses the power of acquiring territory, either by conquest or by treaty."

[1] 1 Peters, 511.

In accordance with this principle we have seen our power stretch far beyond our shores and take possession of insular territories; it has made it possible for the United States to enter upon its career of expansion and in consequence to take its place as one of the great powers of the world.

When Marshall ascended the bench as Chief Justice of the United States, the first wave of reaction had set in against the concentration of power in the Federal Government. Strength and power had been the requisites scarce a dozen years before to deliver the country from anarchy, but now they seemed, to the reactionary spirit, destined to be the means of subverting liberty and establishing monarchy and tyranny, and under the party cry of liberty and self-government the Democratic-Republicans had triumphed. When Marshall laid down the ermine along with his life, the country was just beginning to witness the second reaction against too great power in the central government. South Carolina and Nullification were the logical successors of the Virginia and Kentucky Resolutions; Calhoun and the Fort Hill address, of Roane and the Richmond *Enquirer*.

The Federalist principles had beyond question persisted in the interpretation of the Constitution at the hands of the Court and even in the political branches they found a quiet acceptance in practice. Had not the baleful influence of slavery cast its shadow over the land and produced a "peculiar institution," demanding support from every possible source, even from the Constitution itself, it is highly probable that the great work of Marshall, in establishing the national principles and doctrines of the

Constitution, would have sufficed to determine for all time the nature of the Union. Never would it have been necessary to draw the sword in final arbitrament.

VII
Andrew Jackson. Growth through Democratization

ANDREW JACKSON

1767. Mar. 15.		Born near boundary line between North and South Carolina.
1784–88.		Studied law in Salisbury, N. C.
1788.		Licensed to practice law.
1791.		District Attorney for the Mero District.
1796.		Delegate to State Constitutional Convention.
		First Representative in Congress from Tennessee.
1797.		Elected to U. S. Senate.
1798–1804.		Judge of Supreme Court of Tennessee.
1801.		Major-General of State Militia.
1813–14.		War with Creek Indians.
1814.	May 31.	Appointed Major-General in U. S. Army.
1815.	Jan. 8.	Battle of New Orleans.
1817.	Dec. 17.	Took personal command of U. S. troops.
1819.	Feb. 8.	Congress sustains his action in Florida.
1822.		U. S. Senator from Tennessee.
1824.		Candidate for President.
1825.		Resigned from Senate.
1828.		Elected President.
1832.	July.	Vetoed Bill rechartering National Bank.
	Nov.	Re-elected President.
	Dec.	Nullification Proclamation.
1837.		Retired from public life.
1845.	June 8.	Died at the Hermitage.

VII

Andrew Jackson. Growth through Democratization

THE success of democracy in the election of Jefferson in 1800 was only partial. It meant merely that the country repudiated the extremes to which the Federalists were driving the national development. A desire to preserve the complete independence of local self-government, which the Democratic-Republicans professed to believe was imperilled by the strengthening of the central government, united with the carefully cultivated sentiment that the Federalists were monarchists, or at least aristocrats, and that they feared and distrusted the people, gave to the movement organized by Jefferson the semblance of democracy. To the extent that it professed a belief in the wisdom of the multitude and a respect for local self-government as the bulwark of liberty, it was more democratic than its opponent; but it would be a great mistake to imagine that its professions were such as to-day would be regarded as consistent with thorough-going democracy. Jefferson's belief in the people had back of it always the supposition that the people would be wise enough to suffer themselves to be led by men like himself,—men thoroughly imbued with the ideals of democracy, and fitted by their training to carry them out far better than the people could do it for themselves. There was still present the belief in the superiority of the Virginia Dynasty as the people's leaders.

The democracy of Jefferson, moreover, was far removed from that modern tenet of the faith which demands the suffrage as the inalienable right of man. At that period property and educational qualifications, not inconsiderable in extent, were required almost universally both for office-holders and voters. The democracy was in reality based on property, and the limited body thus enfranchised was expected to yield itself to the wisdom of approved leaders.[1]

The Jeffersonian revolution was after all very limited in its radicalism. Yet the Federalists dreaded its weakening effect on the centralizing tendencies of the Federal Government. Their apprehension on this score was exceeded by their fear of the rule of the masses, of the fickleness and passion of "democracies," and of those characteristics which literature had made classic through reference to the Greek city-states and the Italian republics as models.

None of their fears was realized. The fundamental principles of the government were continued unchanged by the Democratic-Republicans, the essential character of the Union was unassailed; only its tone and complexion were altered; a dull gray replaced the black; expenditures civil, military, and naval were cut down, but Louisiana was purchased. Nor did passionate and hasty democracy sweep away all the barriers and overleap all the hindrances erected in the Constitution against the immediate triumph of the popular will; there was only a half-

[1] H. J. Ford, *Rise and Growth of American Politics*, p. 132 *ff.*

hearted attack upon the Judiciary as the bulwark of a defeated party against the complete supremacy of its rival. There was less ceremony and more of simplicity, a change which was greatly facilitated by the transfer of the seat of government from the most fashionable city of the Republic to the dreary wastes of the newly laid-out city of Washington. Yet on the whole things moved on much as they had done before; men of the same general type and of the same general social position continued in control. The real aristocracy of education and training remained as before the leaders of thought and action. Democracy had triumphed, but in theory rather than in practice; and another generation must arise under other conditions before the "People" should come into their own.

These new conditions were many, but none of them contributed so much to the development of new ideas in respect to the government as did the settling of the country beyond the Alleghanies; and of these new conditions and new theories respecting government, Andrew Jackson was the unconscious embodiment. Born in 1767, so near the border line between North and South Carolina that his most exhaustive biographer and Jackson himself are at variance as to which State shall have the honor of his birthplace, he was early made to feel the hardships of the War for Independence, which in the end caused the death of his mother and his two brothers, inflicted upon him, child though he was, wounds and imprisonment, and engendered in his heart a fierce hatred of the British which sought and won its revenge at New Orleans.

His father, a Scotch-Irishman from Carrickfergus, County Antrim, Ireland, who had come over in 1765, had died a few days before Jackson's birth, so that the close of the Revolution found him an orphan, dependent upon his mother's relations. His training was that of the frontier settlement and his education of the most meagre sort.[1] The stories of his early years give little promise of the future; they show a dashing, dare-devil spirit, with little of serious purpose and less of serious effort, living the wild, free life of an outpost of civilization where sustenance was easy and refinement impossible. In 1784 he began the study of law at Salisbury, N. C., but even then life did not become too serious. He was the gayest and most careless of all the young blades, fond of horse-racing and cock fighting and spending no small part of the four years at Salisbury in these pursuits.

Admitted to the bar in 1788, he was in 1791 appointed District Attorney for the Mero district, comprising the settled portions of North Carolina that lay beyond the mountains. The eastern part of this district had just been through the anarchy of the abortive efforts to establish the "State of Franklin," and the western portion, reaching as far as Nashville, was suffering from almost daily attacks by the lurking savages. Many settlers everywhere along the Western boundary of civilization, as it slowly pushed its way toward the Pacific,

---

[1] Lives by Parton, Sumner, Buell, and Colyar. Also see C. H. Peck, *The Jacksonian Epoch;* W. MacDonald, *The Jacksonian Democracy,* and C. E. Merriam, *American Political Theories.*

Andrew Jackson

degenerated into a condition not far removed from that of the savage. The restraints of civilization became unbearable and, like the deer and the Indians, they kept just ahead of the advancing line of settlement.[1] In such a community Andrew Jackson began his career as an officer of the State; he performed his duties fearlessly, if not always with wisdom, and in 1796 he was elected the first Representative from the new State of Tennessee. A year later he was appointed Senator to succeed Blount who had been expelled. His career as a Senator was of short duration, for he resigned his seat in 1798 and in the same year was made " Judge of the Superior Courts " of Tennessee.

A man less suited for the position in an older civilization can scarcely be imagined. Yet there were no serious complaints against his decisions. Force of will and violence of temper commanded respect in a society where the restrictions of law weighed lightly, where the security of life and property were less dependent on law than on individual effort, and where the code of honor found imitation and reproduction in a travesty of the original.

Jackson ended his services on the bench in 1804. By this time he had firmly established himself in the raw community as a man who could and would do things, without fear either of individuals or of society; he had fought his duels, raced his horses, and matched his game-cocks; he had married a lady without observing proper care in determining whether she had been legally divorced, and had thereby laid up for himself a wealth of slander and heart-burn-

[1] Sumner (ed. of 1899), p. 6 *ff*.

ing for the future; he was thoroughly representative of the crude life of the times in that section, both in his social and political ideals and relations. He had been charmed by Burr, the fallen idol of democracy, and had been enlisted in assisting his preparations till suspicion of their treasonable intent was aroused; at the time of the trial, to which he had been summoned as a witness, he delivered a public harangue in defence of Burr and in derogation of General Wilkinson. This course of conduct meant that he was deeply alive to the importance of the Mississippi, as was all the Southwest, and as deeply in sympathy with all efforts to unite Louisiana more closely to the Union, and that the name of democracy was sweet to his ears. But to him democracy meant something very different from what it meant to men of the Democratic-Republican school of the more populous States along the coast. The free life of the Southwest afforded no suitable atmosphere in which to hedge democracy about with checks and chains. Rather did it afford almost perfect conditions for the development of ideas of complete local self-government and equality with respect to the participators in it. Small and infrequent was the assistance rendered any political community by a larger and superior community; the smaller desired nothing from the larger, and independence of external control was regarded as a matter of course and of right.

In a society dependent upon itself for the food it eats, the clothes it wears, and the implements and utensils which its civilization demands, there was small chance for the development of sharply marked classes, or for social and political distinctions. The right to vote was regarded as inherent in every free white man, and the ability to fill a political office as commensurate with the right to vote. In a self-reliant and self-assertive social life, where complex political problems were unknown, and where the administration of a rude system of justice and taxation constituted the bulk of political activity, it was natural that any ordinary man should be regarded as fit for the position, and that such positions should rotate from one member of the community to another, that as many as possible might enjoy the social distinction and emoluments. Rotation in office, short terms, equality in ability to fill the offices, and universal suffrage were the commonplaces of political thought in the Tennessee of Jackson's earlier life, and he himself the embodiment of these principles.[1]

It is important to gather some impression of the general conditions under which Jackson grew up, and to perceive what were the forces at work upon him and the Western country, for his place in our constitutional development is due to the influence he exerted upon the spirit of the government, and to the principles of administration that he introduced into it. He placed upon it the distinctive character of his own thought and feelings. Not a word of the Constitution did he change, and but one new idea of constitutional law did he advance, and yet his administrations mark a turning-point in the development of our institutions. He infused into them the spirit and practices of real democracy, the ideals of equality, of the supremacy of the people, and of rotation in office, and finally he introduced into the

[1] Merriam, *op. cit.*, p. 176 *ff.*

national administration the most vicious of our political evils, the "spoils system."[1] Not less pronounced was the lofty position of supremacy over the other departments of government to which he raised the Executive, but this elevation was personal and transitory and was due to the indomitable will of the "old Hero," not to any lasting forces.

Retiring from the bench in 1804 Jackson became a merchant and farmer and bade fair to spend the remainder of his life as an inconspicuous member of society. Chance saved him, for having been elected Major-General of the State Militia in 1801, the Creek war gave the first opportunity for the display of those military talents which carried him steadily forward to the battle of New Orleans and eventually to the Presidency. Jackson's military career interests us only in so far as it brought into display the perseverance and iron will of the man. His own sickness and the wretched support given by the government could not baffle or discourage him; in the face of almost insuperable difficulties he held his steady course toward the goal; his imperious nature refused to acknowledge defeat either at the hands of nature or of superior numbers. His qualities of leadership won the unfaltering allegiance of his soldiers, and the victory over Pakenham placed him among the notable figures of the country. Made a Major-General in the regular army, he undertook in 1818 the war against the Seminoles and, disregardful of international amenities, he invaded Spanish territory and hung British subjects.

[1] *Cf.* MacDonald, *op. cit.*, p. 56 *ff*, and Sumner, *op. cit.*, p. 187 *ff*.

From 1819 his political reputation grew apace through the skilful management of that master wire-puller, William B. Lewis, and his availability as a presidential candidate to succeed Monroe was carefully cultivated. The "Era of Good Feeling" under Monroe had produced a partyless condition of factional fights among the leaders. Clay, Crawford, Calhoun, Jackson, and John Quincy Adams divided the hosts among them.[1] Calhoun succeeded in combining the opposing forces upon himself for Vice President, and of the others, Jackson, as the candidate of the People, received the largest number of electoral votes, but not a majority of all. The election was therefore thrown into the House of Representatives, where Clay's overwhelming influence was turned to Adams and the cry of "bargain and corruption" arose, to pursue Clay with deadly effect for the remainder of his life.[2] Jackson had at first protested against his name being presented as a candidate on the ground of his age, but having been defeated by unfair means, as it seemed to him, although he had the largest electoral and popular vote, his whole being was fired with a desire to be revenged upon his enemies, and the "Jackson men" became a party seeking to right a wrong that had been done him and the people.

At the same time parties were beginning to reshape themselves out of the personal factions, and the Jackson men, claiming to be the lawful heirs and successors of the true Jeffersonian principles, appropriated the name of Democrats. Jackson's nomi-

---

[1] *Cf.* Sumner, *op. cit.*, p. 92 *ff.*
[2] *Cf.* Schurz, *Life of Henry Clay*, i., 254 *ff.*

nation and election in 1828 were marked by a variety of innovations in political life. In the first place, the Congressional Caucus as a nominating agency passed out of existence with the nomination of Crawford in 1824. It had already fallen into disrepute as an undemocratic institution which deprived the people of their free choice of a Chief Magistrate. Jackson's first nomination was made by the legislatures of his own and of other States, and by popular assemblies everywhere. His second nomination was so well assured as to be unnecessary, but his opponents, who had by this time become consolidated under the leadership of Clay, held a national nominating convention which has grown into the highly developed modern organization for that purpose.[1]

The election of Jackson brought far reaching changes in the whole atmosphere of government, the effects of which we still feel. It was hailed as the triumph of the People; at last they had come into their own, and the smallest remnants of opposition to the reign of the popular sovereign were to be swept away forthwith. Jackson regarded himself as peculiarly the representative of the people and their wishes, and the idea grew upon him with the successive years of his Presidency. Through him the people had spoken in unmistakable fashion and therefore his wishes must prevail. Before him in this representative capacity the other branches of government must give way. The Executive, to his mind, incorporated the highest expression of the will of the people and that will must be obeyed. It was a con-

---

[1] *Cf.* Ostrogorski, *Democracy and the Organization of Political Parties*, ii., 1–207.

ception that fitted in well with the domineering temper and quality of his own mind.

The democratic simplicity of the traditional Jefferson, riding alone to the Capitol and hitching his horse outside while he went in to take the oath of office, is parodied in the gaping multitudes who crowded into the city and into the White House with the bold air of ownership when Jackson came into power. Through four years the "people" had been cajoled into believing themselves the victims of an infamous plot of their enemies to keep them out of that control of the government which was their due. The necessary counterpart of such teaching was the prospect that, with Jackson's election, everything would be turned over into their hands, and in a vague sort of way the ignorant multitude foreshadowed to itself some direct pecuniary benefit from the success that had been won. Filled with such ideas, the common people poured into Washington to see and touch and handle that which had come into their possession.[1] Their numbers were swelled by the great crowd of hungry office-seekers who, from every quarter of the country but chiefly from the South and West, came clamoring for the rewards that had been dangled before their eyes during the campaign. The more refined elements of society looked on aghast and affrighted at the mob in homespun, with a hot-tempered, passionate, and at times lawless military hero as their leader, and feared for the safety of property and republican government.

The political ideals of the newly settled West had

[1] *Cf.* MacDonald, *op. cit.*, p. 43 *ff.*

triumphed over the more conservative elements of the East. Democracy in practice as well as in principle was seeking realization, and in Jackson it had found the man fitted above all others to effect the desired result. He was of humble birth and circumstances; he had risen by his own strength and owed his success to no fortuitous circumstances. Brave, determined, self-willed, passionate in hatred and in friendship, making every difference of view assume the attitude of personal opposition, neglectful of law if it stood in the way of his desires, he was yet honest, sincere, and fervently patriotic, and furnished the great unthinking masses a hero whom they could worship, not as they had worshipped "the Sage of Monticello," afar off for his wisdom, but as "the old Hero" of the Hermitage, for his honesty. The people trusted him and, backed by their trust and reliance, he worked the third revolution in our history. Jackson, no less than Jefferson, was brought into office on an anti-Hamilton platform, though it was not so called. The Federalists as a party had disappeared and more than twenty years before, J. Q. Adams had joined the Democratic-Republicans, but the anti-Jackson men, the men whom Clay led, and the Adams administration stood for the same general principles and policies that had characterized Hamilton.

Jackson's fiercest fight was against the Bank of the United States; not the original bank whose legality Hamilton had so warmly defended and Jefferson as warmly attacked, but another on the same plan that the Democratic-Republicans had been forced to charter in 1816. Jackson's second administration became on the surface almost a fight between the classes, a fight between the rich and the poor. Certain it is that the body of the people was made to feel that it was a death struggle with the money-power which had not yet acquired the title of Wall Street; that unless " Nick " Biddle and his infamous institution were destroyed, the national life would be corrupted beyond hope and republican government would disappear, a prey to plutocracy. Against this dreadful calamity it was every plain man's duty to take his stand behind the banner of General Jackson.[1]

That facts are stranger than fiction is perhaps more often illustrated in politics than elsewhere. Jackson, heralded and fought for as the saviour of the country, proclaimed as the one man capable of contending successfully with the corruption in the government, and himself convinced of his mission, did more to degrade and corrupt and pollute our political life than any man before or since. Honest beyond all question, he made possible the greatest dishonesty and incompetency. Such an unlooked-for and unhappy result followed hard upon the practice of rewarding party services with public places. Jackson was not the inventor of the spoils system; it had already been tried with success in the States and he merely introduced it into our national life. Much as Jackson's own personality tended to strengthen the Executive, the patronage much more increased his power but only as a member of a party; it decreased his efficiency and destroyed his disinterested position. The President could no longer pretend to follow the example of Washington and be the impartial Presi-

[1] *Cf.* Sumner, *op. cit.*, chaps. viii., x., and xi.

dent of the whole country. He became more and more the head of a party.

The forces of democracy had been steadily gathering strength since the close of the Revolution and we may congratulate ourselves that the way had been prepared for their peaceful introduction. The influence of Jackson upon our national life was, however, far from being altogether bad. His ideals were not less far removed from those of Jefferson than they were from that extreme section of the Democratic party which was beginning to identify local self-government with the protection of slavery. Jackson and Calhoun soon found themselves widely separated on the question of the nature of the Union. With Jackson, to be sure, the attempt of South Carolina to nullify a law of the Federal Government had the appearance very largely of an attempt to defy his own authority, to thwart him personally. His defence of the Union assumed to a measurable degree the appearance of a defence of his position as Chief Executive, and his toast "The Union, it must be preserved!" rang both with patriotism and personal feeling. His proclamation [1] of December 10, 1832, asserted a doctrine of national supremacy which brought consternation to the Nullifiers, who trusted to his Southern sympathies to incline him in their favor.[2] There was no doubt in his mind of the right or of the power of the Federal Government to maintain itself against the spirit of disunion, and he challenged in sharpest terms the upholders of the heresy of Nullification. The whole power of the gov-

[1] For the text of Jackson's Proclamation see the Appendix.
[2] *Cf.* Sumner, *op. cit.*, chaps. ix. and x.

Andrew Jackson

ernment was to be put in motion to secure the enforcement of the laws, should resistance by force be tried.

Difficult as it may be to speculate with accuracy upon what might have been, it would seem in this case safe to believe that had Jackson refused to entertain the idea of a compromise, had he joined with Webster in the belief that now was the time to test the strength of the Federal Government,[1] the terrible conflict of the Civil War might possibly have been averted. No other State stood ready to join South Carolina in 1832 in a movement to withdraw from the Union. The South had not yet been set apart in thought and feeling from the rest of the country; it had not yet been made to feel its own homogeneity and the need of concerted action in defence of its peculiar labor. Had the precedent been set in 1832 of vigorous action against all efforts to dissolve the Union, there would have been no excuse for the feeble admission of 1860 that, though there was no right of Secession, the Federal Government was nevertheless lacking in all constitutional means to maintain its own existence against the unlawful attempt of a State to withdraw.[2] Had force been used against South Carolina in 1832, there is little likelihood that it would have been necessary against eleven States in 1861. Yet it must ever remain to Jackson's credit that he sounded the true note of national supremacy and gave support to a growing sentiment that from 1861 to 1865 became supreme.

[1] *Cf.* Lodge's *Daniel Webster*, p. 222.
[2] *Cf.* President Buchanan's message of December, 1860, *Messages and Papers of the Presidents*, v., 635 *ff.*

Reference has already been made to Jackson's attitude toward the other branches of the government. He considered himself in a very special sense the direct representative of the people's wishes, and the courts, no less than Congress, were made to feel the force of Executive independence. John Marshall still presided over the Supreme Court during most of the years of Jackson's administrations; he typified the extremest form of the anti-democratic tendencies and was therefore highly objectionable to Jackson. But aside from personal antipathy and political creed, Jackson could not brook any interference with the triumphant progress of democracy as embodied in himself and his position. He claimed, therefore, an equal right with the Supreme Court to judge of the constitutionality of laws. Had he not sworn to support the Constitution, and was it not his duty to support it as he understood it? That the President has a right to pass an opinion upon the constitutionality of a bill presented for his signature is unquestioned, but when a law has been definitely settled through years of practice and repeated decisions, it is no longer within the province of the Chief Executive to pass judgment. Jackson, then, must be condemned for his violent assumption of the unconstitutionality of the Bank, and his attacks upon the institution from this standpoint were unwarranted. Still more is his attitude toward the Court in the case of the Cherokee Nation *v.* the State of Georgia to be condemned.[1] The chief value of the Court lies in the fact that, as Hamilton said, it is will, not force. This is at once its strength and its weakness,

[1] *Cf.* J. W. Burgess, *The Middle Period*, p. 220 *ff.*

and unless the Executive power of the government be used unreservedly in its support, it must inevitably fall into disrepute and lose its independence. No more destructive principle could have found expression on Jackson's lips than that contained in his famous remark with reference to this case: "John Marshall has made his decision; now let him enforce it."[1] To carry out such a policy consistently would utterly overthrow the system of checks and balances so carefully devised by the separation of the powers of government and reduce the courts to a position of subserviency to the Executive. Fortunately it is a principle which has not found imitation among Jackson's successors.

With Jackson's retirement from the Presidency, the balance that had been disturbed by his personal character was restored and the Executive power sank back into its normal position. The forces of democracy, however, had come to stay and, while the rawness of methods and of individuals gradually disappeared, the principles of political equality as manifested in the suffrage and the civil service continued in undiminished strength.

[1] Horace Greeley, *The American Conflict*, i., 106.

VIII

Daniel Webster. Growth through Rising National Sentiment

DANIEL WEBSTER

1782.	Jan. 18.	Born in Salisbury, N. H.
1797–1801.		At Dartmouth College. Taught school in Maine.
1805.		Admitted to Bar.
1812.		Opposed War of 1812.
1813.		Representative in 13th Congress.
1814.		Re-elected to Congress.
1816.		Moved to Boston.
1818.		Dartmouth College Case.
1820.		Member of State Convention.
1823–27.		Member of Congress. Opposed tariff of 1824.
1827.		Elected U. S. Senator.
1828.		Voted for "Tariff of Abominations."
1830.	Jan. 20 and 26.	Replies to Hayne.
1833.		Re-elected U. S. Senator.
	Feb. 16.	Replied to Calhoun.
1839.		Re-elected to Senate.
1841.		Resigned from Senate.
		Appointed Secretary of State.
1843.		Resigned.
1845.		Elected to Senate.
1850.		Secretary of State.
1852.	Oct. 24.	Died at Marshfield, Mass.

VIII

Daniel Webster. Growth through Rising National Sentiment

WEBSTER was born in a small New Hampshire village on January 18, 1782; he was, therefore, seven years old at the time of the adoption of the Constitution. So intimately is his name associated with this document that it is pleasing to think that the whole of his responsible existence was spent under it. He belonged to the first generation of Americans who knew no other form of government than that established by the present Constitution. He felt himself to be a citizen of the Union, not of the America of the Revolution. It was a generation that had not felt the evils of a loose Confederacy, nor the full force of State pride and State patriotism; it could not recall the conflicting opinions and the resultant compromises of the Philadelphia Convention. It knew that Union meant prosperity and it found in the Constitution both the cause and the justification of the Union. Webster's generation was reared in that era when men, no matter how widely they might differ in their views of the Constitution, were a unit in their devotion and loyalty to the instrument itself. It was nourished on that almost blind worship of the Constitution which followed so quickly after its adoption by all the States. North and South alike felt the force of the rising national sentiment; South Carolina no less than Massachusetts, offered homage at the shrine of the Constitution. Federalist and Republican could unite in a self-sufficing admiration of the new form of government, for after it was adopted, the fight was thenceforth within the Constitution.

Such at least was the case in Webster's early years; not until he was well into middle life did South Carolina proclaim Nullification, yet even then protesting that such a measure was constitutional and consistent with the retention of its place within the Union. Death mercifully came to him nine years before South Carolina led the way of Secession out of the Union, to maintain which he had given freely and fully of his wonderful gifts of intellect and oratory his whole life long.

In estimating Webster's influence upon the development of our Constitution, it may be helpful to sketch briefly the course of a few of the most important events of the period embraced within the span of his maturity, for, unlike the actual framers of the Constitution, Webster was not so much maker, as upholder; he interpreted it through the part he played in the history of his times. He was the living embodiment of the national spirit and he first gave adequate expression to the "slow results of time"; he first voiced for the new generation the new spirit that had come as a result of a multitude of causes.

When the Virginia and the Kentucky Resolutions sent abroad their warning note of danger against the Alien and Sedition Acts, and the reaction against the overreaching nature of Federalist tendencies was rising to its full strength, Webster was in the midst of his teens [1]; the triumph of Jefferson came with the completion of his college career, and the year of his majority witnessed the Louisiana Purchase. The first Embargo Act followed within two years after his admission to the bar, and his opposition to the War of 1812 secured his election to the Thirteenth Congress; there he was at once placed upon the Committee of Foreign Affairs of which Calhoun, an eager advocate of the war, was chairman. He was reelected to the Fourteenth Congress and still continued his opposition to the war; in the same Congress he declared himself opposed to the principle of protection.[2]

This opposition to a war which did more than anything up to that time to strengthen the national sentiment and to elevate the Union above the States, and to protection, whose zealous champion he afterwards became, presents, in its contradictions, a very striking parallel to the career of Calhoun. The course of Calhoun, however, was just the reverse of that of Webster. Elected a member of Congress for the first time in 1811, Calhoun straightway assumed, along with Clay, the leadership of that powerful group of young men then entering public life, and forced on peace-loving President Madison the war with England. As late as 1816 Calhoun was an avowed ad-

[1] For lives of Webster see Lodge, McMaster, and Hapgood.
[2] Lodge, p. 55 *ff*.

vocate of protection and internal improvements, both distinctly national doctrines in their effects. The subsequent career of Calhoun as the greatest opponent of a strong central government and the leading exponent of the rights of the individual States, is no more contradictory than that of Webster in filling just as conspicuously the opposite rôle of advocate of a strong central power and of opponent of State Rights.

The Missouri Compromise was entered into while Webster had temporarily withdrawn from national politics because of his removal to Boston from his native State. His re-entry into Congress, as a Representative from Massachusetts, came in 1823 and in the following year he opposed the "Tariff of 1824" in a remarkably brilliant speech. In 1827 Webster entered the Senate, the scene of his worthiest labors and his greatest triumphs. The change that was coming over his views, a change that may be attributed perhaps to the changed conditions of his life, was evidenced in his support of the "Tariff of Abominations" in 1828; from this time forth Webster was a consistent supporter of the policy of protection.[1]

The years following his election to the Senate to his death in 1852 were crowded with events of the highest importance in which he played a principal part. The election of Jackson to the Presidency, with the final success of the democratic movement; the threat of Nullification in South Carolina, which called forth the memorable replies to Hayne and to

[1] Lodge, *op. cit.*, p. 154 *ff*, and F. W. Taussig, *The Tariff History of the United States*.

Daniel Webster

Calhoun; the question of the right of petition so valiantly fought and won by J. Q. Adams; the first mutterings of the slavery question that grew rapidly into a demand, on the one side for extension, and on the other for extinction; the annexation of Texas; the questions regarding the power of Congress in the Territories, and the admission of new States with slavery or without, are sufficient to illustrate the historical movements of the times and to give indication of the opportunities presented of influencing the national development.[1]

Time and space forbid a detailed study of Webster's speeches on all these questions, richly as such study repays the student, whether of oratory or of the principles of our government. Neither can we pause to trace the economic influences that were daily marking off North and South more distinctly from each other. Suffice it to say that slavery early disappeared in the North, manufactures and free labor flourished, while in the South, cotton and slavery seemed linked in perpetual bonds to the exclusion of practically all industries save agriculture. The West, from its spirit of self-reliance as well as from its economic conditions, found itself far more closely united in sympathy and interest with the North than with the South.

Webster grew up in the atmosphere of Federalist principles, though the Federalist party went down in lasting defeat before he was old enough to cast a ballot. Though the party died, its principles lived. They were incorporated in the very structure of the

[1] *Cf.* T. H. Benton, *Thirty Years' View*, and J. W. Burgess, *The Middle Period*.

government which the Democratic-Republicans dared not tear down; their victory in 1800 could only check, not undo, what had already been done. The Federalist principles, moreover, found constant application and expansion at the hands of Marshall and the Judiciary. Webster's first great argument on the Constitution was made before the Supreme Court with Marshall presiding. It was in the celebrated Dartmouth College case in 1818 when Webster was thirty-six years old. A graduate of Dartmouth, he found peculiar pleasure in defending the chartered rights of this institution of which he said, " It is . . . a small College. And yet there are those who love it." [1]

The point at issue was whether the charter of the college was a contract; if so, then certain statutes passed by the Legislature of New Hampshire, modifying the charter, were null and void because in violation of the Constitution which lays upon the States a very positive limitation. The prohibition is contained in the following words. " No State shall . . . pass any bill of attainder, *ex post facto* law, or law impairing the obligations of contracts." [2]

The court was thoroughly in sympathy with the position taken by Webster. In the case of Fletcher *v.* Peck,[3] decided in 1810, the Court had held that the term " contract " included both those agreements already executed and those still to be executed; that " a grant or conveyance is an executed contract, the obligation of which continues binding upon the

[1] Quoted, Lodge, *op. cit.*, p. 90.
[2] Art. i., Sec. 10.
[3] 6 Cranch, 87.

grantor." These principles the Court now applied in the Dartmouth College case to the charter of a private corporation and the New Hampshire laws were declared unconstitutional. Though often cited as the case which established the inviolability of contracts under the Constitution, in reality the question decided was whether the charter was a contract for the security and disposition of property, or a grant of political power which might be recalled at the pleasure of the State. In accepting the former view, the Court strengthened its position as the supporter of the nation against the States and increased the reputation of Webster as a constitutional lawyer.

The great opportunity, however, for Webster to stand forth as the exponent of the idea of national unity came when the doctrine of Nullification was proclaimed in South Carolina. Then it was that he delivered his wonderful speeches in support of the Constitution as the basis of a perpetual Union, as a real instrument of government by which a national state had been created. Of his two most noted speeches, the reply to Hayne was the first and was delivered in 1830.[1] Nominally on the Foote Resolution in the Senate, which looked to the restriction of the sale of public lands, it in reality dealt with the paramount question of the nature of the Federal Union. Senator Hayne of South Carolina had taken advantage of the opportunity presented by the Foote Resolution to give expression to the growing separatist feeling in his State, a feeling which owed its immediate origin to the Tariff of 1828 and which

[1] In *Writings and Speeches of Daniel Webster* (National Edition), vi., 3 *ff.*

found its culmination in the Nullification Ordinance of 1832.[1] To Webster fell the task of replying in behalf of that great body of the people who believed in the necessity of Union for the preservation of Liberty—a necessity to which he gave expression in the closing words of his peroration, " Liberty *and* Union, now and forever, one and inseparable."

The reply to Hayne was delivered almost without preparation, yet the truth is that his whole life had been, as he said, a constant preparation. Day by day he had gathered together thoughts, impressions, ideals of national unity, and on this occasion he reached the zenith of his career as statesman and as orator. Other speeches in behalf of the Constitution followed, but none of them quite equalled this first attempt to set forth the nature of the Union as it had developed under the Constitution.

In a consideration of the questions raised in this debate we must remember that they were not new; they were as old as the Constitution itself, for they found expression in the Convention which framed it and in the State conventions which adopted it; they arose in the Virginia and Kentucky Resolutions which sought to interpret it, in the Hartford Convention and in the decisions of the Supreme Court in some of its most famous cases. They were now presented in new form and as a result of new causes and conditions; they were presented more concretely and as a practical question which demanded settlement. Not since the days of the Constitutional Con-

---

[1] *Cf.* C. W. Loring, *Nullification, Secession, Webster's Argument, and the Kentucky and Virginia Resolutions,* and E. P. Powell, *Nullification and Secession in the United States.*

vention had the issue been brought to a test, and even now the final trial was postponed as a result of the efforts of the "Great Compromiser," Henry Clay. For another generation South Carolina allowed the doctrine of Nullification to sleep—to sleep and wake, changed in form but not in substance. Nullification transformed into Secession shows itself in its true light of revolution in the Civil War.

The great problem to be solved was the nature of the Federal Union; around it were gathered all the other questions so hotly debated back and forth; whether the Constitution was a compact, creating a league of sovereign States, or a supreme law constituting a supreme government within the sphere of the powers conferred upon it; whether the Constitution was the creature of the States, or of their governments, or of the people of the United States as a whole, as the preamble declared; whether the individual States, as sovereigns, were the final judges of the powers conferred by the Constitution, or whether that power was vested in the general government in the appropriate organ. These are the questions upon whose solution such a wealth of argument was poured out, and which called forth the loftiest eloquence our country has produced.

Webster bore off the palm of victory in this debate, whether in the field of oratory or of argument; as an orator he was without a peer, and his logic carried conviction to the hearts of the great mass of the people because he thought as they thought, because he represented the growing spirit of nationalism which saw safety in Union; because he looked forward to a brilliant future of united action and not backward to an era of disunion, as the goal of his ambition for his country. He sought to support his conception of the nature of the Union from the Constitution itself and from its provisions he drew the proofs in support of his positions. He went back, to be sure, to the proceedings of the Convention, to the arguments of the *Federalist,* and to the State conventions, but always with the impression that the arguments deduced from history are subsidiary in character, that the true source of information upon the nature of the document is the Constitution itself, what it then was and what it had come to mean.

To a certain extent Webster was caught in the toils of the legal formalism of the age; he was deeply influenced by the worshipful attitude toward the Constitution that had held sway so long over the people and thought there could be no safer guide to its meaning than the words of the instrument itself. Herein lay the weakness of his reply to Hayne. Its strength and its power upon the people were due to the fact that it made clear to them what had been hazy; it formulated in faultless style the vague conceptions of the times; it crystallized the national tendencies and became a part of the people's life and thought, their storehouse of argument upon which they were to draw in succeeding years.

The Tariff of 1832, though it lowered some of the duties, reasserted the principle of protection and therefore was equally as obnoxious to the South, and to South Carolina in particular, as was the "Tariff of Abominations" of four years previous. Acting in accordance with her previously declared intention, on

November 24, 1832, South Carolina passed the Ordinance of Nullification,[1] declaring the tariff unconstitutional, and null and void within her territory, and the Legislature proceeded by a series of acts to render its execution impossible without recourse to arms.

On December 10th, President Jackson issued his Proclamation that rang with the spirit of his famous toast, " The Union, it must be preserved! " The supremacy of the national government was heralded in no uncertain terms, and to maintain it, he declared that the armed forces of the United States would be used, if necessary, to carry into effect the laws which the Ordinance of Nullification had declared null and void. Calhoun, the foremost champion of Nullification, resigned his office of Vice-President and was elected a member of the Senate, there to support the cause of South Carolina.

It was but natural that Webster and Calhoun should lead the opposing forces in this fight and the clash soon came on the Force Bill, a measure to confer on the President the powers necessary to secure the enforcement of the law in South Carolina. In his exposition of the doctrine of Nullification, Calhoun surpassed Hayne in the logic and power of his speech as the master does the pupil. But Webster's reply on the 16th of February, " The Constitution not a Compact of Sovereign States,"[2] equalled neither in oratorical power nor logical strength his reply to Hayne.

Calhoun's strength, as Webster's weakness, was in

[1] See Appendix for the text of the Ordinance.
[2] *Writings*, vi., 181 *ff.*

history. What the Constitution meant in 1789 was the foundation of Calhoun's argument, and it was difficult to controvert his position that the Constitution was a compact, and was so regarded by its framers. The support he drew from the Virginia and Kentucky Resolutions, the frequent threats of dissolution in the early days of the Union, and the action of the Hartford Convention rendered his position a strong one. What the Constitution was in 1789, that it was in 1832; such was the conclusion of Calhoun and it was difficult to see how the conclusion could be avoided. There had been few amendments and they had looked rather toward his view than away from it. How, then, was it possible that the nature of the instrument had changed? Was there some subtle process of transformation by which the nature of things was changed without changing their appearance? Was the Constitution the same and not the same?

Webster likewise attempted to take the same attitude toward the Constitution and sought to show from history that it had always been what it then was. He would have been wiser to have disregarded history, and to have accepted the Constitution as being the instrument of National Union the people then considered it, for in this lay his true strength, and his appeals to history only weakened an otherwise impregnable position.

The reply to Calhoun, however, supplemented that to Hayne and the two together did more than anything else, perhaps, to mould the sentiment of Union, to give it form, consistency, and coherency in the years of severe trial that were to come. In this, as

Daniel Webster

in the former speech, there is the appeal to the words of the Constitution itself. He draws upon them to support his principal contention. What does it proclaim itself to be, a compact or a constitution, which, in the words of Hamilton, is only "another name for power or government"? It is a constitution, an instrument of government. "The Constitution, sir, is not a contract, but the result of a contract; meaning by contract no more than assent. Founded on consent, it is a government proper. . . . The people have agreed to make a Constitution; but when made, that Constitution becomes what its name imports. It is no longer a mere agreement." [1]

Futhermore the Constitution itself is authority for the statement that it was ordained by the people of the United States, not by the States as such. But here Webster failed to note that the original preamble declared that "We, the people of the States of New Hampshire, Massachusetts, etc.," and that the names of the several States were omitted and the form, "We, the people of the United States," was adopted because of the uncertainty as to which States would adopt the Constitution, and the fact that it would become binding upon such States when adopted by nine.[2] Even as it stands, the expression, "We the people of the United States," is capable of a twofold interpretation, and Webster's opponents were not slow to seize upon the one favorable to their view.[3] To a calmer generation it would appear futile to

[1] *Writings*, vi., 201.

[2] *Documentary History of the Constitution*, iii., 444, and Madison, *Writings*, iii., 92 and 422.

[3] Johnston, *American Political History*, ed. by James A. Woodburn, i., 47.

attempt to derive a conclusive argument from either view.[1]

Having established, then, the position that the Constitution is not a compact among sovereign States, but a law and ordinance of government, established by the whole people, just as the State constitutions are established by the people of the States, Webster advances to his next point. This law declares itself to be supreme. "This Constitution, and the laws of the United States which shall be made in pursuance thereof . . . shall be the supreme law of the land; and the judges in every State shall be bound thereby, anything in the constitution or laws of any State to the contrary notwithstanding."[2]

The practical question which presented itself was: Who had the right to decide in the case of a controversy between the States and the central government regarding the extent of the powers conferred upon the latter? All agreed that the Federal Government was one of strictly limited powers and that it could exercise only those rights which had been expressly delegated to it, but as to the extent of those powers there must arise differences of opinion. The doctrine of Nullification asserted that each State, in its sovereign capacity as a party to the contract, had the right to determine whether or not Congress had exceeded its powers in the passage of any law, and having determined the question in the affirmative, possessed the further right of declaring such law unconstitutional, and so null and void within the

[1] *Cf.* Merriam, *op. cit.*, p. 284 *ff.*
[2] Art. vi.

limits of such State.[1] Webster admitted that this would be the case if the Union were only a league, resting on a compact, but having proved, to his own satisfaction at least, that the Constitution was no compact but the supreme law of the land, it followed "both by necessary implication and by express grant," that the Federal Government was the final and conclusive judge of its own powers. Only so can the Constitution be supreme.[2]

The exercise of this power by the central government might take place in either of two ways. First, in the determination of all cases that might arise under the Constitution and laws of the United States, the national Judiciary is declared by the Constitution to be supreme. "As to the cases . . . which do not come before the courts, those political questions which terminate with the enactments of Congress, it is of necessity that these should be ultimately decided by Congress itself."[3] If not, and each State is to decide for itself, then the dilemma confronts us that "what is law in one State is not law in another. Or, if the resistance of one State compels an entire repeal of the law, then a minority, and that a small one, governs the whole country."[4] The power of ultimate and final judgment is one that must be entrusted to the national government under the security of the responsibility of members of Congress to the people.

The right of each State to declare null and void

[1] *Cf.* Calhoun's *Works*, ii., passim.
[2] Webster, *Writings*, vi., 213.
[3] *Ibid.*, vi., 219.
[4] *Cf. Ibid.*, vi., 196.

a law it deemed unconstitutional, was declared by the supporters of Nullification to be a constitutional right and one that might be exercised while the State still remained in the Union. Such a condition, which Webster characterized as "half allegiance and half rebellion," he proved conclusively was and could be ultimately nothing but revolution, open rebellion, to be maintained by force of arms.[1] So convincing was his argument that a later generation was compelled to admit its truth and Secession replaced Nullification. But Secession was admittedly revolutionary, extra-constitutional, of which the justification could be found only in the appeal to the inherent right of all peoples to change their form of government when the evils they endure become intolerable.

The arguments of both sides rested in large part upon the phraseology of the Constitution itself; the appeal to history for justification made by each was better founded in the case of Calhoun than of Webster, but Webster's argument prevailed with the body of the people because it interpreted the Constitution in the light of the popular feeling of the day. There was unquestionably a time when Calhoun's argument would have touched a more responsive chord than Webster's, but that time was past. The generation of Nullification knew no State outside of the Union; knew not the States, discordant, warring, as in the days of the Confederation. The States of the West knew no other existence than that within the Union and desired no other. Their spirit had been, almost without exception, national in its character and manifestations, as though the fact that the Western Terri-

[1] Webster, *Writings*, vi., 192 *ff*.

tory had been a bond of union in the days of the Confederation, had left its stamp upon the disposition of the States formed from it. The North and the West could not conceive of the right of a State to destroy the Union, as Nullification and Secession would inevitably have destroyed it. Hence came the well-nigh universal response with which the noble argument of Webster was met throughout these sections.

Webster's attitude with regard to the Bank was but another indication of his general position, one more evidence of his general stand with respect to the powers of the national government.[1] Though Webster had stood with Jackson in sustaining the Union against the destructive doctrine of Nullification, he could not join him in what he deemed a foolish, if not a criminal, attack on the United States Bank. Webster felt no scruple as to the constitutionality of the Bank and was convinced of its value to the country; Jackson's antagonism to it he regarded in the light of a personal hatred, aroused by the belief that the Bank was a political machine in the hands of his enemies, and his action in reference to it as a gross violation of the Constitution. Webster joined in passing the Resolution of Censure, the expunging of which from the records of the Senate became the most ardent desire of all Jackson men.

From the days of Nullification to the day of Webster's death, the great issue before the country was slavery.[2] In the very year that Webster made

[1] For Webster's speeches on the Bank, see *Works*, vi., vii., and viii.
[2] *Cf.* A. B. Hart, *Slavery and Abolition*, 1831–1841.

his reply to Calhoun, the National Anti-Slavery Society was established and Abolition became an active principle. Webster was in no sense an abolitionist. In his fiercest condemnations of slavery, there is never a hint of abolition. Against the slave trade, against the extension of slavery, against the institution of slavery itself, he might hurl his most savage attacks, but never without recognition of the position that had been assured it by the Constitution. The desire to uphold the Union and the Constitution was as strong in Webster on March 17, 1850, as on February 16, 1833, but his idea as to the means had changed. In 1833 he was bitterly opposed to the compromise mediated by Clay and declared " that the time had come to test the strength of the Constitution and the government." [1] In 1850, facing a united and menacing slave power, the strongest political force in the country, he deemed it wise to yield to its demands and not forbid slavery in the new Territories. Such a concession seemed to offer the only hope of preserving the Union. To forbid slavery, moreover, in these Territories was useless, and he " would not take pains uselessly to reaffirm an ordinance of nature, nor to re-enact the will of God." [2]

Early and late he sought to guard against Secession and war; in 1833 he was willing to put South Carolina to the test, but in 1850 he would set the threatening agitation at rest and ensure a final and conclusive settlement by yielding. But peace was not to be secured through an attempt to silence the agitation; the narcotic of constitutional guarantees

[1] Quoted in Lodge, *op. cit.*, p. 222.
[2] *Writings*, x., 84.

was no longer effective in deadening the moral conscience, and a decade later, the men of the North remembered only the Webster of the earlier days—the man who voiced a nation's cry for life; the man to whom Liberty meant Union and Union meant Liberty, "one and inseparable, now and forever!"

IX

John C. Calhoun.   Retardation through Sectional Influence

JOHN C. CALHOUN

1782.	March 18.	Born in Abbeville district, S. C.
1802-04.		At Yale.
1807.		Admitted to Bar.
1808.		Elected to State Legislature.
1811.		Elected as Representative to Twelfth Congress.
		Advocated war with Great Britain.
1816.		Advocated Tariff and Bank Bill.
1817–1825.		Secretary of War.
1824.		Vice-President.
1828.		Vice-President.
		"The South Carolina Exposition."
1832.		Resigned Vice-Presidency and became Senator.
		Nullification measures.
1835.		Re-elected to Senate.
1836.		Opposed reception of anti-slavery petitions.
1842.		Resigned, to take effect March 3, 1843.
1844.		Secretary of State.
1845.	March 4.	Retired from Cabinet.
	Dec. 1.	Took seat in Senate again.
1849.		"Address to the People of the South."
		"A Disquisition on Government."
		"A Discourse on the Constitution and Government of the United States."
1850.	March 31.	Died at Washington.

IX

John C. Calhoun. Retardation through Sectional Influence

NO two names in American history are more closely associated than those of Webster and Calhoun; no names are more often mentioned in conjunction and no careers present more startling contrasts. North and South, Union and Secession, Free and Slave, are summed up in these two men,—in their lives, their characters, and their public acts.

In time they were contemporary in the strictest sense, for both were born in the year 1782, and they died within two years of each other, Calhoun in 1850 and Webster in 1852. Both were graduates of New England colleges, for Calhoun, though born in South Carolina, was not satisfied with the limited opportunities offered by the South and so sought the larger advantages of Yale where he graduated in 1804.[1] Later he studied law at the then prominent law school at Litchfield, Connecticut. Both men entered public life at about the same time, both were members of the House and of the Senate, both were members of Cabinets, and both were aspirants for the Presidency; Calhoun, moreover, was twice elected Vice-President.

[1] Lives by H. von Holst and Gaillard Hunt.

Calhoun entered public life in 1808 as a member of the State Legislature, having already demonstrated the logical character of his mind and his sound mental equipment by an unusually rapid rise to prominence at the bar. Three years later he was elected a member of the Twelfth Congress. Henry Clay had at the same time been elected a member of the House and was chosen Speaker. Clay appointed Calhoun a member of the Committee on Foreign Relations and the Committee elected him chairman. Both Clay and Calhoun were new men in the House, though Clay had served a few months in the Senate, and their elevation to the two most important positions in it is explicable only on the ground of their well-known view on the question of a war with England.[1] The West and the South were eager for the war, while New England opposed it. The latter was more jealous of the growing influence of the other sections in national affairs than zealous for the national honor, especially when its defence meant a loss to her commercial interest.

Clay and Calhoun drew in with their first breath the vigorous air of the new democracy of the West, alive with the spirit of nationality; they were the product of a new era, the advance guard of a new order of things in our political life, and they swept away with ruthless hand the statesmen of the older generation, the leaders who had developed out of the revolutionary struggle. Mr. Bagehot has told us how, in English politics, it has seemed at times that a whole generation of statesmen, who have grown old in their leadership and who have held on long beyond their

[1] *Cf.* Von Holst, *John C. Calhoun,* p. 15 *ff.*

allotted years, drops off all at once and its place is taken by a new and younger generation. Instead of a gradual process of removal which leaves no break, there is an abrupt severance as though a whole generation had been passed over.

Some such condition existed at the opening of the Twelfth Congress. Madison had succeeded to the Presidency in 1809, in regular line of promotion from the Secretaryship of State, bringing with him all the traditions of a former period and perpetuating the principles and practices of other times. But with the coming of Clay and Calhoun and their brilliant following of young men, the scene changes. Madison, to be sure, continues to be President, but he is in no sense leader as Jefferson had been; the principal rôle has passed from the Executive to Congress, and interest centres around the Speaker and the Chairman of the Committee on Foreign Relations; they assume the leadership and force on an unwilling President a party war.

Webster entered Congress two years later than Calhoun and as an opponent of the war with England. The conflict with Calhoun that lasted nearly forty years began at once. Fate seemed to have created these two to play the rôles of opposing champions, for each changed his position with respect to the great issues before the country and thus remained ever upon opposing sides. Calhoun was at this time and continued for some years to be, an advocate of measures and of principles that were of a strongly nationalizing character.[1] To these Webster found

[1] Von Holst, *op. cit.*, p. 26 *ff*. For Calhoun's early speeches *cf. Works*, ii., ed. by R. K. Cralle.

himself opposed. Calhoun was eager for a war that did more than all else that had preceded it, to create a national feeling. Webster's first political success came from his hostility to this war. Both were influenced here, as throughout their lives, by the atmosphere around them, though it is Calhoun who now feels the throb of the great nation's life in his pulses while Webster is under the domination of New England's antipathy to the war. Calhoun advocates a tariff and internal improvements; Webster opposes them. As time went by influences were at work which eventually brought them again, but with positions reversed, into opposition upon these same questions. Calhoun ceases to advocate a tariff and internal improvements; Webster ceases to oppose them and becomes their advocate. Calhoun ceases to think of national welfare before State interests; Webster comes to think first and always of national union and greatness. Calhoun begins to see in national strength a menace to liberty, in too close a union a danger to freedom; Webster sees safety only in union and beholds the blessings of liberty imperilled by the sovereignty of the States.

During the eight years of Monroe's administration, Calhoun was Secretary of War and showed himself an administrator of a high order; in 1824 and again in 1828 he was elected Vice-President. It was during these years of administrative work that Calhoun's opinions began to change, and it is much to be regretted that his activities were not such as to call out expressions of his opinions, that we might with greater certainty trace the progress of the change. This much seems sure: that when Calhoun returned to South Carolina in 1828 after the passage of the "Tariff of Abominations," he had been so long away from, and had gotten so far out of touch with, the people of the State that he was unprepared for the great change that had come over them. The representations made to him by the leading men who visited him at his home at Fort Hill made a deep impression upon him [1]; it did not seem possible, as he brooded over the distressing economic condition thus presented to his attention, that the framers of the Constitution could ever have intended that a single State or several States should suffer from national legislation, as he believed South Carolina was then suffering from the tariff; and as he himself said, "he turned to the Constitution to find a remedy." The result was the "South Carolina Exposition," [2] in which Calhoun set forth for the first time a thorough-going programme of Nullification.

The Virginia and Kentucky Resolutions of 1798 were claimed as the lawful source of the doctrine, and the great name and fame of Jefferson were adduced in its support. Despite Madison's protest against the use of Jefferson's name "as a pedestal for this colossal heresy," [3] the possibility of reading into the Resolutions the meaning Calhoun attached to them remained and contributed its share toward strengthening the sentiment. The time, however, was not yet ripe for more than a formal declaration. There was a hope that the tariff, through its inequal-

---

[1] *Cf.* D. F. Houston, *A Study of Nullification in South Carolina.*
[2] *Works*, vi., 1 *ff.*
[3] Madison, *Letters and Other Writings*, iv., 229.

ities, would prove unendurable to the North as well as to the South, and that Jackson, a Southerner and a State-Rights man, would favor its repeal.[1] Meanwhile the efforts of Calhoun were directed to strengthening his position and to consolidating the forces that were to sustain him.

Calhoun's hope of relief through Jackson soon proved vain, for though the duties of 1828 were lowered, the principle of protection was reaffirmed in the Act of 1832. The time had now come for a more active programme of resistance, for a trial of the doctrines that had been proclaimed as a threat. South Carolina, through a convention, passed in November the Ordinance of Nullification,[2] declaring the tariff laws "null, void, and no law, nor binding upon South Carolina, her officers and citizens," and threatening Secession if force should be used in the attempt to execute them. The Legislature of the State met in the same month and proceeded to prepare for war and to resume the powers which had been expressly granted to the Government of the United States in the Constitution.

Calhoun was the guiding spirit in South Carolina's every action, and soon after President Jackson had issued his famous proclamation of December 10th, in which he declared his fixed intention to carry out the law in the face of all opposition, Calhoun resigned the Vice-Presidency and was elected to the Senate, there to fight the losing battle of State-Rights and Slavery for the remainder of his life.

If Calhoun had believed that Jackson would sup-

[1] Von Holst, *op. cit.*, 82 *ff.*
[2] See Appendix.

port South Carolina, or at least not oppose her by force, because of his Southern sympathies, or if he trusted that because Jackson had failed to support the Supreme Court's decision in the Cherokee Indian case, he would follow a similar course of inaction on the present occasion, he was far from a correct interpretation of the situation or of Jackson's character. It was doubtless a great satisfaction to Jackson to leave unexecuted a decision of his old enemy, John Marshall; it was an opportunity to enforce the lesson that Federalist principles were no longer to be the order of the day; a notice that the long predominance of the Court was at an end; that Jackson as well as Marshall would act as interpreter of the Constitution whenever it became necessary from the standpoint of Executive action. Had he not sworn to uphold the Constitution, and to keep his oath must he not uphold it as he understood it?

Hatred of Marshall confirmed him in inaction in the Cherokee case. The conditions were exactly reversed in the case of South Carolina. Calhoun he hated with even more violence than he did Marshall,[1] and this hatred led him to proclaim a stronger national sentiment than he could well maintain when Nullification no longer threatened. Jackson was determined to have his will. Action in the one case and inaction in the other were alike to him, so his imperious will might have its way, and contradictory constitutional doctrines easily found lodgment in the "old Hero's" breast when passion stirred it.

The result of the conflict between South Carolina

[1] *Cf.* Hunt, *op. cit.*, p. 112; Von Holst, *op. cit.*, p. 84, and Sumner's *Andrew Jackson*, p. 196 *ff.*

and the Federal Government added another to the many compromises in our constitutional history. Both sides claimed the victory which belonged clearly to neither. For the time being, Calhoun had accomplished what he immediately desired, for the tariff was to be reduced. But his interpretation of the Constitution was not accepted, and the spirit of nationality continued to increase in strength till it reached its final triumph in the Civil War.

Early in the year 1833, Calhoun in fulfilment of his object in entering the Senate, stated in masterly fashion the interpretation of the Constitution that underlay Nullification.[1] Lacking in the fire that made Webster's eloquence overpowering, Calhoun was, nevertheless, a great orator to whom men listened with rapt attention. His deep earnestness, logical precision, keen analysis, and almost prophetic vision of the future, when added to the fact that he spoke as the unquestioned representative of the South and its peculiar interests, lent a gravity and impressiveness to his words, second to that inspired by none.

Calhoun was no longer national in his feelings and sympathies; he had repudiated all his earlier national views and was become the representative of a section and its interests. Yet his love for his country and for the Union was intense, but it was love for a kind of Union that was dead. With almost his last breath he proclaimed his love for it and would save it from destruction at the hands of those who called themselves its friends.[2] The word he most wished engraved on his tombstone was Nullification, for it

[1] *Works*, ii., 197 ff.
[2] *Ibid.*, iv., 577.

meant the freedom of South Carolina and of every other State from oppressive measures on the part of the general government; it meant the liberty of the States, and the preservation of the Union in its original form. To him the Union of Webster's desire meant tyranny, and tyranny meant rebellion and dissolution of the Union. If the Union was to be saved, it could only be by reverting to its original form from which there had been so wide a departure.

Led on by his zeal for his State, for the South, and its institution of slavery, he could see no safety in any form of Union in which the minority could not protect itself against the majority, in which a State could not defend its reserved rights by being itself the judge whether or not these rights had been infringed. It was self-evident, he thought, that to make the Federal Government the judge of its own powers was to make its discretion, not the Constitution, the measure of those powers, and to place every right and liberty of the States at the mercy of this discretion, and to destroy the true nature of the Union. He believed in a Confederation of sovereign States, united by a compact for certain specific purposes. The Constitution he regarded as such a compact among sovereign States and it was not difficult to find abundant warrant for his view in the words of the framers of the document.[1]

If the Constitution was a compact, then, argued Calhoun, the Union was a Confederation and not a Federal State. The only result of an agreement was an agreement, and not, as Webster declared, " a gov-

[1] *Cf. Works*, i., 111 *ff. Discourse on the Constitution and Government of the United States.*

ernment proper." The general government was merely the agent of the States and when the agent exceeds his authority, when the general government passes a law that one of the parties to the compact considers unconstitutional, that party may declare such law null and void. If the right of Nullification were recognized, the majority would be more willing to listen to reason, and would be forced to accommodation. It was a constitutional right to be exercised for the preservation of the Union; only by its use could the members of the Union live together in peace. After Nullification, the last resort of an injured State was Secession!

Calhoun proclaimed himself a Democrat of the strictest sect and doubtless he believed that he was; yet the foundation of all his political belief rests upon the rejection of the corner-stone of democracy, the belief in the principle of the supremacy of the majority. From the days of the Constitutional Convention there had been an incongruous alliance of men of conflicting views. In the Convention itself, the men of the small-State party, advocates of State-Rights, allied themselves in the main with the advocates of democracy; the alliance was made permanent by Jefferson and carried to the point of absurdity by Calhoun.[1] State-Rights and democracy are in an irrepressible conflict and the strictest of the strict constructionists was a Democrat in name only! The great principles of modern democracy, the equality of all men, the rule of the numerical majority, and manhood suffrage did not kindle his soul with a glow of enthusiasm. He was an aris-

[1] Oliver, *Alexander Hamilton*, p. 151.

tocrat in feeling and belief, though he would have been the last to admit it. He believed himself a Democrat because he cheated himself with words; the shadow, not the substance of democracy, pleased his fancy; the outward form, not the inner reality of his principles, was democratic.

To soften the sharp edge of Nullification and the rule of a minority, Calhoun developed the idea of a "concurrent majority."[1] The rule of a numerical majority he regarded as capable of the greatest tyranny. Had he not experienced its evil effects in South Carolina? For protection against such possible tyranny, he would put it in the power of the minority to protect itself, or rather he would do away with the rule of the numerical majority and in its place he would set an intricate system for the representation of interests, so that both numbers and interests must concur in all legislation.

The application of such a principle, as Webster rightly declared, was to substitute the control of the minority for that of the majority, and to overthrow democracy as it had been known and accepted since the formation of the Constitution. However excellent the idea of the concurrent majority may have been, it was not democratic and it was folly to call by the name of democracy a theory which, when applied to the Federal Government, rendered it possible for a few States to prevent all action on the part of the government.

To some extent, Calhoun as well as Webster, sought the proofs of his view of the nature of the Union in the Constitution itself, but he differed from

[1] *Works*, i., 27 *ff.*

Webster in that with him the argument from the Constitution itself is subsidiary in character; it is not the primary and fundamental proof; that is to be found in the principle that underlies all governments. Calhoun starts with a radical departure from the principles of the school of political philosophy that had gone almost unquestioned for so many years and that had been the faith of the "Fathers" of the Constitution. The doctrine of the social contract as the basis of society and of government had been almost universal among English-speaking peoples since the days of John Locke; for the French it had been a national fetish since Rousseau. Calhoun rejected this theory and under the influence of the changed basis of the world's philosophical thought, of which he himself was perhaps unconscious, he harkens back to Aristotle and declares that man is by nature a political animal and must live in society if he live at all.[1]

The rejection of the contract theory of society sounds paradoxical in a man who personifies the contract theory of the Constitution. If there is any one fact about Calhoun's political ideas that is more widely known than any other, it is that he believed the Constitution was a compact. The same belief was held by the majority of the members of the Constitutional Convention and the Constitution was repeatedly declared to be both a social compact for the establishment of society, and a political contract for the institution of a particular kind of government. From the general principle of the natural

[1] *Works*, i., 1 *ff.*

law school, that unanimity was necessary to establish the contract, the principle was deduced that it could not be dissolved except by unanimous consent; in this fashion an argument had been drawn by Madison to demonstrate the change that had been brought about in the nature of the Union by the adoption of the present Constitution.

Such a view was utterly at variance with Calhoun's theory; for him society was natural and necessary; some form of political organization was essential; the choice was not between government and no government, but between the various forms of government[1]; the Constitution, therefore, could not be a contract for the establishment of society but of government. From this standpoint Calhoun was relieved from the necessity of refuting the general argument regarding the unanimity necessary for the dissolution of the contract. Further, if the Constitution was not a social contract, then it did not necessarily follow that the contracting parties were the individuals living under it, and it became a relatively easy matter to construct an argument from the historical circumstances surrounding the making and the adoption of the Constitution, which set forth in very plausible, not to say convincing, form, the view that the contracting parties were the sovereign states.[2]

It has been said with a great deal of truth that if you admit the correctness of Calhoun's premises, you cannot consistently reject his conclusions. The character of his mind was extremely logical—too logical

[1] *Works,* i., 2.
[2] *Ibid.,* i., 111.

to permit of his being a really great statesman, for his devotion to logical sequence led him to lose sight of the movements of history, which do not always fall within the bounds of a logical course. Even had Calhoun's view been the correct one at the time of the adoption of the Constitution, it was no longer so. There had been developed a strong national feeling that had availed itself of the possibilities of the Constitution to realize itself in the forms and practices of a national state. Calhoun failed to take account of this feeling or imagined, for a time at least, that it could be turned back in its course.

However much one may differ from Calhoun in his views of the nature of the Union, the time is past when anything but the most patriotic motives can be attributed to him. Narrow, twisted, perverse, even sectional, as his views may have been, to him they were genuine and begotten of an intense love for what he regarded as the only true and lasting form of Union. Our regret must be that his conception of patriotism was so distorted. He saw in a league of States, in a confederacy, all those guarantees of liberty and security which we regard as the peculiar blessing of an "indissoluble union of indestructible States."

The rejection by Calhoun of the principle of the social contract as the basis of society had a far deeper significance for his whole conception than at first sight would be apparent. It indicated not only a change of view regarding the nature and origin of society, but also a complete change in the entire philosophical basis of his thought; it denoted the assumption of a new standpoint from which to judge of political phenomena, it marked the beginning of the organic theory as it was awakened, first by the historical, and later by the biological, character of men's thought, working under the influence of evolution. In place of the purely mechanical conception of society, which placed the union of its atoms in an act of will, in a legal volition, Calhoun set the immutable principles of human nature and distinguished sharply between the action of law and of nature.[1]

With this distinction in mind, Calhoun declared the Constitution to be a compact and that the only result of a compact was a compact. Nowhere is the fundamental difference in thought between Webster and Calhoun more clearly shown than in this particular. Webster, grasping the full significance of the national sentiment that had been developed under the Constitution, yet stands upon the same plane of thought regarding the nature of political action as did the makers of the Constitution, and maintained that the Constitution was a compact, if thereby no more is meant than agreement, but the result of that agreement is a government. Calhoun, from the new standpoint of all his thought, also declared the Constitution to be a compact, but the conclusion he draws is that the only result of a contract is a contract, and that therefore no State could have been created by the Constitution, but only an alliance whose common agent was the Federal Government.

Madison lived long enough to see the confusion that was arising from this use of old words with a

[1] *Cf.* McLaughlin, *The Social Compact and Constitutional Construction*, in *American Historical Review*, April, 1900.

new meaning. To the one side, contract was the old and immemorial fashion in which governments had been set up, the fashion that had been consecrated by the Declaration of Independence. To the other, it was impossible that a contract should do more, or be more, than a contract at law, which confessedly could not create anything by its terms save obligations upon the parties.

To the followers of Calhoun the Constitution, then, was a contract or compact which united sovereign states into a league, thereby imposing upon them certain obligations and conferring upon them certain rights and duties. The measure of the obligation must rest in the judgment of the contracting parties. A sovereign State was the final judge of its own competence; sovereignty meant the final and ultimate power of judgment; it was, therefore, one and indivisible;—to divide it was to destroy it.[1] The issue was sharply drawn and the old theory of a divided sovereignty was rejected. Was the Federal State sovereign or did sovereignty lie in the individual States? Calhoun did not hesitate to ascribe sovereignty to the individual States and to deny to the Union all right and title to such a power. That he was wrong only war could settle, and that only for the future!

No consideration of Calhoun's influence upon the history of our constitutional development can omit a review of his position on slavery. We have seen that in his earlier years he was strongly national in his thought and feeling, while in his later years under

---

[1] *Works*, i., 146; "Sovereignty is an entire thing;—to divide, is,—to destroy it." *Cf.* Madison, *Letters, etc.*, iv., 61 and 419.

the name of Union, he sought to give power to a section and was forced to replace a national ideal by that of a confederacy. The cause of this change was slavery, that "peculiar institution" whose security became the passion of his life. Its existence he at first defended, as did most other men of the South, as an institution protected by the Constitution; but subtle forces were at work which transformed the ideas of the South. Slavery came to be regarded not merely as an economic necessity, guaranteed by the Constitution, but as a "positive good," as Calhoun so often asserted.[1]

Convinced of the necessity of slavery, his every effort was devoted to its defence. Inspired with a love of his country, he predicted with the voice of a seer the conflict that must come unless slavery were secured beyond the possibility of disturbance. To save the Union and to render slavery safe, he proclaimed Nullification in 1833; to guarantee the permanence of equality between the North and the South, to maintain that equilibrium he regarded as essential, he became Secretary of State in 1844 for the express purpose of bringing Texas into the Union; to maintain the same equilibrium he opposed the admission of California as a free State and, when his efforts to prevent it proved unavailing, his voice was that of a Cassandra, proclaiming swift destruction to ears that heeded not. With his last words in the Senate, three weeks before his death, he uttered a final appeal to his countrymen to avoid the dangers of disunion that threatened from all sides. His remedy was an amendment to the Constitution,

[1] Von Holst, *op. cit.*, p. 164 *ff.*

which, as was afterwards discovered, provided for a double Executive, a Northern and a Southern President, each with a power of veto upon legislation hostile to his section. An idle and visionary scheme! A chimera in the realm of constitutional law! A last attempt to avoid the irrepressible conflict by legislative enactment, to smother a growing moral sentiment beneath constitutional formalism, to prevent disunion by destroying the nation!

X

Abraham Lincoln. Growth through Civil War

ABRAHAM LINCOLN

1809.	Feb. 12.	Born in Kentucky.
1816.		Removed to Indiana.
1830.		Removed to Illinois.
1832.		Elected captain of volunteers in Black Hawk War.
1833.		Postmaster in New Salem.
1834.		Deputy surveyor of Sangamon County.
1834–42.		Representative in State Legislature.
1837.		Admitted to Bar. Settled in Springfield.
1847–49.		Representative in Congress.
1854.		Representative in State Legislature.
1858.		Douglas debates.
1860.		Elected President.
1861–65.		Civil War.
1863.	Jan. 1.	Issued Emancipation Proclamation.
1864.		Re-elected President.
1865.	April 14.	Shot by John Wilkes Booth in Ford's Theatre, Washington.
	April 15.	Died.

X

Abraham Lincoln. Growth through Civil War

THE ten years following Calhoun's death brought a startling fulfilment of his prophetic utterances on the slavery question. The Compromise of 1850 resulted in only a temporary cessation of the agitation; the effort to silence the voice of an awakening moral conscience by legislation proved futile, and in 1854 the Kansas-Nebraska Bill, repealing the Missouri Compromise and throwing open to slavery vast regions of the Northwest, more than undid all the good that had been accomplished by the compromises of former years. The fight for "bleeding Kansas" stirred both North and South to a depth before unknown and aroused hatreds and animosities that boded ill for the nation's future. The fratricidal strife which Calhoun had foreseen was already imminent, and the vision he had shuddered at would soon be realized unless some solution of the question of the extension of slavery could be reached. Douglas's doctrine of "Squatter Sovereignty" proved a delusion. Its sole merit was that it furnished the occasion that made Lincoln a national figure.

Born in Kentucky of a family which he himself designated as of the second rank, Lincoln early moved with his parents to Indiana and later to Illinois.[1] The story of his poverty and privation, of his struggle for an education under the most adverse circumstances and of his final success is so well known as not to need recounting. Bred of a non-slaveholding stock and reared among a free-State people, Lincoln had from early manhood a deep-rooted conviction of the evils of slavery. As time passed, this moral conviction was strengthened and took shape politically in a literal acceptance of the words of the Declaration of Independence that "all men are created equal." These words became the inspiration of all his political action from his entrance into politics to his tragic death in 1865.

After a brief term of service in the State Legislature, Lincoln was elected as a Whig to a seat in the House of Representatives in 1846. His attitude toward the Mexican War was what might have been expected. Though he was willing to support it with his vote when it came to a question of men or supplies, he was unwilling to accept the view that the war was one of defence and undertaken solely because of Mexican aggression. Such an attitude violated his every instinct of justice and his course of opposition rendered his re-election impossible.[2] From this time till his nomination for Senator by the Republicans of Illinois in 1858, Lincoln pursued

---

[1] For biographies, see Nicolay and Hay, J. T. Morse, Jr., and Ida M. Tarbell.

[2] For the so-called "Spot Resolutions," see *Works*, i., p. 318; Mexican War Speech, i., 327.

the practice of law without acquiring more than a moderate reputation or success. He had, however, firmly established a reputation for good sense and good humor, for large-mindedness, and for an unselfish honesty that won for him the affectionate nickname of "Honest Abe."

Lincoln's views on slavery were well known. He hated it as an institution and regarded its continued existence as a curse upon a free country, yet he saw no means of getting rid of it except by the action of the slaveholding States themselves. The Constitution had recognized its existence; this very recognition had been part of the price paid for Union and he believed in keeping the bargain.

Within each State the general government had no control over domestic institutions, but within the national Territories he thought the matter was quite different. There was no reasonable doubt to his mind that Congress, from the Ordinance of 1787 till the Kansas–Nebraska Bill of 1854, had had the power and had exercised it, of prohibiting slavery in the Territories.[1] The "Fathers" of the Constitution, he thoroughly believed, were persuaded of the evil of slavery and that its existence would be of short duration. Had the Constitution not forbidden the foreign slave trade after the year 1808? Had not the Northwest Territory been made free forever? Was there not every reason to believe that emancipation would take place in the South as it had done in the North? That the framers of the Constitution could have wished to perpetuate slavery was incredible to him. How much less could they have

[1] *Cf.* speech at Peoria, Oct. 16, 1854, *Works*, ii., 190 *ff.*

intended to extend it! But the repeal of the Missouri Compromise by the Kansas-Nebraska Bill threw open the Territories to the possibility of slavery; the Dred Scott decision went a step further and proclaimed the impotency, both of Congress and of the territorial Legislatures, to prohibit slavery within the national domain.

Dred Scott, it will be recalled, was a slave who had been taken by his master from Missouri into a free Territory, and after several years spent there had been brought back to Missouri.[1] He entered suit for his freedom and the case went to the Supreme Court on a question of jurisdiction. Chief Justice Taney in delivering the judgment for the Court did not confine himself to the immediate question at issue, but, after declaring that Dred Scott was not a citizen in the meaning of the Constitution and therefore had no right before the Court, went on to establish the doctrine that slaves were property, that the Constitution provided that no man could be deprived of his life, liberty, or property without due process of law, and that therefore it was beyond the competence of Congress or of the territorial Legislatures to forbid the carrying of slaves, the owner's property, within the limits of any Territory. By the obiter dicta of this decision the free Territory was no longer free; by it slavery was extended to all the Territories, whether they desired it or not, and only when a Territory became a State could it abolish slavery within its limits.[2]

---

[1] For the decision, see 19 Howard 393. See abstract in the Appendix.
[2] *Cf.* Johnston, *American Political History*, ii., p. 169 *ff.*

It was the evident intention of the Court to attempt a final solution of the slavery question. The attempts of the Executive and of Congress to effect a permanent settlement had proved only partially successful, and in the mind of the Court, as of the rest of the country, it was most desirable that some final settlement should be reached, so that peace might come again. The folly of the Supreme Court's attempt to give final form by judicial decision to the great moral and political question involved soon became apparent. It was not only the throwing open of free Territory to slavery that stirred men like Lincoln to determined opposition to the political results of this decision.[1] They were equally opposed to the doctrine which would rob the slave of his character as man and condemn him forever to the position of a mere chattel. Lincoln's moral sense rebelled against the idea and the history of his country taught him that the Declaration of Independence meant what it said, and that its " all men are created equal," included negroes as well as whites. And none could deny the presence of free negroes at the time of the adoption of the Constitution or that they had continued to that day.

Lincoln regarded the Dred Scott decision as the second step in a movement by the South to make the whole country slave; the first was the repeal of the Missouri Compromise by which free Territories were thrown open to slavery, the Dred Scott decision marked a further advance in depriving Congress and the Territories of the right to forbid slavery within their limits; the third and last step he apprehended

[1] *Works*, ii., 321 *ff*.

would be to throw open to slavery by judicial decision or by congressional enactment not only the free Territories but the free States as well.[1]

The possibility of such a culmination to the process of slavery extension filled him with horror, and he eagerly took advantage of the formation of the new Republican party to be among the first to espouse its principles and to ally himself with the party which its opponents delighted to stigmatize as "black." His position in Illinois and his relation to the party brought him the Republican nomination in 1858 for Senator to contest the seat then filled by Senator Douglas.[2]

The rivalry of Lincoln and Douglas had begun in their early manhood and continued till the election of 1860; it was a rivalry in love as well as in politics, in character and disposition as well as in policies of national welfare. Douglas far outstripped his competitor in the early stages of their careers, and while Lincoln was still an unknown country lawyer in central Illinois, Douglas was one of the leaders of the Senate and a figure of national prominence. As a Northern Democrat, Douglas had fathered the Kansas-Nebraska Bill and the repeal of the Missouri Compromise in 1854; he was the author of the doctrine of "Popular Sovereignty" which asserted for the Territories the right to determine for themselves whether or not slavery should be permitted within their borders; no one espoused more heartily than he the dicta of the Dred Scott decision, though he

[1] *Works*, iii., 3 *ff*.
[2] *Cf*. Nicolay and Hay: *Abraham Lincoln; A History*, ii., 135 *ff*.

failed to perceive the logical contradiction between that decision and his pet doctrine of "Popular Sovereignty."

Lincoln, on the other hand, was touched by the rising tide of opinion against the extension of slavery; he was in no sense an abolitionist, for he recognized the constitutional guarantees of slavery as a domestic institution within the States, but he believed in the right and power of Congress to forbid its presence in the Territories.

A series of joint debates was arranged between these champions of opposing principles, and the Lincoln-Douglas Debates of 1858 are second only to the Webster-Hayne Debates in the political annals of our country.[1] Lincoln was defeated but in losing the Senatorship he won the Presidency.

The debates centred around the great question at issue, that of the extension of slavery. Douglas upheld the principle of "Popular Sovereignty" and the Dred Scott decision. Lincoln grasped the inconsistency of Douglas's position and propounded to him a series of questions the answers to which disclosed the inconsistency and placed Douglas in a dilemma from which he could not extricate himself except at the cost of losing the support either of the North or of the South. The most famous of these questions and the one central to the discussion was in the following words: "Can the people of a United States Territory, in any lawful way, against the wishes of any citizen of the United States, exclude slavery from its limits prior to the formation of a State constitution?" To admit that it could, would be

[1] For the debates, see *Works*, iii., 200-347, iv., and v., 1-85.

to reject the Dred Scott decision and to alienate the South. To deny that it could not, was to demolish his own doctrine of Popular Sovereignty and to lose the support of the North. Douglas chose the former, though he sought to conceal it under the guise of the principle of "unfriendly legislation," which came to be known as the "Freeport heresy."[1] By this, Douglas meant that, though the people of a Territory could not by statute exclude slavery, yet that slavery could not exist in a Territory without friendly legislation, legislation of such a character as to call into being the exercise of the police power to protect it.

It was the answer Lincoln had been seeking; at a conference of Republican leaders the night before the Freeport debate, Lincoln, according to tradition, was urged not to ask this question, for fear he would lose the prize for which he was contending. "I am killing larger game," he said; "the battle of 1860 is worth a hundred of this."[2] Lincoln was right in his prophecy. The South would never accept for President a man who had proclaimed such a doctrine. Senator Benjamin of Louisiana, in a speech in the Senate on May 22, 1860, accused Douglas of having broken faith with the South and fitly described the situation when he said: "The Senator from Illinois faltered. He got the prize for which he faltered; but lo, the prize of his ambition slips from his grasp because of the faltering which he paid as the price for the ignoble."[3]

[1] For Lincoln's questions, see *Works*, iii., 273–4, and for Douglas's idea of "unfriendly legislation," iii., 297.

[2] Nicolay and Hay, ii., 160.

[3] *Congressional Globe,* first session 36th Congress, 1859–1860, p. 2241.

The result of these debates made Lincoln a figure of national prominence and the candidate of his party for the Presidency two years later. There could be no mistaking the attitude of Lincoln and of the Republican party toward slavery in this campaign. The issue was clearly stated in the party platform; the defence of the principles of the Declaration of Independence, "the maintenance inviolate of the rights of the States, and especially the right of each State to order and control its own domestic institutions according to its own judgment exclusively," as "essential to that balance of power on which the perfection and endurance of our political fabric depend"; the condemnation of the new dogma "that the Constitution, of its own force, carries slavery into any or all of the territories of the United States," as "a dangerous political heresy," "revolutionary in its tendency, and subversive of the peace and harmony of the country," and that "the normal condition of all the territory of the United States is that of freedom."[1]

Slavery was recognized as a peculiar domestic institution, wholly subject to the control of the individual States within their borders, but equally subject to the control of Congress within the Territories; it was an evil and therefore to be restricted to its present area, that in the course of time it might die out altogether, but so long as any State desired to retain slavery, it might do so free from molestation from the Federal Government.

In his Cooper Union speech of February 27, 1860,

[1] T. J. McKee, *National Conventions and Platforms*, pp. 113–114.

Lincoln struck to the heart of the differences between the sections.[1] It was the nationalization of slavery. "Holding as they [the Southern people] do that slavery is morally right and socially elevating, they cannot cease to demand a full national recognition of it, as a legal right and a social blessing. Nor can we justifiably withhold this on any ground save our conviction that slavery is wrong." "Wrong as we think slavery is, we can yet afford to let it alone where it is, because that much is due to the necessity arising from its actual presence in the nation." The fight must be made against the extension of slavery; free soil must remain free in the Territories lest it should cease to be free in the States.

The period from the election in November to the inauguration in March was one of great doubt and uncertainty. South Carolina waited only long enough to hear the result before setting in motion the machinery to effect Secession, and on December 20th, the Convention proclaimed the Ordinance of Secession,[2] whereby the old ties were severed and the Union destroyed so far as South Carolina could effect it. Before the 4th of March, seven States had seceded and had established the Confederate States of America, had chosen officials, had made preparations for organizing an army and navy, had seized the property of the United States within their limits and were offering to treat for a peaceable separation.[3]

The practical question assumed a different form with the completion of Secession and the commence-

[1] *Works*, v., 293 *ff.*
[2] See Appendix.
[3] *Cf.* J. W. Burgess, *The Civil War and the Constitution.*

ment of hostilities. It was no longer the extension of slavery; it was the preservation of the Union. President Buchanan had been weak and vacillating; he had denied, in his message of December, 1860,[1] the right of a State to secede, but at the same time had as emphatically denied the right of the Federal Government to employ force against any State that might attempt Secession. Driven by the aggressive policy of the Secessionists, he had been obliged later to take a firmer stand with respect to the power of the Union to execute its laws and to retain control of its property even at the risk of war.

Lincoln's inaugural address was unwavering on the question of the extension of slavery[2]; there must be no compromise on the question of its restriction, but equally must there be no encroachment upon its existence within the States. But slavery for the moment had ceased to be the great issue. It had yielded to Secession. Could a State lawfully withdraw from the Union? Was the nature of the Union such that it could not prevent its own destruction? Were the States joined in mere alliance or in the indissoluble bond of a Federal State? This was the question, agitated since the foundation of the Republic, which at last was to be put to the test of war. The threat of three quarters of a century had at length become a reality!

Lincoln's attitude toward Secession was clear from the start, and the words of his first inaugural characterized it as rebellion and revolution. The Union

---

[1] *Messages and Papers of the Presidents*, v., 635 *ff*. *Cf.* Burgess, *The Civil War and the Constitution*, i., 82 *ff*.
[2] *Works*, vi., 169 *ff*.

of the States he regarded as perpetual. Never had any government had a provision for its own destruction embodied in its organic law, and, even if the Constitution were a contract, it could not peaceably be dissolved without the consent of all. "One party to a contract may violate it—break it, so to speak; but does it not require all to lawfully rescind it?"[1] But to Lincoln's mind the Constitution was not a contract by which sovereign States had been leagued together. It was only the last step in the process of union which had begun in 1774. "The Union is much older than the Constitution," he asserted, and one of the declared objects of the establishment of the Constitution was "to form a more perfect Union." The same opinion he elaborated in his first message to Congress in language that is familiar to all. "The States have their status in the Union, and they have no other legal status. If they break from this, they can only do so against law and by revolution. The Union, and not themselves separately, procured their independence and their liberty . . . The Union is older than any of the States, and, in fact, it created them as States."[2]

The conclusions that Lincoln drew from these premises are evident. Secession was a sophism, resting upon the fallacy that there was at some former time a number of sovereign States, a number of political communities without a political superior, which mutually surrendered a portion of their rights, but not their sovereignty, and having retained this, might, therefore, legally withdraw from the Union

[1] *Works*, vi., 174.
[2] *Ibid.*, vi., 315.

by resuming the powers granted to it. Lincoln's theory left no ground for the legal dissolution of the Union. If the States never had any existence outside the Union, if "the Union is older than any of the States, and, in fact, . . . created them as States," then they can have rights outside of it only by destroying it, by revolution, by rebellion. Furthermore it follows that Secession Ordinances are null and void, and have no legal effect whatever upon the relation of a State to the Union. That relation persists so long as the Union continues, and the destruction of the Union must come from violence and not from law, for "no government proper ever had a provision in its organic law for its own termination." Secession was rebellion and must be put down with all the power of a government fighting for its life.[1]

The Union was not only historically and legally an indissoluble one, but also "physically speaking, we cannot separate." It was not possible to "build an impassable wall" between the sections; they could not, like divorcées, "go out of the presence and beyond the reach of each other"; they must remain face to face.

Thus bluntly did Lincoln make known his attitude toward the seceding States. They were still in the Union and could not get out of it till they had successfully resisted its efforts to execute its laws within their boundaries, till the right of revolution had once more been appealed to with success. The duty of a President holding such views was clear; the use of the military and naval forces of the Union to secure

[1] *Cf.* Johnston, *op. cit.*, ii., 280 *ff*. *The Secession Movement.*

obedience to its laws was imperative; the calling into activity of the war-power became his most solemn duty.

The way in which Lincoln met Secession and his appeal for the preservation of the Union thrilled the masses of the North with a patriotic zeal, deep and far reaching. The precious heritage of Union was endangered, the great experiment of republican government was threatened with failure,—had failed many said, —and ancient liberties and recent greatness could be preserved only by the preservation of the Union. For the time being slavery and all its vexed problems that had held the boards for nearly half a century, sank into the background; a greater and a nobler issue than the extension of slavery was to be decided; the single sentiment of Union filled the minds of the North to the exclusion of all else. Only a few extremists still talked of abolition or of peaceable dissolution.

The exercise of the war powers by the Executive led almost at once to a temporary military dictatorship. Under the pressure of circumstances and the plea of necessity, the President, first on his own responsibility and then with the sanction of Congress, assumed the exercise of powers which destroyed on the one hand the old balance between the States and the nation and between the departments of government, and on the other overstepped almost all the guarantees of liberty to the individual, while the theory of delegated powers lost all real importance in the presence of national peril.

This dictatorship enabled Lincoln to perform his first great service to the Constitution, that of preserving its very existence, of settling in favor of the Union the divergent views which reached back to the Constitutional Convention, and of making of us for all time a sovereign nation, a single political people.

Though slavery had been pushed aside at the outbreak of war, it could not long remain in the background. It daily became more evident that the fundamentally different views of North and South on all manner of topics were somehow or other rooted in slavery. It was clear that the nation must be wholly free or wholly slave before there could be the homogeneity of thought and feeling necessary for a true Union. Nor was it less clear that the success of the war was intimately connected with the continued existence of slavery. So long as slavery continued, it was possible for the South to put its maximum fighting strength in the field and depend for its support upon the produce of slave labor. Likewise the North was estopped by the existence of the institution from employing the blacks in its military forces. All these considerations bore with great weight upon Lincoln's attitude as expressed in his inaugural. It might be true that so long as peace existed, the Federal Government could not touch slavery in the States, but with the outbreak of the war, new powers not previously contemplated came into play. The doctrine of the " war-powers " of Congress and the Executive received a rapid and none too careful development.[1] Men did not scrutinize too closely the constitutionality of measures whose

[1] *Cf.* W. A. Dunning, *Essays on the Civil War and Reconstruction*, p. 1 *ff.*

object was the maintenance of the Constitution itself. Lincoln gave expression to this attitude in characteristic fashion in speaking of the suspension of the writ of Habeas Corpus by Executive order when he asked: "Are all the laws but one to go unexecuted, and the government itself to go to pieces lest that one be violated?"[1]

Emancipation by proclamation of the President was the result of this growth of powers.[2] Avowedly a war measure, it was made applicable only to those districts in revolt on the first day of January, 1863. The war for the Union gained great moral strength when it became also a war for liberation, and the Emancipation Proclamation takes rank, along with the Declaration of Independence, as the second great charter of American freedom. As the latter was insufficient to secure the blessings of the liberty it proclaimed and needed to be supplemented by an instrument of government giving form and stability to its ideals, so the Emancipation Proclamation, bringing freedom to new millions, needed to be supplemented by constitutional amendments to give it lasting efficiency. Lincoln did not live to see any but the first of the new amendments, the thirteenth, take form; by it slavery and involuntary servitude, except as a punishment for crime, were forever banished from the land.

Two great ideas filled Lincoln's mind: Union and Liberty. But the Union was more precious than the liberty of the slaves. Fiercely as he hated slavery,

[1] *Works*, vi., 309.
[2] *Ibid.*, viii., 161, and Johnston, *op. cit.*, ii., 389 *ff*. *Emancipation*. For the text, see the Appendix.

he would nevertheless save the Union at the cost of its continued existence. As slavery was the price of the first acceptance of the Constitution, so he was willing to make it a part of the second bargain for its preservation. But it was not to be. The South refused all offers of guarantees for its inviolability within the borders of any State. The slaveholding States seemed bent on nothing short of rule or ruin, on nothing less than the complete acceptance of slavery everywhere or a violent dissolution of the Union. When this became evident, Lincoln seized the opportunity to save the Union by destroying slavery.

Lincoln's view of Reconstruction followed naturally from his belief in the indissoluble character of the Union.[1] The States could not possibly withdraw from the Union. The rebellion was the work of certain persons who had seized control of the State governments and had unlawfully made use of them for the purposes of the rebellion. So soon, then, as the Federal Government should reassert its authority, so soon as the rebellion should be put down and loyal governments be set up, the old relations would likewise be re-established. The States had never been out of the Union; they could not, therefore, be brought back into it.

In accordance with this idea Lincoln proclaimed the so-called "ten per cent. plan," by which it was provided that any State whose citizens had been in rebellion, might be reconstructed as loyal, when a number equal to ten per cent. of those who had voted in the election of 1860 should take the oath of

[1] *Cf.* C. H. McCarthy, *Lincoln's Plan of Reconstruction.*

allegiance to the United States, and should proceed to elect state officials and national representatives.[1] A government so constituted Lincoln declared would be recognized by the Executive as a member of the Union, and several States were so constituted and recognized.

The difficulties of Reconstruction, however, were not to be settled in any such simple fashion. Congress had its own notions about the method of procedure which were radically different from those of President Lincoln, and as the Constitution gives each House the exclusive right of judging of the qualifications of its members, mere Executive recognition of a reconstructed State would not be sufficient to reinstate it completely in its old position; it might still be kept out of its representation in the legislative councils of the nation.

How this difference of opinion between the President and Congress might have been settled but for the assassination of Lincoln, it is impossible to say, but surely it would have been settled in some way that would have spared the South those bitter years of political debauchery, that would have spared our country's history the darkest blot upon its record for political sagacity—" Reconstruction."

[1] *Works,* ix., 218 *ff.*

XI

Thaddeus Stevens. Growth through Reconstruction

THADDEUS STEVENS

1793. April 4.		Born in Danville, Vt.
1814.		Graduated from Dartmouth College.
		Removed to Pennsylvania. Studied law.
1829.		Supported anti-Masonic party.
1833–35. 1837–42.	}	Representative in Pennsylvania Legislature.
1838.		Member of State Constitutional Convention.
1842–49.		Practised law in Lancaster.
1849–53.		Representative in Congress.
1859–68.		Representative in Congress.
1861.		Chairman of Committee on Ways and Means.
1866.		Chairman of House Committee on Reconstruction.
1868.		Chairman of Committee of Impeachment of Andrew Johnson.
Aug. 11.		Died in Washington.

XI

Thaddeus Stevens. Growth through Reconstruction

WITH the death of Lincoln and the accession of Andrew Johnson to the Presidency the period of Reconstruction may be said to have begun. The new President declared his intention of following out the plan laid down by his predecessor. That plan had not met with the approval of Congress even when advocated by Lincoln [1]; much less would it do so when tried by a man of Johnson's antecedents and character. Within the space of a few weeks after he took the oath of office, Johnson and Congress were in bitter opposition. Johnson at first had breathed out fire and slaughter against the " rebels " who must be taught, he said, what it meant to be traitors. Soon, however, he began to court the favor of the South and in proportion as his suit prospered, the fear of the radical Republicans was aroused that, if the seceded States should be restored on the Lincoln-Johnson plan, with no further guarantees of their good conduct in the future or of the security of the freedmen, the Democrats might easily gain control

---

[1] *Cf.* J. W. Burgess, *Reconstruction and the Constitution*, p. 15.

of Congress and the fruits of victory be lost both to the nation and to the party.

The leader of the radicals and of Congress in the fight with Johnson was Thaddeus Stevens of Pennsylvania. At the extra session of Congress which met on July 4, 1861, Stevens was appointed Chairman of the Committee on Ways and Means. This Committee performed at that time the duties now performed by the various appropriation committees as well, so that the enormous task devolved upon Stevens both of providing revenue and of determining how it should be spent. This position he filled throughout the war and became, in the words of Blaine, " the natural leader who assumed his place by common consent."

Stevens was born in Vermont in 1793 and was therefore at the outbreak of the war at the advanced age of sixty-eight.[1] After graduating from Dartmouth College in 1814 he had moved to Pennsylvania, first to teach school at York and then to practise law at Gettysburg and Lancaster. For fifteen years he followed with success the practice of his profession without evincing any particular interest in politics and only in 1833, at the age of forty, did he receive his first election. It was to the Pennsylvania House of Representatives in which he continued to serve until 1842. During this period Stevens established his ability to lead a legislative body by his caustic wit and brilliant oratory. His speech in 1835 in favor of free schools was a remarkable effort which changed a hostile majority, not only in the House but also in the Senate, the mem-

[1] Lives by McCall and Callender.

bers of which had crowded into the House to hear him, and which firmly established the great public school system of the State.[1]

During these years his views on slavery took shape in their final form. Living near the dividing line between the free and the slave States, he was a constant witness to the struggles of the unhappy slaves to escape from bondage and to the action of the Fugitive Slave Law in dragging them back into captivity. As a lawyer he was always ready to lend his aid in their defence, and as a member of the Constitutional Convention in 1838, he opposed all discriminations against any man on account of his color and refused to sign the proposed constitution because it limited the right of suffrage to "white citizens."[2] At about the same time Stevens attended a convention at Harrisburg which proposed to save the Union by repressing the anti-slavery agitation. His views were radically opposed to such an attitude, and by his ridicule and his arguments he drove the convention into an adjournment without action.

In 1849 Stevens was elected a member of the national House of Representatives, at an age when most men are beginning to contemplate the end of their active careers. His real career, however, was not yet beginning, for after serving two terms he retired from Congress, as it then seemed for good, and did not return till six years later. When first elected to Congress, Stevens had at once assumed the leadership of the small band of Free-Soilers and extreme Whigs, and in the slavery contests during his two

[1] S. W. McCall, *Thaddeus Stevens*, p. 37.
[2] *Ibid.*, p. 48.

terms, he was unwavering in his hostility to the institution. The close of the Mexican War and the acquisition of new territory brought the question of the extension of slavery to the front as it had not been since 1820. California quickly filled up with a non-slaveholding population and immediately adopted a constitution forbidding slavery and asked for admission as a free State. If California should be admitted as a free State, the hope of the slave States to profit by the war would be greatly lessened. The fairest portion of the newly acquired territory would be lost to them. It is small wonder, then, that the admission of California was so vigorously opposed.

An ever present cause of irritation between the sections of the country was the Fugitive Slave Law by which "persons held to service or labor" were to be returned to those to whom they owed the service or labor. In the North it was detested and its enforcement was hindered in every lawful and in some unlawful ways. Any other course seemed to imply complicity in the horrors of slavery, a newly awakened moral sensitiveness rebelled at the constitutional safeguards of the evil, and personal liberty laws abounded. In the South, on the other hand, the idea that slavery was a "positive good" had become very generally accepted and this positive good was guaranteed to them by the solemn compact of the Constitution itself. Every failure to return a fugitive slave was not only the occasion of direct financial loss to the owner, but also was a violation of the most sacred obligation. The attitude of the North toward slavery bore infinitely more hardly upon the South than did the actual loss of the slaves. It was a constant accusation against their whole ethical and moral system. It was like a goad in the flanks that finally drove them into an unmanageable revolt.

When Congress met in December, 1860, the revolt was already in progress; Secession conventions had been summoned in more than one Southern State and the Senators from South Carolina had resigned their seats. President Buchanan, in his message to Congress on the day of its assembling, combined a rebuke for " the long continued and intemperate interference of the Northern people with the question of slavery," [1] and for the agitation which had produced its " malign influence upon the slaves, and inspired them with vague notions of freedom," with a justification of the action of the South that came as from the lips of one of them. Furthermore he asserted his belief that Congress was powerless to prevent the dissolution of the Union, that " the sword was not placed in their hands to preserve it by force." In Congress itself the old spirit of compromise still ruled. Both Senate and House appointed committees of reconciliation and the extent to which the North was willing to go to preserve the Union seems incredible in view of the victory of the Republican party at the polls.[2] Repeal of personal liberty laws, revision of the Fugitive Slave Law to the point of endangering the liberty of free white men, and an amendment to the Constitution forever removing the possibility of an amendment which would interfere with slavery in the

[1] *Messages and Papers of the Presidents*, v., 635 *ff.*
[2] Burgess, *op. cit.*, i., 96; and McCall, *op. cit.*, p. 121 *ff.*

States unless such amendment should originate in a slave State and be ratified by every State in the Union, were the concessions proposed but without avail. Only on the question of the extension of slavery did the Republicans stand firm.

The adoption of such measures as these would have riveted the chains of slavery till the millennium if the Constitution could control. The folly was that men did not see that the time for compromise was past; that former compromises had postponed only to increase the evils they sought to cure; that the life of the nation could not be regulated by the law, no matter how solemnly compacted, if the life of the nation be at stake. Secession was already full grown. The Confederacy was an established fact. A Constitution had been proposed, Jefferson Davis elected President, and a Congress assembled before the compromise measures passed the House, and the separation had been declared to be "perfect, complete, and perpetual."

Thaddeus Stevens desired no compromise; the time had come to determine whether or not Secession was a lawful act. If so, he said, "then the Union is not worth preserving for a single day." But he utterly repudiated the right of a State to withdraw and exulted in the election of Lincoln, though he should "see this government crumble into a thousand atoms." His opposition to compromise had no effect and the man who should lead Congress through the crisis "sat by, protesting and threatening, waiting for his time to come."[1]

[1] McCall, p. 124.

That time was not long delayed. Lincoln had summoned Congress to meet on July 4th. War had begun with the firing on Fort Sumter, and when Congress met there was urgent need of both men and money. Stevens, as chairman of the Ways and Means Committee, was supreme in all financial legislation. From this point of vantage, he was soon recognized as the leader in Congress and more and more it followed his guidance. With the death of Lincoln, Stevens's influence, which had been decisive in legislation, became dominant. During Reconstruction, Stevens so long as he lived, was dictator in the House and leader of his party.

By disposition and by training Stevens was a radical. There was no element of compromise in him and from the first he held a consistent theory regarding the position of the Southern States and the treatment that should be accorded them.[1] That theory is in the main well known. The seceding States were in rebellion and their supporters should be dealt with as rebels. The right of revolution was comprehensible to his mind, but the right of Secession was abhorrent. The Union must be preserved at any cost, nor need too great thought be bestowed upon the strict legality of the means employed. The powers of the Federal Government, he argued, were limited only by the necessities of the occasion when the maintenance of its own existence was at stake. So eager was he to render support to the President, that, within a week after Congress assembled, the money asked for by the Administration had been granted, and within a few days more the necessary bills for rais-

[1] McCall, p. 191.

ing the enormous sums demanded had been introduced and passed.

The "Crittenden Resolution" which declared that "the war is not waged in any spirit of oppression, or for any purpose of conquest or subjugation," or to interfere with "the rights or established institutions" of the seceded States, but to "preserve the dignity, equality, and rights of the several States unimpaired," passed both Senate and House with scarcely a dissenting Republican vote save that of Stevens.[1] The nation, he thought, should not hamper itself in any particular with reference to the conduct of the war or the results which might flow from it. By the opening of the next session the principle of the resolution had been so far violated, that the House adopted a motion of Stevens to lay it on the table when it was proposed to reaffirm it.

In this same session a bill was introduced to confiscate the property "used for insurrectionary purposes" and to free the slaves who were employed in any military or naval service against the Government. Both proposals were much to Stevens's liking. The object of the war was "to subdue the rebels," and confiscation of "rebel" property found favor with him both as a measure of war and as a means of punishment. Stevens has been called vindictive, but his vindictiveness was not blood-thirsty; he would punish by taking away property, but not life. He would weaken the enemy by depriving him of the means of support. The laws of war should govern in a rebellion. The rights of the seceded States under the Constitution had been lost by their Secession

[1] McCall, p. 148.

and the constitutional guarantees of slavery destroyed. This was more advanced ground than the House was yet willing to take and the bill was rejected; it was not long, however, till Congress assumed the position now advocated by Stevens.[1]

Stevens was one of the few members of Congress who did not seek to justify every step by some construction of the Constitution, however strained or fanciful. He early recognized the fact that no provision for a civil war had been incorporated in the Constitution, and that in the war in progress the United States was compelled to fight for existence. In that struggle paper barriers must be swept away. Secession had destroyed the Constitution in the seceding States and the great task of the Union was to restore its sway over them. He would not be scrupulous about the constitutionality of the means when the end was the establishment of the Constitution. He recognized, as did few others, that the time for fine-spun theories had passed, and that the need for success was greater than that for legality of procedure.

For two generations the American people had been blind worshippers of the Constitution. They had thought to find in it a solution for all the political problems that confronted them, if only their worship were blind enough, with the result that metaphysics had taken the place of common sense, and the best intellects of the country had been devoted to the barren attempt to determine by subtle processes of constitutional construction the course of mighty moral and political forces. Stevens perceived this

[1] McCall, pp. 149–50.

clearly and with his characteristic directness, broke away from the mental bondage of the times and proclaimed a doctrine of force. The Constitution had been exalted above the Union. He sought to restore it to its proper place, and in the attempt he would be guided by the needs of the situation rather than be hampered by constitutional doctrines.

Illustrations of Stevens's attitude toward the Constitution are abundant throughout the war. At its very inception he advocated the issue of legal tender notes as being within the province of the Federal Government.[1] Such a power had not been expressly enumerated in the Constitution, but every power necessary to carry out the granted powers had been conferred upon it. In the Constitutional Convention, with respect to this power it had been left " to the exigencies of the times to determine its necessity," and Congress had the power to judge whether or not this necessity had arisen.

An even clearer illustration may be seen in his attitude toward the admission of the new State of West Virginia.[2] This mountainous district of " The Old Dominion " did not share with the rest of the State its feeling toward Secession. It proceeded, therefore, to organize a State government and to elect representatives to Congress. That so small a portion of the people of Virginia should claim to represent the whole State was absurd, so it was determined to apply for admission as a new State. Here, however, an apparently insuperable obstacle was encountered, for the Constitution provides that no new States

[1] McCall, p. 152 *ff.*
[2] *Ibid.*, p. 190 *ff.*

shall be formed from the territory of an old one, without the latter's consent. Many were not unwilling to argue that the Legislature of the new State was the Legislature of Virginia, and so could give the necessary consent to its own dismemberment. Such a viewpoint Stevens rejected as ridiculous on the face of it. He wished it plainly understood that he was not "being deluded by the idea that we are admitting this State in pursuance of any provision of the Constitution." It was preposterous to maintain that two hundred thousand people, segregated in a single district, could represent more than a million in the rest of the State, who were themselves organized in their own form of government. The State of Virginia, therefore, had never given its consent to the separation. This was no objection to Stevens's mind to admitting the new State, for in accordance with his general view, the Constitution had ceased to be applicable to the seceded States, and therefore the observation of its provisions with respect to them was unnecessary.

This was his view of the constitutional status of the seceded States from the beginning of the war to his death.[1] It was the view consistently advocated by him in the days of Reconstruction and the view finally adopted by the nation in its legislation.[2] The Confederate States, he asserted, had established a power which the United States had recognized by the proclamation of a blockade of the Southern

[1] Johnston, *American Political History*, ii., 440. "From the outbreak of the Rebellion until the end of reconstruction but two parties consistently maintained a consistent theory, the Democratic party and Thaddeus Stevens."
[2] McCall, *op. cit.*, p. 261 and p. 274.

ports; the Constitution, therefore, had not the slightest application to them, nor its obligations the slightest effect upon them; likewise its protection no longer extended to them. In short the relations of the two parties to this civil war could not be regulated by the law of the land but by the law of nations; the parties, he declared, "stand in precisely the same predicament as two nations who engage in a contest," and this principle he applied to Reconstruction with the result that he was brought into immediate conflict with the theories of Lincoln and Johnson.

In his first inaugural Lincoln had declared that " in contemplation of universal law and of the Constitution, the Union of these States is perpetual "[1]; and in the last speech he ever made, one on Reconstruction on April 11, 1865, while avoiding the theoretical question as to whether the seceded States had ever been out of the Union, he took the position that they were out of their proper practical relation with the Union, and that "the sole object of the government, civil and military, in regard to those States is to again get them into that proper practical relation."[2]

With such a view Stevens was utterly out of sympathy and his hostility to the theory of Lincoln, as Johnson attempted to carry it out, was bitter and determined. Lincoln's plan of Reconstruction was simple in the extreme and rested upon the position that the States as such could not secede; that what had taken place was that certain citizens of the seceded States were in insurrection against the United

[1] *Works*, vi., 169.
[2] *Ibid.*

States, and in carrying out their plans had gotten possession of the State governments. All that was necessary to reconstruct them was to restore the governments to the hands of loyal citizens. Lincoln perceived that such a Reconstruction would be limited to the establishment and recognition of such governments by the Executive. Congress must still determine whether or not the representatives from these reconstructed States should be admitted to its halls.

The question of Reconstruction had not become acute when Lincoln was assassinated. The whole strength of the nation had been directed towards the successful completion of the military struggle. With Lee's surrender at Appomattox, the Confederacy was practically at an end, and President Johnson was at once confronted with the settlement of this vexed question: a settlement that had of necessity been postponed till the close of the war. Serious consideration of the question, however, had been in progress during the course of the contest. In fact Congress and the President had come to a deadlock on the subject in 1863.

Stevens had early arrived at the conclusion which Congress now proceeded to enforce in opposition to the plan of the President. If the rights of the seceding States had been destroyed, they were, at the conclusion of the war, "conquered provinces," and it would rest with the conqueror to determine upon what conditions they might be restored to the enjoyment of those rights.

Under the plan of Reconstruction which President Johnson promulgated within six weeks after his inauguration, which was substantially Lincoln's plan, the Southern States rapidly amended their constitutions so as to bring them into harmony with the new conditions, and in a short time their Legislatures were in session and their representatives to Congress chosen.

Had the Southern States been content to let the negro alone, all might have gone well, but they at once began to pass laws discriminating against the freedmen.[1] These laws were of such a character as to arouse the fear in the North that the negroes were being virtually reinslaved and that the fruits of victory were in grave danger of being lost. Emancipation was about to be robbed of its efficacy through the action of the newly erected State governments, and a profound distrust of the President and his policy was excited in the North because of his leniency toward the South. In proportion as he was conservative, Congress became radical. The opinion rapidly gained ground that the freedmen must be armed with the ballot to protect themselves and to continue the Republican party in power.[2] Equally rapidly the Johnson plan of Reconstruction was discredited with Congress. The way was opened for radical action which was destined to bring the President to the bar of the Senate and to subject the South to years of humiliation and suffering.

The spirit of the radical reaction was Thaddeus Stevens; aged and infirm, with body bent under the years of struggle so that at times he had to be carried into the House, he still retained a strength of

[1] Burgess, *Civil War and Reconstruction*, p. 44.
[2] Johnston, *op. cit.*, ii., 447.

will, clearness of purpose, and keenness of wit that made him dictator of the House and master of the radical sentiment of the country.

Immediately upon the assembling of Congress in December, 1865, Stevens proposed the appointment of a committee composed of nine Representatives and six Senators to investigate the conditions in the South and " report whether they or any of them are entitled to be represented in either House of Congress." Stevens was made House Chairman of the Committee on Reconstruction and from this time to his death, in 1868, he devoted his chief efforts to bring about Reconstruction in accordance with his own views.[1]

Whether the States were within or without the Union, he was firmly convinced that Reconstruction could not take place by Executive action alone, but that it must be a concurrent act of the President and of Congress. The Reconstruction that had already taken place by Executive action was, therefore, invalid, unless it should receive the sanction of Congress. If any hope ever existed that Congress would concur in the Lincoln-Johnson plan, it vanished in the face of Johnson's utter disregard of Congress, his denunciation of the Reconstruction Committee, and his egotistical belief in himself as the leader of the people and defender of the Constitution. With an overwhelming majority at his back, Stevens was able to carry his measures over the President's veto, and in a short time the Freedman's Bureau Bill and the Civil Rights Bill had become law in this manner.

In the same session of Congress Stevens intro-

[1] McCall, *op. cit.*, 258; and Burgess, *op. cit.*, 57 *ff.*

duced into the House the Fourteenth Amendment for submission to the States for adoption. The Thirteenth Amendment, abolishing slavery, had already been adopted and had found no stronger advocate than Thaddeus Stevens. But the Thirteenth Amendment seemed insufficient to furnish protection to freedmen in their civil rights, and hence the need of the Fourteenth Amendment, establishing their citizenship and guaranteeing them against the abridgment of their "privileges or immunities as citizens of the United States"; against the deprivation "of life, liberty, or property, without due process of law," and affording to all "the equal protection of the laws." Representation was to be apportioned according to the population, but should be reduced in proportion as the right to vote was denied to any male citizen twenty-one years of age, except as a punishment for crime. A disability, that could be removed by a two-thirds vote of Congress, was placed upon all who had held office before the war, had taken an oath to support the Constitution of the United States, and had subsequently engaged in the rebellion against the Union.[1] The validity of the national debt was established, and payment of all debts incurred "in aid of insurrection or rebellion against the United States, or any claim for the loss or emancipation of any slave" was forever forbidden.

At the same time a bill was introduced by Stevens providing that when the Fourteenth Amendment had become a part of the Constitution and had been ratified by "any State lately in rebellion," and such State should have adopted a constitution and laws in

[1] *Cf.* Burgess, *op. cit.*, p. 78.

accordance therewith, it should be admitted to representation in Congress. The bill, however, was not acted upon and before the opening of the next session, Johnson had disgraced himself "swinging around the circle,"[1] the congressional elections had gone overwhelmingly against him, and his cause was lost. The radical sentiment was on the increase and when Congress met in December, Stevens had nothing to fear from the President's veto. He was in complete control of the situation and immediately began to carry out in legislation the theory respecting the seceded States that he had advocated since Lincoln reconstructed Louisiana on the ten per cent. plan. The "conquered province" theory was triumphantly carried out, and Reconstruction was made the result of Congressional and not Presidential action.

The two ideas, that Reconstruction was the business of Congress, and that the seceded States had lost their rights under the Constitution, had been cherished by Stevens from the beginning and in the report of the combined House and Senate committee referred to above, his views had found expression. The argument that the seceded States had never been out of the Union was refuted in the following language: "If rebellion succeeds, it accomplishes its purpose and destroys the Government. If it fails, the war has been barren of results, and the battle may be still fought out in the legislative halls of the country. Treason, defeated in the field, has only to take possession of Congress and the cabinet."[2] To the radical Thaddeus Stevens, such a possibility

[1] McCall, *op. cit.*, p. 280.
[2] Quoted, McCall, *op. cit.*, 274.

was abhorrent, almost impious. In his eyes the seceded States were rebels and should be made to pay the penalty of rebellion. They should be made to feel that the greatest civil war on record was not "barren of results." The victors could and should prescribe such conditions to the vanquished as would secure forever the grand result of freedom to the blacks.

The Southern legislatures, with the exception of that of Tennessee, had contemptuously rejected the Fourteenth Amendment and with it the mild conditions that had been proposed. Deluded by the hope that President Johnson would win in his contest with Congress and unwilling to brand with infamy the leading men in the South, or to proclaim with their own mouths that they had been in error, the States had rejected Reconstruction on the terms of the Fourteenth Amendment.[1] Whether or not a different course would have been pursued had they realized what the radical element, once in power, had in store for them, is matter of speculation merely.

During the campaign the feeling in favor of negro suffrage grew apace. Before the close of the preceding session, Stevens had made a powerful speech in its advocacy. The force of his appeal was increased by the fact that it seemed not unlikely that it would be his last effort, as his health was very poor. When Congress assembled in the autumn of 1866, there was little delay in putting into effect the verdict of the country that had been rendered in the recent elections. Congressional Reconstruction was at once substituted for Executive. Military

[1] Burgess, *op. cit.*, p. 106.

governments were established over the Southern States, and as a condition of their re-entry into the Union, universal suffrage for the blacks as well as for the whites was added to the conditions of the preceding session. Negro suffrage had to be incorporated in the State constitutions and the Fourteenth Amendment in the national Constitution before the States should "be declared entitled to representation in Congress."[1]

Upon the basis of Stevens's ideas, Reconstruction was eventually carried out. The South entered upon a period of political anarchy and debauchery which it seems incredible that thinking men should not have foreseen and have shrunk from aghast. Could Stevens have lived to witness the entry of the last seceded State into the Union, even his vindictive spirit must have felt that the "traitors" had paid their due.

The logical outgrowth of this legislation was the Fifteenth Amendment which Stevens, however, did not live to see. It secured, so far as the forms of law could effect it, that the right to vote should not be denied "on account of race, color, or previous condition of servitude."

The last important act of Stevens's life was the attempted impeachment of President Johnson.[2] For the first and only time in our history, the President of the United States was presented at the bar of the Senate by the House of Representatives. The interest of the trial for us is in its effects upon our constitutional theory. It determined finally the

[1] McCall, *op. cit.*, p. 275 *ff.*
[2] *Ibid.*, p. 323, and Burgess, *op. cit.*, p. 157.

futility of attempting to use impeachment as a "political proceeding." If it were possible for the Senate and the House, when two-thirds of their members differed from the President, to remove him from office by the political practice of impeachment, the stability of the Executive would be lost and the balance of the powers of government be destroyed.

On August 11, 1868, Stevens died, but the radical spirit which he typified lived after him. It stands to-day imprinted on our statute books in the legislation of the War and Reconstruction, and has found enduring form in the amendments to the Constitution. But the will-o'-the-wisp of universal suffrage no longer lures us toward the destruction of our institutions. We have realized that it is impossible to lift from "barbaric ignorance" by the ballot, or to endow with political wisdom by the gift of the suffrage. Suffrage is a privilege, not a right, and like liberty, can be enjoyed only by those who have passed through the struggle to win it by their merit. We view with complacency the practical nullification of negro suffrage as secured by the Constitution. Rather than try to work the cumbersome machinery of amendment to undo what required such a wrench of the national life to achieve, we tolerate the violation of the letter of the law of which the spirit is dead.

XII
Theodore Roosevelt. Growth through Expansion

THEODORE ROOSEVELT

1858.	Oct. 27.	Born in New York City.
1880.		Graduated from Harvard.
		Student at New York Law School.
1882–84.		Republican member of New York Assembly.
1884.		Candidate for Speaker of Assembly.
		Delegate to Republican State Convention.
		Delegate-at-large to Republican National Convention at Chicago.
1884–86.		Lived on ranch in North Dakota.
1886.		Candidate for Mayor of New York City.
1889.		Appointed on U. S. Civil Service Commission.
1895.		Resigned.
1895–97.		President of Board of Police Commissioners of New York City.
1897.	April.	Appointed Assistant Secretary of U. S. Navy.
1898.	May.	Commissioned Lieutenant-Colonel of the 1st U. S. V. Cavalry.
		Promoted to Colonelcy.
1899–1900.		Governor of New York.
1900.	Nov. 6.	Elected Vice-President.
1901.	Sept. 14.	Became President upon death of McKinley.
1904.		Elected President.

XII

Theodore Roosevelt. Growth through Expansion

WHEN Reconstruction was over and the Hayes–Tilden election had reached its partisan conclusion, the result was acquiesced in by all from a strong desire for peace. The turbulence that had succeeded upon the years of actual warfare was little less exhausting than the strife of battle. It interfered with national development of every character so seriously that by 1877 men were willing to secure peace at almost any price. For two decades thereafter the nation gave itself over unrestrainedly to commerce and the development of its natural resources.[1] Railways sprang up all over the country and were united into great systems; enormous aggregates of capital were gathered into corporations and corporations into trusts; business lost its local and assumed a national character. The spirit of commercialism and the love of gain were the gods of the hour, to be worshipped with the sacrifice of moral character and business principles.

[1] For the period 1877–1897, see Sparks, E. E., *National Development*, 1877–1885; and Dewey, D. R., *National Problems*, 1885–1897.

The reaction from the high moral tone and severe stress of the slavery agitation and emancipation came with the greater disaster because of their previous strength. The moral stamina of the nation seemed impaired; new standards of ethics and of conduct arose in the world of affairs, which winked at the offences of corporation officials and condoned their violations of law as if there were a difference between private and official conduct, as if officials were as soulless as the corporations they represented. The same tendency showed itself in the field of government: with the lessening of the tension, corruption crept in.

With the return of peace, moreover, there set in a steady process of readjustment in the functions of government. The various departments settled back into their normal extent. In the earlier part of the war Lincoln had expanded the power of the Executive into a dictatorship to save the Union. Before its close the dictatorship had passed to Congress, which far exceeded the normal limits of its action and assumed the direction of the whole course of the government. Combined with the Judiciary, the Executive and the Legislative branches of the government had stretched federal powers beyond the limits previously conceived, and State and divided sovereignty were replaced by an unquestioned national supremacy.[1]

The sovereignty of the nation has remained, but the high tide of Executive and Legislative encroachment began to recede shortly after the close of the

[1] *Cf.* Dunning, *Essays on Civil War and Reconstruction,* the first two chapters.

war, and from 1878 to 1898 men felicitated themselves upon the ease with which the powers of the national government could be expanded to meet a crisis and then sink back into their normal condition as of course. In such a spirit men preferred to see the government do too little rather than too much.

From the standpoint, then, of our constitutional development in its larger phases, we may regard the years from 1878 to 1898 as the seven lean years that followed upon the seven fat years of the Civil War. Something of the plethora of previous high living was lost and a more normal condition supervened. There was, nevertheless, a development going on, but so quietly and unobtrusively as to be almost unnoticed, which lay chiefly in the field of property rights as influenced by the presence of corporations.

This purely commercial era was followed by the Spanish War, which marked the latest stage in our national expansion and ushered in Imperialism.[1] The possession of colonial dependencies has brought many new and grave questions for solution, while the economic and social problems which the commercial and industrial development had produced, have become more aggravated and acute. The problems of Imperialism have been linked with those of our economic development and to many, colonial empire has been synonymous with wider markets. As the issues of Imperialism have become less absorbing, those of Industrialism have become more pressing. The nation at large has been touched by the

[1] See Latané, J. H., *America the World Power*, 1897–1907; also Giddings, F. W., *Democracy and Empire;* Hobson, J. A., *Imperialism, A Study;* and Jordan, D. S., *Imperial Democracy.*

growing strength of the social consciousness, by the increasing demands for an enlarged conception of social welfare, and has given ear to the socialistic tendencies of the day.

The last ten years, therefore, may properly be designated as years of expansion, both territorial and commercial. For the first time in our history we have attempted to govern over-sea possessions and for the first time we have become a factor of consequence in the politics of the world. We are no longer isolated, but stand shoulder to shoulder with the great nations of the earth.[1]

No name has been more intimately associated with this period of our national life than that of Mr. Roosevelt. In its earlier phases, to be sure, he was not the most commanding figure nor was he in a position to guide and direct affairs, though he participated in them. Yet he has identified himself so completely in word and in deed with the war and its results, both while it was in progress and subsequently, that he may justly be regarded as representative of its ideals. Since the first problems of Imperialism have been met and the attention of the country has been directed to the social and economic evils attendant upon our commercial development, he has stood at the front. For the past seven years he has held first place in the public eye, and the " Roosevelt Policies " have been the guides of government action[2]; his influence has been the determining force

[1] *Cf.* Coolidge, A. C., *The United States as a World Power.*
[2] *Cf. The Roosevelt Policy: Speeches, Letters, and State Papers Relating to Corporate Wealth and Closely Allied Topics*, 2 vols., N. Y., 1908; and *The Roosevelt Doctrine, Being the Per-*

Theodore Roosevelt

and in him is personified the spirit of our development since 1898.

The career of Mr. Roosevelt is so well known that a detailed exposition of it is unnecessary.[1] He was born in New York City in 1858, was graduated from Harvard in 1880, served as a member of the New York State Assembly from 1882 to 1884, and in 1886 was an unsuccessful candidate for Mayor of New York City; three years later he was appointed by President Harrison a member of the National Civil Service Commission on which he served for six years, resigning to become President of the Board of Police Commissioners of New York City for two years. As Assistant Secretary of the Navy, Roosevelt entered national politics in 1897, and in the following year was appointed Lieutenant-Colonel, then Colonel, of the "Rough Riders" in the Spanish War and was elected Governor of New York. In 1900 he was elected Vice-President and upon the death of President McKinley, became President of the United States on September 14, 1901. In 1904 he was elected President.

His life may be epitomized in the phrase "doing things," and the most prominent characteristic of the government he has guided would find suitable expression in the same words. This activity of the government has been present in the fields both of territorial expansion and industrial combination, but we must recognize that the nearer we stand in point of time to the things the government is doing, the

---

sonal *Utterances of the President on Various Matters of Vital Interest*, N. Y., 1904.

[1] *Cf.* Riis, *Theodore Roosevelt, the Citizen.*

more difficult it is for us to pass a correct judgment upon them, to estimate the forces producing them, and to determine their results. No attempt will be made to predict the final results as they shall take shape in our constitutional life, or to estimate conclusively the relation that Roosevelt will bear to the changes, but it seems possible to indicate some of the general tendencies and to show how they are modifying our constitutional life and habit. It is quite another matter to determine how lasting will be the present movements or how deep-seated are the transformations now in progress.

The expansion that came as a result of the Spanish War was essentially different from that which had preceded. Beginning with the purchase of Louisiana, the westward growth of the national territory had been steady and natural. It came through settlement, through the pushing out of the borders of civilization into country hitherto unoccupied, or at best in the possession of Indian tribes or of scattered Spanish settlements. The government of the new territory was exercised over men of the same race, with the same ideals and the same traditions respecting liberty and authority; the virgin soil of the West was occupied by the steady advance of the same civilization. The expansion of 1898 imported new conditions and new problems. It was not mere extension, but at a single bound we crossed the sea and took possession of territory already held by peoples with a civilization essentially different from our own; the new task was set us of incorporating these radically different elements into our national life, and even yet their final status is matter of discussion. We have undertaken a previously untried work—that of teaching an Oriental people the art of self-government.

The framers of the Constitution could not possibly have foreseen such an expansion and therefore they made no specific provision for it, but following out the general lines of previous national development, we have found warrant in the existence of a national state for the performance of this function of government as an integral part of state life. In accordance with this view, we have moulded our constitutional practices with reference to our dependencies. They are in our national life, but they are not a part of it. For certain purposes they are our territory, while for certain other they are not. Their citizens are not citizens of the United States, though they are entitled to its protection. The Constitution does not follow the flag, though the fundamental rights of liberty are not to be denied to the inhabitants of our dependencies. We may hold and govern dependent territories; a republic, we may nevertheless rule over subjects.[1]

Self-government is rightly regarded as of the essence of modern political liberty. No people is free that cannot and does not govern itself, it matters not how large a sphere of action is left to individuals by their rulers. By many it has been deemed fatal to liberty for a free people to rule over subjects; the exercise of arbitrary power reacts upon the liberty of those exercising it and there is a lessening of

[1] *Cf.* Latané, *America, the World Power*, p. 133 *ff;* and the *Insular Cases*, 182 U. S. Supreme Court Reports, 1 *ff;* 183 U. S. 151 *ff* and 176 *ff.*

the spirit of true freedom. Men cannot consistently claim the right to rule themselves and not grant to others the same right. Inconsistency and inequality, in politics as elsewhere, tend toward uniformity, and as in the science of finance the worse metal will drive the better out of circulation, so in the world of political relations the baser coinage of despotic rule puts to flight the pure mintage of individual liberty.

It cannot be successfully denied that to some extent the truth of this view has been demonstrated in our own case, though the loss of liberty we have experienced is to be felt rather in the general attitude of the government toward the individual than in any concrete loss we have suffered through statutory enactment.[1] The centralizing tendencies of the Federal Government have been increased and the uneven balance between the States and the nation has been rendered still greater. With alarming frequency the government has undertaken new services for the people and the more government does, the louder is the demand for fresh acts of paternal care. The spirit of individual initiative is weakened and the desire for collective activity grows apace.

Within the Federal Government itself, the position of the President has profited most by Imperialism.[2] Both in domestic affairs and in foreign relations he has assumed a far more commanding position than heretofore. Though Congress has the right to pass

[1] *Cf.* Jordan, David Starr, *Imperial Democracy*, and Hobson, J. A., *Imperialism, A Study*.
[2] Wilson, Woodrow, *Congressional Government*, Preface to the 15th Ed., p. xi. *ff.*

all laws regulating the government of national territory, in the earlier stages of acquisition it has been the President, through the army, who has governed it, and even after Congress has legislated there still remains an extensive field for Executive action and discretion. Our position as a world power has likewise contributed to the elevation of the Executive in proportion as it has enlarged and complicated our relations with other powers. In both the external and the internal policy of the government, President Roosevelt was peculiarly fitted by temperament to make the influence of the Executive felt to a degree seldom attained in our history. In this respect he stands with Jackson and Lincoln; each of them exalted the power of the Executive to a place of predominance in our scheme of government.

The influence, then, of our recent territorial expansion has been twofold: on the one hand, it has tended to strengthen the power of the Executive and of the Federal Government, to accentuate the centralizing tendency that is present in every modern government and in every stage of governmental activity from city to nation; on the other, it has rounded out the constitutional development of the country on the side of national sovereignty. The Civil War wrought sad havoc in the fine-spun theories of delegated and strictly limited powers, of divided sovereignty and of the nice adjustment of the parts of government over against each other. The President and Congress by turns assumed a preponderance that destroyed all equilibrium, and the Federal Government acted on the theory of national sovereignty and the necessity of preserving the Union as the only limit of its powers.

These extensions of power were, nevertheless, regarded as usurpations and as justified only by the circumstances; they were to be tolerated only so long as the conditions that produced them should continue operative. Thus it happened that a process of readjustment set in after the return of normal conditions and, save for the questions which the actual result of the war had settled, there was little to mark the previous expansion of the powers and the unsettling of relationships. The nature of the Union was at length fixed but the determination seemed to bring little change. The States no longer claimed to be sovereign, but the existence of sovereignty in the nation left the every-day relations of the States to the Union in much the same condition as previously. Their influence, however, was lessened and their individual positions were less commanding, and in proportion as they have lost, the Federal Government has gained, in the esteem in which it is held by the people. As the one has fallen the other has risen, till a lively fear is entertained by many that a real danger threatens from this quarter. When Mr. Root spoke of wiping out State lines,[1] champions of a new kind of State-Rights arose on every hand to execrate the dangerous tendency of centralization.

A large part of the increase of Federal powers has come as a result of our colonial policy which has both elevated and strengthened the position of the nation, without effecting a corresponding change in that of the States. The holding of dependencies by the nation has reacted in a twofold manner on the nation itself; it has brought a vivid consciousness of

[1] In New York City, 1906.

a new phase of nationality to our Union and vastly increased the activities of that Union. The process of the development of our national feeling has been a long and a difficult one and it is only since the acquisition of our colonies that we have experienced its full extent; since then we have acquiesced more fully in the view that the limits of action set to the sphere of the Federal Government are not to be measured with the foot-rule of strict construction and delegated powers, but are to be meted out generously with the yardstick of true nationality.

President Roosevelt was the leader in bringing to our conscious realization this sense of nationality; the sense that we have at last reached our majority and have been admitted to an equal place and an equal voice in the family of nations. He has attempted to awaken a corresponding sense of the national duties and responsibilities that accompany national maturity. We must mean what we say and be prepared to make it good, if we would fill a man's place in the world. We must love peace and pursue it, but at the same time be prepared for war. We must be ready and willing to assume the responsibilities that result from our foreign policy if we would make that policy respected.[1] Thus it is that he pleads for a stronger navy and army; that he restores the peace of the world through his mediation; that he reformulates the Monroe Doctrine and, regretting the Pacific Blockade of Venezuelan ports in 1903, anticipates similar action in San Domingo by arranging that the United States shall collect the revenue and herself apply it to the liquidation of

[1] *The Roosevelt Policy, passim.*

the debts; that he seizes a questionable opportunity to secure territorial concessions that make the building of the Panama Canal a possibility; that he secures the participation of the United States in a European conference on Morocco and the admission of the South and Central American states to the Second Hague Conference.

If Mr. Roosevelt may be regarded as typical of the development that has resulted from territorial expansion, and as embodying the nationalizing forces of Imperialism, even more may he be regarded as the soul of the constitutional changes which have resulted from modern industrial conditions. He has stood in the forefront, pointing the way to ever increasing activity on the part of the Federal Government. To vary the figure, he has lashed Congress and the country with repeated blows from the Presidential message, urging and reurging the enactment of measures of a great variety, nearly all of them characterized by an expansion of power or an extension of function on the part of the government, and touching the industrial life of the country.[1] The old ideals of government in general, and of our government in particular, are declared no longer adequate. New economic and social conditions demand new courses of action on the part of the government and from the peculiar character of our government, with its division of power between the States and the nation, it has been declared necessary, from the nature of our economic development, that the Federal Government should undertake the new functions.

The old ideal of individualism found expression in

[1] *The Roosevelt Policy, passim.*

the economic world in the theory of free competition; it was regarded as sound economic doctrine that unrestricted competition would work out best in the end, both for individuals and for industry. The part of the law was to provide merely that competition should be unrestricted; having provided a clear field, let the contestants fight it out and the individual with the greatest amount of energy, shrewdness, strength, perseverance, and talent would triumph, to the benefit of himself and of society. Such a view comported well with the conditions of a society, simple in its structure and organization, wherein the contestants were measurably equal; wherein individuals struggled with individuals and success was due to a natural superiority, but it has proved inadequate to modern industrial conditions, with their great complexity of relations and with the competing factors on a plane far from equal. The law, instead of affording a free field for equal competitors, has itself produced the gravest inequality through the creation of group persons, corporations, with which the individual finds it increasingly difficult to compete successfully. Success is no longer due to the natural talents of the individual but to the natural talents, plus the fortuitous advantages accruing to groups of individuals through the corporation.

To meet the organizations of capital, labor, too, has been organized [1]; the trust and the labor union are new and controlling factors in the modern industrial world; through them a large part of society finds itself separated into opposing camps, each fighting for existence. The clash of these divergent

[1] *Cf.* Dewey, *op. cit.*, p. 40 *ff.*

interests has often been severe and prolonged. The strike and the lockout are familiar proceedings, while the boycott and blacklist have attained a notoriety for lawlessness and oppression, as detestable as the unwarranted use of the injunction and Pinkerton detectives.

Meanwhile the interests of the public at large have been disregarded with unpardonable indifference by both sides. In an age of such highly developed specialization of industries and consequent greater dependence of man upon man for the means of existence, it is not solely capital and labor that have a vital interest in their disputes; the circle of those affected is a constantly widening one, and the steady and uninterrupted pursuit of those industries touching the public welfare is of so great importance to the community, that it welcomes the settlement of an anthracite coal strike through the interposition of the personal influence of the President, and canvasses the question of government ownership of natural resources, when limited in extent and essential to modern life.

The individual has sunk his individuality in large measure in the corporation on the one hand and the labor union on the other; individualism and free competition as the basis of industrialism have given way to combination. While this change has been in progress, the public welfare has suffered and the interests of the community have been disregarded because our theories of government and economics have not squared with practice, and the whole foundation of society, of law, and of government has been affected. We have clung to individualism in the field of government and deserted it in the field of business, and the inevitable result has followed. The law has proved inadequate to the task set it and government has failed in some of its primary obligations to its citizens. The "predatory rich" no less than the walking delegate, have trampled upon the rights of individuals and of society; corporations and labor unions have menaced the safety and prosperity of society, until the people, at length awakened to the dangers of the situation, have attempted to put a hook in the nose of these great Leviathans.

No one perceived these dangers more clearly than President Roosevelt and no one has been more strenuous in seeking to remedy them, in order that equality of opportunity for both labor and capital might be secured, and that every man, to use his own words, might get "a square deal." [1] No one with less courage would have cast himself so boldly upon the people for support, and his constant appeals to them have ranged him with Jefferson and Jackson as a believer in the ultimate wisdom of the mass of mankind. No one who was not both leader of his party and of the nation could have succeeded.

The only possible solution of the problem lay in the performance by the government of its legitimate function of maintaining a free field, of its first duty of equal justice to all, though in doing so it might depart very far from the old ideals of *laissez-faire* and be compelled to strengthen its powers and extend its functions. Such a result was in entire harmony with Roosevelt's whole theory of government, which combines the trust of Jefferson in the people with

[1] *The Roosevelt Policy*, i., 158.

Hamilton's belief in the efficacy of government as a means of progress. He typifies a triumphant and confident democracy which is bent on making government an instrument of the general welfare to an extent hitherto only dreamed of. Jefferson led the forces of the people to an attack upon government that they might conquer and curb it, lest it destroy their liberties. They would weaken it, that it might not harm them. Jackson captained the hosts of the country to win possession of the government from which they had been unjustly excluded; and once in possession, they sought to crush out the Bank as an agency of oppression. The danger from government was still present to their minds, though it was because government was in the hands of the enemies of the people. When President Roosevelt assumed the reins of government, it was to lead the people in an attack upon the money power that had gotten possession of the government somewhat as in the time of Jackson, but, unlike either Jefferson or Jackson, the desire to secure control came not from fear of the government, but from the belief that government should be an organ for the advancement of the interests of society, that it should actively and consciously strive to promote the welfare of the community. Instead, therefore, of being afraid of government as an instrument of oppression and being jealous of the extent of its sphere, he sought to control it that he might widen its scope to meet the needs of an awakened social consciousness. Like James Wilson, he desired the foundation of all authority to flow from the people, but he desired that authority to be strong.

So far as the Federal Government was concerned, the period since the Civil War had witnessed a retrogression rather than a progression in the extent of its services to the community; it had lagged behind the needs of the country; almost no serious attempt had been made to control the great combinations of capital and labor. The most urgent considerations demanded that the public should not be made a prey of either, and protection could be secured through no other agency than that of government, for no other was strong enough. From the peculiar character of our constitutional arrangements, with its dual system of government, and from the national extent of the combinations, the logical and legal source of the power to exercise the necessary protection must lie in the Federal Government.

The country at large acquiesced in this view and a rapid succession of measures followed, each tending to increase the power and the extent of the control of the Federal Government over the daily life of the citizens.[1] But the extent of the change can no more be measured by the laws upon the statute book than could that effected by the election of Jefferson or Jackson. It is a change of ideals, and its ultimate effect upon our constitutional life and practices can be estimated only by subsequent generations.

The source of the government's power over so large a part of our industrial activity lies in its control of interstate commerce, and that clause of the Constitution conferring the control has been the authority for most of the legislation of recent

[1] *Cf.* Pierce, Franklin, *Federal Usurpation*, and Stimson, J. F. *The American Constitution.*

years which smacks of paternalism and even of socialism.

The need for uniformity in the regulation of commerce between the States and with foreign nations was one of the leading causes for summoning the Constitutional Convention and elaborating a new Constitution. The jealousies and discriminations of the States against each other had produced a deplorable and unendurable condition, which made it necessary that all commerce not within a single State should be put under the control of the Federal Government. The power to regulate interstate and foreign commerce has always been a source of great strength to the national government, for the expansion of commerce has necessitated a corresponding expansion of the activities of government. The development of great corporations, both for production and for transportation, has made interstate commerce a marvel of complexity. To meet the new conditions laws have been passed looking to their regulation by the Federal Government. A supervision of this character has necessitated the creation of a host of government inspectors and commissions, that has gone far toward justifying the extreme individualist in asserting that we are in danger of erecting a government, **not of laws but of men.**

Appendix

THE DECLARATION OF INDEPENDENCE

In Congress, July 4, 1776

The Unanimous Declaration of the Thirteen United States of America

WHEN in the Course of human events, it becomes necessary for one people to dissolve the political bands which have connected them with another, and to assume among the Powers of the earth, the separate and equal station to which the Laws of Nature and of Nature's God entitle them, a decent respect to the opinions of mankind requires that they should declare the causes which impel them to the separation.

We hold these truths to be self-evident, that all men are created equal, that they are endowed by their Creator with certain unalienable Rights, that among these are Life, Liberty, and the pursuit of Happiness. That to secure these rights, Governments are instituted among Men, deriving their just powers from the consent of the governed, That whenever any Form of Government becomes destructive of these ends, it is the Right of the People to alter or to abolish it, and to institute new Government, laying its foundation on such principles and organizing its powers in such form, as to them shall seem most likely to effect their Safety and Happiness. Prudence, indeed, will dictate that Governments long established should not be changed for light and transient causes; and accordingly all experience hath shown, that mankind are more disposed to suffer, while evils are sufferable, than to right themselves by abolishing the forms to which they are accustomed. But when a long train of abuses and usurpations, pursuing invariably the same Object, evinces a design to reduce them under absolute Despotism, it is their right, it is their duty, to throw off such Government, and to provide new Guards for their future security.—Such has been the patient sufferance of these Colonies; and such is now the necessity which constrains them to alter their former Systems of Government. The history of the present King of Great Britain is a history of repeated injuries and usurpations, all having in direct object the establishment of an absolute Tyranny over these States. To prove this, let Facts be submitted to a candid world.

He has refused his Assent to Laws, the most wholesome and necessary for the public good.

He has forbidden his Governors to pass Laws of immediate and pressing importance, unless suspended in their operation till his Assent should be obtained; and when so suspended, he has utterly neglected to attend to them.

He has refused to pass other Laws for the accommodation of large districts of people, unless those people would relinquish the right of Representation in the Legislature, a right inestimable to them and formidable to tyrants only.

He has called together legislative bodies at places unusual, uncomfortable, and distant from the depository of their Public Records, for the sole purpose of fatiguing them into compliance with his measures.

He has dissolved Representative Houses repeatedly, for opposing with manly firmness his invasions on the rights of the people.

He has refused for a long time, after such dissolutions,

The Declaration of Independence

to cause others to be elected; whereby the Legislative Powers, incapable of Annihilation, have returned to the People at large for their exercise; the State remaining in the mean time exposed to all the dangers of invasion from without, and convulsions within.

He has endeavored to prevent the population of these States; for that purpose obstructing the Laws for Naturalization of Foreigners; refusing to pass others to encourage their migration hither, and raising the conditions of new Appropriations of Lands.

He has obstructed the Administration of Justice, by refusing his Assent to Laws for establishing Judiciary Powers.

He has made Judges dependent on his Will alone, for the tenure of their offices, and the amount and payment of their salaries.

He has erected a multitude of New Offices, and sent hither swarms of Officers to harass our People, and eat out their substance.

He has kept among us, in times of peace, Standing Armies without the Consent of our legislature.

He has affected to render the Military independent of and superior to the Civil Power.

He has combined with others to subject us to a jurisdiction foreign to our constitution, and unacknowledged by our laws; giving his Assent to their Acts of pretended Legislation:

For quartering large bodies of armed troops among us:

For protecting them, by a mock Trial, from Punishment for any Murders which they should commit on the Inhabitants of these States:

For cutting off our Trade with all parts of the world:

For imposing taxes on us without our Consent:

For depriving us in many cases, of the benefits of Trial by Jury:

For transporting us beyond Seas to be tried for pretended offences:

For abolishing the free System of English Laws in a neighboring Province, establishing therein an Arbitrary government, and enlarging its Boundaries so as to render it at once an example and fit instrument for introducing the same absolute rule into these Colonies:

For taking away our Charters, abolishing our most valuable Laws, and altering fundamentally the Forms of our Governments:

For suspending our own Legislatures, and declaring themselves invested with Power to legislate for us in all cases whatsoever.

He has abdicated Government here, by declaring us out of his Protection and waging War against us.

He has plundered our seas, ravaged our Coasts, burnt our towns, and destroyed the lives of our people.

He is at this time transporting large armies of foreign mercenaries to compleat the works of death, desolation, and tyranny, already begun with circumstances of Cruelty & perfidy scarcely paralleled in the most barbarous ages, and totally unworthy the Head of a civilized nation.

He has constrained our fellow Citizens taken Captive on the high Seas to bear Arms against their Country, to become the executioners of their friends and Brethren, or to fall themselves by their Hands.

He has excited domestic insurrections amongst us, and has endeavored to bring on the inhabitants of our frontiers, the merciless Indian Savages, whose known rule of warfare is an undistinguished destruction of all ages, sexes, and conditions.

In every stage of these Oppressions We have Petitioned for Redress in the most humble terms: Our repeated Petitions have been answered only by repeated injury. A Prince, whose character is thus marked by every act which may define a Tyrant, is unfit to be the ruler of a free People.

Nor have We been wanting in attention to our British brethren. We have warned them from time to time of attempts by their legislature to extend an unwarrantable jurisdiction over us. We have reminded them of the circumstances of our emigration and settlement here. We have appealed to their native justice and magnanimity, and we have conjured them by the ties of our common kindred to disavow these usurpations, which would inevitably interrupt our connections and correspondence. They too have been deaf to the voice of justice and of consanguinity. We must, therefore, acquiesce in the necessity, which denounces our Separation, and hold them, as we hold the rest of mankind, Enemies in War, in Peace Friends.

We, therefore, the Representatives of the United States of America, in General Congress, Assembled, appealing to the Supreme Judge of the world for the rectitude of our intentions, do, in the Name, and by Authority of the good People of these Colonies, solemnly publish and declare, That these United Colonies are, and of Right ought to be Free and Independent States; that they are Absolved from all Allegiance to the British Crown, and that all political connection between them and the State of Great Britain, is and ought to be totally dissolved; and that as Free and Independent States, they have full Power to levy War, conclude Peace, contract Alliances, establish Commerce, and to do all other Acts and Things which Independent States may of right do. And for the support of this Declaration, with a firm reliance on the Protection of Divine Providence, we mutually pledge to each other our Lives, our Fortunes, and our sacred Honor.

JOHN HANCOCK.

New Hampshire—Josiah Bartlett, Wm. Whipple, Matthew Thornton.

Massachusetts Bay—Saml. Adams, John Adams, Robt. Treat Paine, Elbridge Gerry.

Rhode Island—Step. Hopkins, William Ellery.

Connecticut—Roger Sherman, Sam'el Huntington, Wm. Williams, Oliver Wolcott.

New York—Wm. Floyd, Phil. Livingston, Frans. Lewis, Lewis Morris.

New Jersey—Richd. Stockton, Jno. Witherspoon, Fras. Hopkinson, John Hart, Abra. Clark.

Pennsylvania—Robt. Morris, Benjamin Rush, Benja. Franklin, John Morton, Geo. Clymer, Jas. Smith, Geo. Taylor, James Wilson, Geo. Ross.

Delaware—Caesar Rodney, Geo. Read, Tho. M'Kean.

Maryland—Samuel Chase, Wm. Paca, Thos. Stone, Charles Carroll of Carrollton.

Virginia—George Wythe, Richard Henry Lee, Th Jefferson, Benja. Harrison, Thos. Nelson, jr., Francis Lightfoot Lee, Carter Braxton.

North Carolina—Wm. Hooper, Joseph Hewes, John Penn.

South Carolina—Edward Rutledge, Thos. Heyward, Junr., Thomas Lynch, Junr., Arthur Middleton.

Georgia—Button Gwinnett, Lyman Hall, Geo. Walton.

THE ARTICLES OF CONFEDERATION

Articles of Confederation and Perpetual Union between the States of New Hampshire, Massachusetts Bay, Rhode Island and Providence Plantations, Connecticut, New York, New Jersey, Pennsylvania, Delaware, Maryland, Virginia, North Carolina, South Carolina, and Georgia.

ARTICLE I.—The style of this Confederacy shall be, "The United States of America."

ART. II.—Each State retains its sovereignty, freedom, and independence, and every power, jurisdiction, and right, which is not by this Confederation expressly delegated to the United States in Congress assembled.

ART. III.—The said States hereby severally enter into a firm league of friendship with each other, for their common defence, the security of their liberties, and their mutual and general welfare, binding themselves to assist each other against all force offered to, or attacks made upon them, or any of them, on account of religion, sovereignty, trade, or any other pretence whatever.

ART. IV.—The better to secure and perpetuate mutual friendship and intercourse among the people of the different States in this Union, the free inhabitants of each of these States, paupers, vagabonds, and fugitives from justice excepted, shall be entitled to all privileges and immunities of free citizens in the several States; and the people of each State shall have free ingress and egress to and from any other State, and shall enjoy therein all the privileges of trade and commerce subject to the same duties, impositions, and restrictions as the inhabitants thereof respectively; provided that such restrictions shall not extend so far as to prevent the removal of property imported into any State to any other State of which the owner is an inhabitant; provided also, that no imposition, duties, or restriction shall be laid by any State on the property of the United States or either of them. If any person guilty of, or charged with, treason, felony, or other high misdemeanor in any State shall flee from justice and be found in any of the United States, he shall, upon demand of the governor or executive power of the State from which he fled, be delivered up and removed to the State having jurisdiction of his offence. Full faith and credit shall be given in each of these States to the records, acts, and judicial proceedings of the courts and magistrates of every other State.

ART. V.—For the more convenient management of the general interests of the United States, delegates shall be annually appointed in such manner as the Legislature of each State shall direct, to meet in Congress on the first Monday in November, in every year, with a power reserved to each State to recall its delegates, or any of them, at any time within the year, and to send others in their stead for the remainder of the year. No State shall be represented in Congress by less than two, nor by more than seven members; and no person shall be capable of being a delegate for more than three years in any term of six years; nor shall any person, being a delegate, be capable of holding any office under the United States for which he, or another for his benefit, receives any salary, fees, or emolument of any kind. Each State shall maintain its own delegates in any meeting of the States and while they act as members of the Committee of the States. In determining questions in the United

States in Congress assembled, each State shall have one vote. Freedom of speech and debate in Congress shall not be impeached or questioned in any court or place out of Congress; and the members of Congress shall be protected in their persons from arrests and imprisonment during the time of their going to and from, and attendance on, Congress, except for treason, felony, or breach of the peace.

ART. VI.—No State, without the consent of the United States, in Congress assembled, shall send any embassy to, or receive any embassy from, or enter into any conference, agreement, alliance, or treaty with any king, prince, or state; nor shall any person holding any office of profit or trust under the United States, or any of them, accept of any present, emolument, office, or title of any kind whatever from any king, prince, or foreign state; nor shall the United States, in Congress assembled, or any of them, grant any title of nobility.

No two or more States shall enter into any treaty, confederation, or alliance whatever between them, without the consent of the United States, in Congress assembled, specifying accurately the purposes for which the same is to be entered into, and how long it shall continue.

No State shall lay any imposts or duties which may interfere with any stipulations in treaties entered into by the United States, in Congress assembled, with any king, prince, or state, in pursuance of any treaties already proposed by Congress to the courts of France and Spain.

No vessel of war shall be kept up in time of peace by any State, except such number only as shall be deemed necessary by the United States, in Congress assembled, for the defence of such State or its trade, nor shall any body of forces be kept up by any State in time of peace, except such number only as, in the judgment of the

United States, in Congress assembled, shall be deemed requisite to garrison the forts necessary for the defence of such State; but every State shall always keep up a well-regulated and disciplined militia, sufficiently armed and accoutred, and shall provide and constantly have ready for use in public stores a due number of field-pieces and tents, and a proper quantity of arms, ammunition, and camp equipage.

No State shall engage in any war without the consent of the United States, in Congress assembled, unless such State be actually invaded by enemies, or shall have received certain advice of a resolution being formed by some nation of Indians to invade such State, and the danger is so imminent as not to admit of a delay till the United States, in Congress assembled, can be consulted; nor shall any State grant commissions to any ships or vessels of war, nor letters of marque or reprisal, except it be after a declaration of war by the United States, in Congress assembled, and then only against the kingdom or state, and the subjects thereof, against which war has been so declared, and under such regulations as shall be established by the United States, in Congress assembled, unless such State be infested by pirates, in which case vessels of war may be fitted out for that occasion, and kept so long as the danger shall continue, or until the United States, in Congress assembled, shall determine otherwise.

ART. VII.—When land forces are raised by any State for the common defence, all officers of or under the rank of Colonel shall be appointed by the Legislature of each State respectively by whom such forces shall be raised, or in such manner as such State shall direct, and all vacancies shall be filled up by the State which first made the appointment.

ART. VIII.—All charges of war, and all other expenses that shall be incurred for the common defence, or general welfare, and allowed by the United States, in Congress assembled, shall be defrayed out of a common treasury, which shall be supplied by the several States in proportion to the value of all land within each State, granted to, or surveyed for, any person, as such land and the buildings and improvements thereon shall be estimated, according to such mode as the United States, in Congress assembled, shall, from time to time, direct and appoint. The taxes for paying that proportion shall be laid and levied by the authority and direction of the Legislatures of the several States, within the time agreed upon by the United States, in Congress assembled.

ART. IX.—The United States, in Congress assembled, shall have the sole and exclusive right and power of determining on peace and war, except in the cases mentioned in the sixth Article; of sending and receiving ambassadors; entering into treaties and alliances, provided that no treaty of commerce shall be made, whereby the legislative power of the respective States shall be restrained from imposing such imposts and duties on foreigners as their own people are subjected to, or from prohibiting the exportation or importation of any species of goods or commodities whatever, of establishing rules for deciding, in all cases, what captures on land and water shall be legal, and in what manner prizes taken by land or naval forces in the service of the United States shall be divided or appropriated; of granting letters of marque and reprisal in times of peace; appointing courts for the trial of piracies and felonies committed on the high seas; and establishing courts for receiving and determining finally appeals in all cases of captures; provided that no member of Congress shall be appointed a judge of any of the said courts.

The United States, in Congress assembled, shall also be the last resort on appeal in all disputes and differences now subsisting, or that hereafter may arise between two or more States concerning boundary, jurisdiction, or any other cause whatever; which authority shall always be exercised in the manner following: Whenever the legislative or executive authority, or lawful agent of any State in controversy with another, shall present a petition to Congress, stating the matter in question, and praying for a hearing, notice thereof shall be given by order of Congress to the legislative or executive authority of the other State in controversy, and a day assigned for the appearance of the parties by their lawful agents, who shall then be directed to appoint, by joint consent, commissioners or judges to constitute a court for hearing and determining the matter in question; but if they cannot agree, Congress shall name three persons out of each of the United States, and from the list of such persons each party shall alternately strike out one, the petitioners beginning, until the number shall be reduced to thirteen; and from that number not less than seven nor more than nine names, as Congress shall direct, shall, in the presence of Congress, be drawn out by lot; and the persons whose names shall be so drawn, or any five of them, shall be commissioners or judges, to hear and finally determine the controversy, so always as a major part of the judges who shall hear the cause shall agree in the determination; and if either party shall neglect to attend at the day appointed, without showing reasons which Congress shall judge sufficient, or being present, shall refuse to strike, the Congress shall proceed to nominate three persons out of each State, and the secretary of Congress shall strike in behalf of such party absent or refusing; and the judgment and sentence of the court, to be appointed in the manner before prescribed, shall be final and conclusive; and if any of the parties shall refuse to submit to the authority of such court, or to appear or defend their claim or cause, the court shall nevertheless proceed to pronounce sentence or judgment, which shall in like manner be final and decisive; the judgment or sentence and other proceedings being in either case transmitted to Congress, and lodged among the acts of Congress for the security of the parties concerned; provided, that every commissioner, before he sits in judgment, shall take an oath, to be administered by one of the judges of the supreme or superior court of the State where the cause shall be tried, "well and truly to hear and determine the matter in question, according to the best of his judgment, without favor, affection, or hope of reward." Provided, also, that no State shall be deprived of territory for the benefit of the United States.

All controversies concerning the private right of soil claimed under different grants of two or more States, whose jurisdictions, as they may respect such lands, and the States which passed such grants are adjusted, the said grants or either of them being at the same time claimed to have originated antecedent to such settlement of jurisdiction, shall, on the petition of either party to the Congress of the United States, be finally determined, as near as may be, in the same manner as is before prescribed for deciding disputes respecting territorial jurisdiction between different States.

The United States, in Congress assembled, shall also have the sole and exclusive right and power of regulating the alloy and value of coin struck by their own authority, or by that of the respective States; fixing the standard of weights and measures throughout the United States; regulating the trade and managing all affairs with the Indians, not members of any of the States; provided that the legislative right of any State, within its own limits, be not infringed or violated; establishing and regulating post-offices from one State to another, throughout all the United States, and exacting such postage on the papers passing through the same as may be requisite to defray the expenses of the said office; appointing all officers of the land forces in the service of the United States, excepting regimental officers; appointing all the officers of the naval forces, and commissioning all officers whatever in the service of the United States; making rules for the government and regulation of the said land and naval forces, and directing their operations.

The United States, in Congress assembled shall have authority to appoint a committee, to sit in the recess of Congress, to be denominated " A Committee of the States," and to consist of one delegate from each State, and to appoint such other committees and civil officers as may be necessary for managing the general affairs of the United States under their directions; to appoint one of their number to preside; provided that no person be allowed to serve in the office of president more than one year in any term of three years; to ascertain the necessary sums of money to be raised for the service of the United States, and to appropriate and apply the same for defraying the public expenses; to borrow money or emit bills on the credit of the United States, transmitting every half year to the respective States an account of the sums of money so borrowed or emitted; to build and equip a navy; to agree upon the number of land forces, and to make requisitions from each State for its quota, in proportion to the number of white inhabitants in such State, which requisition shall be binding; and thereupon the Legislature of each State shall appoint the regimental officers, raise the men, and clothe, arm, and equip them in a soldier-like manner, at the expense of the United States; and the officers and men so clothed, armed, and equipped shall march to the place appointed, and within the time agreed on by the United States, in Congress assembled; but if the United States, in Congress assembled, shall, on consideration of circumstances, judge proper that any State should not raise men, or should raise a smaller number than its quota, and that any other State should raise a greater number of men than the quota thereof, such extra number shall be raised, officered, clothed, armed, and equipped in the same manner as the quota of such State, unless the Legislature of such State shall judge that such extra number can not be safely spared out of the same, in which case they shall raise, officer, clothe, arm, and equip as many of such extra number as they judge can be safely spared, and the officers and men so clothed, armed, and equipped shall march to the place appointed, and within the time agreed on by the United States, in Congress assembled.

The United States, in Congress assembled, shall never engage in a war, nor grant letters of marque and reprisal in time of peace, nor enter into any treaties or alliances, nor coin money, nor regulate the value thereof, nor ascertain the sums and expenses necessary for the defence and welfare of the United States, or any of them, nor emit bills, nor borrow money on the credit of the United States, nor appropriate money, nor agree upon the number of vessels of war to be built or purchased, or the number of land or sea forces to be raised, nor appoint a commander-in-chief of the army or navy, unless nine States assent to the same, nor shall a question on any other point, except for adjourning from day to day, be determined, unless by the votes of a majority of the United States, in Congress assembled.

The Congress of the United States shall have power to adjourn to any time within the year, and to any place within the United States, so that no period of adjournment be for a longer duration than the space of six months, and shall publish the journal of their proceedings monthly, except such parts thereof relating to treaties, alliances, or military operations as in their judgment require secrecy; and the yeas and nays of the delegates of each State, on any question, shall be entered on the journal when it is desired by any delegate; and the delegates of a State, or any of them, at his or their request, shall be furnished with a transcript of the said journal except such parts as are above excepted, to lay before the Legislatures of the several States.

ART. X.—The committee of the States, or any nine of them, shall be authorized to execute, in the recess of Congress, such of the powers of Congress as the United States, in Congress assembled, by the consent of nine States, shall, from time to time, think expedient to vest them with; provided that no power be delegated to the said Committee, for the exercise of which, by the Articles of Confederation, the voice of nine States in the Congress of the United States assembled is requisite.

ART. XI.—Canada, acceding to this Confederation, and joining in the measures of the United States, shall be admitted into, and entitled to all the advantages of this Union; but no other colony shall be admitted into the same, unless such admission be agreed to by nine States.

ART. XII.—All bills of credit emitted, moneys borrowed, and debts contracted by or under the authority of Congress, before the assembling of the United States, in pursuance of the present Confederation, shall be deemed and considered as a charge against the United States, for payment and satisfaction whereof the said United States and the public faith are hereby solemnly pledged.

ART. XIII.—Every State shall abide by the determinations of the United States, in Congress assembled, on all questions which by this Confederation are submitted to them. And the Articles of this Confederation shall be inviolably observed by every State, and the Union shall be perpetual; nor shall any alteration at any time hereafter be made in any of them, unless such alteration be agreed to in a Congress of the United States,

The Articles of Confederation

and be afterwards confirmed by the Legislatures of every State.

AND WHEREAS it hath pleased the great Governor of the world to incline the hearts of the Legislatures we respectively represent in Congress to approve of, and to authorize us to ratify, the said Articles of Confederation and perpetual Union, know ye, that we, the undersigned delegates, by virtue of the power and authority to us given for that purpose, do, by these presents, in the name and in behalf of our respective constituents, fully and entirely ratify and confirm each and every of the said Articles of Confederation and perpetual Union, and all and singular the matter and things therein contained. And we do further solemnly plight and engage the faith of our respective constituents, that they shall abide by the determinations of the United States, in Congress assembled, on all questions which by the said Confederation are submitted to them; and that the Articles thereof shall be inviolably observed by the States we respectively represent, and that the Union shall be perpetual.

In witness whereof we have hereunto set our hands in Congress. Done at Philadelphia in the State of Pennsylvania the ninth day of July in the year of our Lord one thousand seven hundred and seventy-eight, and in the third year of the independence of America.

On the part & behalf of the State of New Hampshire.

JOSIAH BARTLETT,   JOHN WENTWORTH, JUNR.

August 8, 1778.

On the part and behalf of the State of Massachusetts Bay.

JOHN HANCOCK,	FRANCIS DANA,
SAMUEL ADAMS,	JAMES LOVELL,
ELBRIDGE GERRY,	SAMUEL HOLTEN.

On the part and behalf of the State of Rhode Island and Providence Plantations.

WILLIAM ELLERY,	JOHN COLLINS.
HENRY MARCHANT,	

On the part and behalf of the State of Connecticut.

ROGER SHERMAN,	TITUS HOSMER,
SAMUEL HUNTINGTON,	ANDREW ADAMS.
OLIVER WOLCOTT,	

On the part and behalf of the State of New York.

JAS. DUANE,	WM. DUER,
FRA. LEWIS,	GOUV. MORRIS.

On the part and in behalf of the State of New Jersey, Novr. 26, 1778.

JNO. WITHERSPOON,	NATHL. SCUDDER.

On the part and behalf of the State of Pennsylvania.

ROBT. MORRIS,	WILLIAM CLINGAN,
DANIEL ROBERDEAU,	JOSEPH REED, 22d July,
JONA. BAYARD SMITH,	1778.

On the part & behalf of the State of Delaware.

THO. M'KEAN,	NICHOLAS VAN DYKE.
Feby. 12, 1779.	
JOHN DICKINSON,	
May 5th, 1779.	

The Articles of Confederation

On the part and behalf of the State of Maryland.

JOHN HANSON,
    March 1, 1781.

DANIEL CARROLL,
    Mar. 1, 1781.

On the part and behalf of the State of Virginia.

RICHARD HENRY LEE,
JOHN BANISTER,
THOMAS ADAMS,

JNO. HARVIE,
FRANCIS LIGHTFOOT LEE.

On the part and behalf of the State of No. Carolina.

JOHN PENN, July 21st, 1778. JNO. WILLIAMS.
CORNS. HARNETT,

On the part & behalf of the State of South Carolina.

HENRY LAURENS,
WILLIAM HENRY DRAYTON,
JNO. MATHEWS,

RICHD. HUTSON,
THOS. HAYWARD, JUNR.

On the part & behalf of the State of Georgia.

JNO. WALTON, 24th July,
    1778.
EDWD. TELFAIR,

EDWD. LANGWORTHY.

THE CONSTITUTION OF THE UNITED STATES

We, the people of the United States, in order to form a more perfect union, establish justice, insure domestic tranquillity, provide for the common defence, promote the general welfare, and secure the blessings of liberty to ourselves and our posterity, do ordain and establish this Constitution for the United States of America.

ARTICLE I.

SECTION I.

All legislative powers herein granted shall be vested in a Congress of the United States, which shall consist of a Senate and House of Representatives.

SECTION II.

The House of Representatives shall be composed of members chosen every second year by the people of the several States, and the electors in each State shall have the qualifications requisite for electors of the most numerous branch of the State legislature.

No person shall be a Representative who shall not have attained the age of twenty-five years, and been seven years a citizen of the United States, and who shall not, when elected, be an inhabitant of that State in which he shall be chosen.

Representatives and direct taxes shall be apportioned among the several States which may be included within this Union, according to their respective numbers, which shall be determined by adding to the whole number of

Constitution of the United States

free persons, including those bound to service for a term of years, and excluding Indians not taxed, three fifths of all other persons. The actual enumeration shall be made within three years after the first meeting of the Congress of the United States, and within every subsequent term of ten years, in such manner as they shall by law direct. The number of Representatives shall not exceed one for every thirty thousand, but each State shall have at least one Representative; and until such enumeration shall be made, the State of *New Hampshire* shall be entitled to choose three, *Massachusetts* eight, *Rhode Island and Providence Plantations* one, *Connecticut* five, *New York* six, *New Jersey* four, *Pennsylvania* eight, *Delaware* one, *Maryland* six, *Virginia* ten, *North Carolina* five, *South Carolina* five, and *Georgia* three.

When vacancies happen in the representation from any State, the executive authority thereof shall issue writs of election to fill such vacancies.

The House of Representatives shall choose their Speaker and other officers, and shall have the sole power of impeachment.

SECTION III.

The Senate of the United States shall be composed of two Senators from each State, chosen by the legislature thereof, for six years; and each Senator shall have one vote.

Immediately after they shall be assembled in consequence of the first election, they shall be divided as equally as may be into three classes. The seats of the Senators of the first class shall be vacated at the expiration of the second year; of the second class, at the expiration of the fourth year, and of the third class, at the expiration of the sixth year, so that one-third may be chosen every second year; and if vacancies happen by resignation or otherwise during the recess of the legislature of any State, the executive thereof may make temporary appointments until the next meeting of the legislature, which shall then fill such vacancies.

No person shall be a Senator who shall not have attained to the age of thirty years, and been nine years a citizen of the United States, and who shall not, when elected, be an inhabitant of that State for which he shall be chosen.

The Vice-President of the United States shall be President of the Senate, but shall have no vote, unless they be equally divided.

The Senate shall choose their other officers, and also a President *pro tempore* in the absence of the Vice-President, or when he shall exercise the office of President of the United States.

The Senate shall have the sole power to try all impeachments. When sitting for that purpose, they shall be on oath or affirmation. When the President of the United States is tried, the Chief Justice shall preside: and no person shall be convicted without the concurrence of two thirds of the members present.

Judgment in cases of impeachment shall not extend further than to removal from office, and disqualification to hold and enjoy any office of honor, trust, or profit under the United States; but the party convicted shall, nevertheless, be liable and subject to indictment, trial, judgment, and punishment, according to law.

SECTION IV.

The times, places, and manner of holding elections for Senators and Representatives shall be prescribed in each State by the legislature thereof; but the Congress may at any time by law make or alter such regulations, except as to the places of choosing Senators.

The Congress shall assemble at least once in every year, and such meeting shall be on the first Monday in December, unless they shall by law appoint a different day.

SECTION V.

Each house shall be the judge of the elections, returns, and qualifications of its own members, and a majority of each shall constitute a quorum to do business; but a smaller number may adjourn from day to day, and may be authorized to compel the attendance of absent members, in such manner, and under such penalties, as each house may provide.

Each house may determine the rules of its proceeding, punish its members for disorderly behavior, and with the concurrence of two thirds, expel a member.

Each house shall keep a journal of its proceedings, and from time to time publish the same, excepting such parts as may in their judgment require secrecy, and the yeas and nays of the members of either house on any question shall, at the desire of one fifth of those present, be entered on the journal.

Neither house, during the session of Congress, shall, without the consent of the other, adjourn for more than three days, nor to any other place than that in which the two houses shall be sitting.

SECTION VI.

The Senators and Representatives shall receive a compensation for their services, to be ascertained by law and paid out of the Treasury of the United States. They shall, in all cases except treason, felony, and breach of the peace, be privileged from arrest during their attendance at the session of their respective houses, and in going to and returning from the same; and for any speech or debate in either house they shall not be questioned in any other place.

No Senator or Representative shall, during the time for which he was elected, be appointed to any civil office under the authority of the United States, which shall have been created, or the emoluments whereof shall have been increased during such time; and no person holding any office under the United States shall be a member of either house during his continuance in office.

SECTION VII.

All bills for raising revenue shall originate in the House of Representatives; but the Senate may propose or concur with amendments as on other bills.

Every bill which shall have passed the House of Representatives and the Senate shall, before it become a law, be presented to the President of the United States; if he approve he shall sign it, but if not he shall return it, with his objections, to that house in which it shall have originated, who shall enter the objections at large on their journal and proceed to reconsider it. If after such reconsideration two thirds of that house shall agree to pass the bill, it shall be sent, together with the objections, to the other house, by which it shall likewise be reconsidered, and if approved by two thirds of that house it shall become a law. But in all such cases the votes of both houses shall be determined by yeas and nays, and the names of the persons voting for and against the bill shall be entered on the journal of each house respectively. If any bill shall not be returned by the President within ten days (Sundays excepted) after it shall have been presented to him, the same shall be a law, in like manner as if he had signed it, unless the Congress by their adjournment prevent its return, in which case it shall not be a law.

Every order, resolution, or vote to which the concurrence of the Senate and House of Representatives may be necessary (except on a question of adjournment) shall be presented to the President of the United States; and before the same shall take effect, shall be approved by him, or being disapproved by him, shall be repassed by two thirds of the Senate and House of Representatives, according to the rules and limitations prescribed in the case of a bill.

SECTION VIII.

The Congress shall have power to lay and collect taxes, duties, imposts, and excises, to pay the debts and provide for the common defence and general welfare of the United States; but all duties, imposts, and excises shall be uniform throughout the United States;

To borrow money on the credit of the United States;

To regulate commerce with foreign nations and among the several States, and with the Indian tribes;

To establish an uniform rule of naturalization, and uniform laws on the subject of bankruptcies throughout the United States;

To coin money, regulate the value thereof, and of foreign coin, and fix the standard of weights and measures;

To provide for the punishment of counterfeiting the securities and current coin of the United States;

To establish post-offices and post-roads;

To promote the progress of science and useful arts by securing for limited times to authors and inventors the exclusive right to their respective writings and discoveries;

To constitute tribunals inferior to the Supreme Court;

To define and punish piracies and felonies committed on the high seas and offences against the law of nations;

To declare war, grant letters of marque and reprisal, and make rules concerning captures on land and water;

To raise and support armies, but no appropriation of money to that use shall be for a longer term than two years;

To provide and maintain a navy;

To make rules for the government and regulation of the land and naval forces;

To provide for calling forth the militia to execute the laws of the Union, suppress insurrections, and repel invasions;

To provide for organizing, arming, and disciplining the militia, and for governing such part of them as may be employed in the service of the United States, reserving to the States respectively the appointment of the officers, and the authority of training the militia according to the discipline prescribed by Congress;

To exercise exclusive legislation in all cases whatsoever over such district (not exceeding ten miles square) as may, by cession of particular States and the acceptance of Congress, become the seat of the Government of the United States, and to exercise like authority over all places purchased by the consent of the legislature of the State in which the same shall be, for the erection of forts, magazines, arsenals, dockyards, and other needful buildings; and

To make all laws which shall be necessary and proper for carrying into execution the foregoing powers, and all other powers vested by this Constitution in the Government of the United States, or in any department or officer thereof.

SECTION IX.

The migration or importation of such persons as any of the States now existing shall think proper to admit shall not be prohibited by the Congress prior to the year

Constitution of the United States

one thousand eight hundred and eight, but a tax or duty may be imposed on such importation, not exceeding ten dollars for each person.

The privilege of the writ of habeas corpus shall not be suspended, unless when in cases of rebellion or invasion the public safety may require it.

No bill of attainder or ex post facto law shall be passed.

No capitation or other direct tax shall be laid, unless in proportion to the census or enumeration hereinbefore directed to be taken.

No tax or duty shall be laid on articles exported from any State.

No preference shall be given by any regulation of commerce or revenue to the ports of one State over those of another; nor shall vessels bound to or from one State be obliged to enter, clear, or pay duties in another.

No money shall be drawn from the Treasury but in consequence of appropriations made by law; and a regular statement and account of the receipts and expenditures of all public money shall be published from time to time.

No title of nobility shall be granted by the United States; and no person holding any office of profit or trust under them shall, without the consent of the Congress, accept of any present, emolument, office, or title, of any kind whatever from any king, prince, or foreign State.

SECTION X.

No State shall enter into any treaty, alliance, or confederation; grant letters of marque and reprisal; coin money; emit bills of credit; make anything but gold and silver coin a tender in payment of debts; pass any bill of attainder, ex post facto law, or law impairing the obligation of contracts, or grant any title of nobility.

No State shall, without the consent of Congress, lay any imposts or duties on imports or exports, except what may be absolutely necessary for executing its inspection laws; and the net produce of all duties and imposts, laid by any State on imports or exports, shall be for the use of the Treasury of the United States; and all such laws shall be subject to the revision and control of the Congress.

No State shall, without the consent of Congress, lay any duty of tonnage, keep troops or ships of war in time of peace, enter into any agreement or compact with another State or with a foreign power, or engage in war, unless actually invaded or in such imminent danger as will not admit of delay.

ARTICLE II.

SECTION I.

The executive power shall be vested in a President of the United States of America. He shall hold his office during the term of four years, and together with the Vice-President, chosen for the same term, be elected as follows:

Each State shall appoint, in such manner as the legislature thereof may direct, a number of electors, equal to the whole number of Senators and Representatives to which the State may be entitled in the Congress; but no Senator or Representative, or person holding an office of trust or profit under the United States, shall be appointed an elector.

[The electors shall meet in their respective States and vote by ballot for two persons, of whom one at least shall not be an inhabitant of the same State with themselves. And they shall make a list of all the persons voted for, and of the number of votes for each; which list they shall sign and certify, and transmit sealed to the seat of government of the United States, directed to the President of the Senate. The President of the Senate shall, in the presence of the Senate and House of Representatives, open all the certificates, and the votes shall then be counted. The person having the greatest number of votes shall be the President, if such number be a majority of the whole number of electors appointed; and if there be more than one who have such majority, and have an equal number of votes, then the House of Representatives shall immediately choose by ballot one of them for President; and if no person have a majority, then from the five highest on the list the said House shall in like manner choose the President. But in choosing the President the votes shall be taken by States, the representation from each State having one vote; a quorum for this purpose shall consist of a member or members from two thirds of the States, and a majority of all the States shall be necessary to a choice. In every case, after the choice of the President, the person having the greatest number of votes of the electors shall be the Vice-President. But if there should remain two or more who have equal votes, the Senate shall choose from them by ballot the Vice-President.] [1]

The Congress may determine the time of choosing the electors and the day on which they shall give their votes, which day shall be the same throughout the United States.

No person except a natural-born citizen, or a citizen of the United States at the time of the adoption of this Constitution, shall be eligible to the office of President; neither shall any person be eligible to that office who shall not have attained to the age of thirty-five years, and been fourteen years a resident within the United States.

[1] This clause of the Constitution has been amended. See twelfth article of the amendments.

In case of the removal of the President from office, or of his death, resignation, or inability to discharge the powers and duties of the said office, the same shall devolve on the Vice-President, and the Congress may by law provide for the case of removal, death, resignation, or inability, both of the President and Vice-President, declaring what officer shall then act as President, and such officer shall act accordingly until the disability be removed or a President shall be elected.

The President shall, at stated times, receive for his services a compensation, which shall neither be increased nor diminished during the period for which he may have been elected, and he shall not receive within that period any other emolument from the United States or any of them.

Before he enter on the execution of his office he shall take the following oath or affirmation:

"I do solemnly swear (or affirm) that I will faithfully execute the office of President of the United States, and will to the best of my ability preserve, protect, and defend the Constitution of the United States."

SECTION II.

The President shall be Commander-in-chief of the Army and Navy of the United States, and of the militia of the several States when called into the actual service of the United States; he may require the opinion, in writing, of the principal officer in each of the executive departments, upon any subject relating to the duties of their respective offices, and he shall have power to grant reprieves and pardons for offences against the United States, except in cases of impeachment.

He shall have power, by and with the advice and consent of the Senate, to make treaties, provided two thirds of the Senators present concur; and he shall nominate, and, by and with the advice and consent of the Senate, shall appoint ambassadors, other public ministers and consuls, judges of the Supreme Court, and all other officers of the United States, whose appointments are not herein otherwise provided for, and which shall be established by law; but the Congress may by law vest the appointment of such inferior officers, as they think proper, in the President alone, in the courts of law, or in the heads of departments.

The President shall have power to fill up all vacancies that may happen during the recess of the Senate, by granting commissions which shall expire at the end of their next session.

SECTION III.

He shall from time to time give to the Congress information of the state of the Union, and recommend to their consideration such measures as he shall judge necessary and expedient; he may, on extraordinary occasions, convene both houses, or either of them, and in case of disagreement between them with respect to the time of adjournment, he may adjourn them to such time as he shall think proper; he shall receive ambassadors and other public ministers; he shall take care that the laws be faithfully executed, and shall commission all the officers of the United States.

SECTION IV.

The President, Vice-President, and all civil officers of the United States shall be removed from office on impeachment for and conviction of treason, bribery, or other high crimes and misdemeanors.

ARTICLE III.

SECTION I.

The judicial power of the United States shall be vested

in one Supreme Court, and in such inferior courts as the Congress may from time to time ordain and establish. The judges, both of the supreme and inferior courts, shall hold their offices during good behavior and shall, at stated times, receive for their services a compensation which shall not be diminished during their continuance in office.

SECTION II.

The judicial power shall extend to all cases, in law and equity, arising under this Constitution, the laws of the United States, and treaties made, or which shall be made, under their authority; to all cases affecting ambassadors, other public ministers, and consuls; to all cases of admiralty and maritime jurisdiction; to controversies to which the United States shall be a party; to controversies between two or more States; between a State and citizens of another State; between citizens of different States; between citizens of the same State claiming lands under grants of different States, and between a State, or the citizens thereof, and foreign States, citizens, or subjects.

In all cases affecting ambassadors, other public ministers and consuls, and those in which a State shall be a party, the Supreme Court shall have original jurisdiction. In all the other cases before mentioned the Supreme Court shall have appellate jurisdiction, both as to law and fact, with such exceptions and under such regulations as the Congress shall make.

The trial of all crimes, except in cases of impeachment, shall be by jury; and such trial shall be held in the State where the said crimes shall have been committed; but when not committed within any State, the trial shall be at such place or places as the Congress may by law have directed.

SECTION III.

Treason against the United States shall consist only in levying war against them, or in adhering to their enemies, giving them aid and comfort. No person shall be convicted of treason unless on the testimony of two witnesses to the same overt act, or on confession in open court.

The Congress shall have power to declare the punishment of treason, but no attainder of treason shall work corruption of blood or forfeiture except during the life of the person attainted.

ARTICLE IV.

SECTION I.

Full faith and credit shall be given in each State to the public acts, records, and judicial proceedings of every other State. And the Congress may by general laws prescribe the manner in which such acts, records, and proceedings shall be proved, and the effect thereof.

SECTION II.

The citizens of each State shall be entitled to all privileges and immunities of citizens in the several States.

A person charged in any State with treason, felony, or other crime, who shall flee from justice, and be found in another State, shall, on demand of the executive authority of the State from which he fled, be delivered up, to be removed to the State having jurisdiction of the crime.

No person held to service or labor in one State, under the laws thereof, escaping into another, shall, in consequence of any law or regulation therein, be discharged from such service or labor, but shall be delivered up on claim of the party to whom such service or labor may be due.

SECTION III.

New States may be admitted by the Congress into this Union; but no new State shall be formed or erected within the jurisdiction of any other State; nor any State be formed by the junction of two or more States or parts of States, without the consent of the legislatures of the States concerned as well as of the Congress.

The Congress shall have power to dispose of and make all needful rules and regulations respecting the territory or other property belonging to the United States; and nothing in this Constitution shall be so construed as to prejudice any claims of the United States or of any particular State.

SECTION IV.

The United States shall guarantee to every State in this Union a republican form of government, and shall protect each of them against invasion, and on application of the legislature, or of the executive (when the legislature cannot be convened), against domestic violence.

ARTICLE V.

The Congress, whenever two thirds of both houses shall deem it necessary, shall propose amendments to this Constitution, or, on the application of the legislatures of two thirds of the several States, shall call a convention for proposing amendments, which in either case shall be valid to all intents and purposes as part of this Constitution, when ratified by the legislatures of three fourths of the several States, or by conventions in three fourths thereof, as the one or the other mode of ratification may be proposed by the Congress, provided that no amendments which may be made prior to the year one thousand eight hundred and eight shall in any manner affect the first and fourth clauses in the ninth section of the first article; and that no State, without its consent, shall be deprived of its equal suffrage in the Senate.

ARTICLE VI.

All debts contracted and engagements entered into, before the adoption of this Constitution, shall be as valid against the United States under this Constitution as under the confederation.

This Constitution, and the laws of the United States which shall be made in pursuance thereof, and all treaties made, or which shall be made, under the authority of the United States, shall be the supreme law of the land; and the judges in every State shall be bound thereby, anything in the Constitution or laws of any State to the contrary notwithstanding.

The Senators and Representatives before mentioned, and the members of the several State legislatures, and all executive and judicial officers both of the United States and of the several States, shall be bound by oath or affirmation to support this Constitution; but no religious test shall ever be required as a qualification to any office or public trust under the United States.

ARTICLE VII.

The ratification of the conventions of nine States shall be sufficient for the establishment of this Constitution between the States so ratifying the same.

> Done in convention by the unanimous consent of the States present, the seventeenth day of September, in the year of our Lord one thousand seven hundred and eighty-seven, and of the independence of the United States of America the twelfth. In witness whereof, we have hereunto subscribed our names.

George Washington, President, and Deputy from VIRGINIA.
NEW HAMPSHIRE—John Langdon, Nicholas Gilman.
MASSACHUSETTS—Nathaniel Gorham, Rufus King.
CONNECTICUT—William Samuel Johnson, Roger Sherman.
NEW YORK—Alexander Hamilton.
NEW JERSEY—William Livingston, David Brearly, William Paterson, Jonathan Dayton.
PENNSYLVANIA—Benjamin Franklin, Thomas Mifflin, Robert Morris, George Clymer, Thomas Fitzsimons, Jared Ingersoll, James Wilson, Gouverneur Morris.
DELAWARE—George Read, Gunning Bedford, Jr., John Dickinson, Richard Bassett, Jacob Broom.
MARYLAND—James McHenry, Daniel of St. Thomas Jenifer, Daniel Carroll.
VIRGINIA—John Blair, James Madison, Jr.
NORTH CAROLINA—William Blount, Richard Dobbs Spaight, Hugh Williamson.
SOUTH CAROLINA—John Rutledge, Charles Cotesworth Pinckney, Charles Pinckney, Pierce Butler.
GEORGIA—William Few, Abraham Baldwin.

Attest: William Jackson, *Secretary.*

AMENDMENTS

ARTICLE I.

Congress shall make no law respecting an establishment of religion, or prohibiting the free exercise thereof; or abridging the freedom of speech or of the press; or the right of the people peaceably to assemble, and to petition the government for a redress of grievances.

ARTICLE II.

A well-regulated militia being necessary to the security

of a free State, the right of the people to keep and bear arms shall not be infringed.

ARTICLE III.

No soldier shall, in time of peace, be quartered in any house without the consent of the owner, nor in time of war, but in a manner to be prescribed by law.

ARTICLE IV.

The right of the people to be secure in their persons, houses, papers, and effects, against unreasonable searches and seizures, shall not be violated, and no warrants shall issue but upon probable cause, supported by oath or affirmation, and particularly describing the place to be searched, and the person or things to be seized.

ARTICLE V.

No person shall be held to answer for a capital or otherwise infamous crime, unless on a presentment or indictment of a grand jury, except in cases arising in the land or naval forces, or in the militia, when in actual service in time of war or public danger; nor shall any person be subject for the same offence to be twice put in jeopardy of life or limb; nor shall be compelled in any criminal case to be a witness against himself, nor be deprived of life, liberty, or property, without due process of law; nor shall private property be taken for public use without just compensation.

ARTICLE VI.

In all criminal prosecutions the accused shall enjoy the right to a speedy and public trial, by an impartial jury of the State and district wherein the crime shall have been committed, which district shall have been previously ascertained by law, and to be informed of the nature and cause of the accusation; to be confronted with the witnesses against him; to have compulsory process for obtaining witnesses in his favor, and to have the assistance of counsel for his defence.

ARTICLE VII.

In suits at common law, where the value in controversy shall exceed twenty dollars, the right of trial by jury shall be preserved, and no fact tried by a jury shall be otherwise re-examined in any court of the United States, than according to the rules of the common law.

ARTICLE VIII.

Excessive bail shall not be required, nor excessive fines imposed, nor cruel and unusual punishments inflicted.

ARTICLE IX.

The enumeration in the Constitution of certain rights shall not be construed to deny or disparage others retained by the people.

ARTICLE X.

The powers not delegated to the United States by the Constitution, nor prohibited by it to the States, are reserved to the States respectively or to the people.

ARTICLE XI.

The judicial power of the United States shall not be construed to extend to any suit in law or equity, commenced or prosecuted against one of the United States by citizens of another State, or by citizens or subjects of any foreign State.

Constitution of the United States

ARTICLE XII.

The electors shall meet in their respective States and vote by ballot for President and Vice-President, one of whom, at least, shall not be an inhabitant of the same State with themselves; they shall name in their ballots the person voted for as President, and in distinct ballots the person voted for as Vice-President, and they shall make distinct lists of all persons voted for as President and of all persons voted for as Vice-President, and of the number of votes for each; which lists they shall sign and certify, and transmit sealed to the seat of the government of the United States, directed to the President of the Senate. The President of the Senate shall, in the presence of the Senate and House of Representatives, open all the certificates and the votes shall then be counted. The person having the greatest number of votes for President shall be the President, if such number be a majority of the whole number of electors appointed; and if no person have such majority, then from the persons having the highest numbers not exceeding three on the list of those voted for as President, the House of Representatives shall choose immediately, by ballot, the President. But in choosing the President the votes shall be taken by States, the representation from each State having one vote; a quorum for this purpose shall consist of a member or members from two thirds of the States, and a majority of all the States shall be necessary to a choice. And if the House of Representatives shall not choose a President whenever the right of choice shall devolve upon them, before the fourth day of March next following, then the Vice-President shall act as President, as in the case of the death or other constitutional disability of the President.

The person having the greatest number of votes as Vice-President shall be the Vice-President, if such number be a majority of the whole number of electors appointed; and if no person have a majority, then from the two highest numbers on the list the Senate shall choose the Vice-President; a quorum for the purpose shall consist of two thirds of the whole number of Senators, and a majority of the whole number shall be necessary to a choice. But no person constitutionally ineligible to the office of President shall be eligible to that of Vice-President of the United States.

ARTICLE XIII.

SECTION 1. Neither slavery nor involuntary servitude, except as a punishment for crime whereof the party shall have been duly convicted, shall exist within the United States or any place subject to their jurisdiction.

SECTION 2. Congress shall have power to enforce this article by appropriate legislation.

ARTICLE XIV.

SECTION 1. All persons born or naturalized in the United States, and subject to the jurisdiction thereof, are citizens of the United States and of the State wherein they reside. No State shall make or enforce any law which shall abridge the privileges or immunities of citizens of the United States; nor shall any State deprive any person of life, liberty, or property, without due process of law; nor deny to any person within its jurisdiction the equal protection of the laws.

SECTION 2. Representatives shall be apportioned among the several States according to their respective numbers, counting the whole number of persons in each State, excluding Indians not taxed. But when the right to vote at any election for the choice of electors for President and Vice-President of the United States, Representatives in Congress, the executive and judicial officers of a State, or the members of the legislature thereof, is denied to any of the male inhabitants of such State, being twenty-one years of age, and citizens of the United States, or in any way abridged, except for participation in rebellion, or other crime, the basis of representation therein shall be reduced in the proportion which the number of such male citizens shall bear to the whole number of male citizens twenty-one years of age in such State.

Section 3. No person shall be a Senator or Representative in Congress, or elector of President and Vice-President, or hold any office, civil or military, under the United States or under any State, who, having previously taken an oath as a member of Congress, or as an officer of the United States, or as a member of any State legislature, or as an executive or judicial officer of any State, to support the Constitution of the United States, shall have engaged in insurrection or rebellion against the same, or given aid or comfort to the enemies thereof. But Congress may, by a vote of two thirds of each house, remove such disability.

Section 4. The validity of the public debt of the United States, authorized by law, including debts incurred for payment of pensions and bounties for services in suppressing insurrection or rebellion, shall not be questioned. But neither the United States nor any State shall assume or pay any debt or obligation incurred in aid of insurrection or rebellion against the United States, or any claim for the loss or emancipation of any slave; but all such debts, obligations, and claims shall be held illegal and void.

Section 5. The Congress shall have power to enforce, by appropriate legislation, the provisions of this article.

ARTICLE XV.

Section 1. The right of citizens of the United States

to vote shall not be denied or abridged by the United States or by any State on account of race, color, or previous condition of servitude.

SECTION 2. The Congress shall have power to enforce this article by appropriate legislation.

JEFFERSON'S OPINION ON THE CONSTITUTIONALITY OF A NATIONAL BANK

. . . .

I CONSIDER the foundation of the Constitution as laid on this ground: That "all powers not delegated to the United States, by the Constitution, nor prohibited by it to the States, are reserved to the States or to the people." (XIIth amendment.) To take a single step beyond the boundaries thus specially drawn around the powers of Congress, is to take possession of a boundless field of power, no longer susceptible of any definition.

The incorporation of a bank, and the powers assumed by this bill, have not, in my opinion, been delegated to the United States, by the Constitution.

1. They are not among the powers specially enumerated: for these are: 1st. A power to lay taxes for the purpose of paying the debts of the United States; but no debt is paid by this bill nor any tax laid. Were it a bill to raise money, its origination in the Senate would condemn it by the Constitution.

2. "To borrow money." But this bill neither borrows money nor insures the borrowing it. . . .

3. To "regulate commerce with foreign nations, and among the States, and with the Indian tribes." To erect a bank, and to regulate commerce, are very different acts. He who erects a bank, creates a subject of commerce in its bills; so does he who makes a bushel of wheat, or digs a dollar out of the mines; yet neither of these persons regulates commerce thereby. . . .

II. Nor are they within either of the general phrases, which are the two following:

1. To lay taxes to provide for the general welfare of the United States, that is to say, "to lay taxes for *the purpose* of providing for the general welfare." For the laying of taxes is the *power,* and the general welfare the *purpose* for which the power is to be exercised. They are not to lay taxes *ad libitum for any purpose they please;* but only *to pay the debts or provide for the welfare of the Union.* In like manner they are not *to do anything they please* to provide for the general welfare, but only *to lay taxes* for that purpose. To consider the latter phrase, not as describing the purpose of the first, but as giving a distinct and independent power to do any act they please, which might be for the good of the Union, would render all the preceding and subsequent enumerations of power completely useless.

It would reduce the whole instrument to a single phrase, that of instituting a Congress with power to do whatever would be for the good of the United States; and, as they would be the sole judges of the good or evil, it would be also a power to do whatever evil they please....

2. The second general phrase is "to make all laws *necessary* and proper for carrying into execution the enumerated powers." But they can all be carried into execution without a bank. A bank therefore is not *necessary,* and consequently not authorized by this phrase.

It has been urged that a bank will give great facility or convenience in the collection of taxes. Suppose this were true: yet the Constitution allows only the means which are *" necessary,"* not those which are merely " convenient " for effecting the enumerated powers. If such a latitude of construction be allowed to this phrase as to give any non-enumerated power, it will go to every one, for there is not one which ingenuity may not torture into a *convenience* in some instance *or other,* to *someone* of so long a list of enumerated powers. It would swallow up all the delegated powers, and reduce the whole to one power, as before observed. Therefore it was that the Constitution restrained them to the *necessary* means, that is to say, to those means without which the grant of power would be nugatory.

. . . .

HAMILTON'S OPINION AS TO THE CONSTITUTIONALITY OF THE BANK OF THE UNITED STATES

The Secretary of the Treasury having perused with attention the papers containing the opinions of the Secretary of State and Attorney-General, concerning the constitutionality of the bill establishing a National Bank, proceeds, according to the order of the President, to submit the reasons which have induced him to entertain a different opinion. . . .

In entering upon the argument, it ought to be premised that the objections of the Secretary of State and Attorney-General are founded on a general denial of the authority of the United States to erect corporations. The latter, indeed, expressly admits, that if there be anything in the bill which is not warranted by the Constitution, it is the clause of incorporation.

Now it appears to the Secretary of the Treasury that this *general principle* is *inherent* in the very *definition* of government, and *essential* to every step of progress to be made by the United States, namely: That every power vested in a government is in its nature *sovereign*, and includes, by *force* of the *term*, a right to employ all the *means* requisite and fairly applicable to the attainment of the *ends* of such power, and which are not precluded by restrictions and exceptions specified in the Constitution, or not immoral, or not contrary to the *essential ends* of political society.

This principle, in its application to government in general, would be admitted as an axiom; and it will be incumbent upon those who may incline to deny it, to prove a distinction, and to show that a rule which, in the general system of things, is essential to the preservation of the social order, is inapplicable to the United States.

The circumstance that the powers of sovereignty are in this country divided between the National and State governments, does not afford the distinction required. It does not follow from this, that each of the portion of *powers* delegated to the one or to the other, is not sovereign with *regard to its proper objects*. It will only *follow* from it, that each has sovereign power as to *certain things,* and not as to *other things.* To deny that the Government of the United States has sovereign power, as to its declared purposes and trusts, because its power does not extend to all cases, would be equally to deny that the State governments have sovereign power in any case, because their power does not extend to every case. The tenth section of the first article of the Constitution exhibits a long list of very important things which they may not do. And thus the United States would furnish the singular spectacle of a *political society* without *sovereignty,* or of a *people governed,* without *government.*

If it would be necessary to bring proof to a proposition so clear, as that which affirms that the powers of the Federal Government, as to *its objects,* were sovereign, there is a clause of its Constitution which would be decisive. It is that which declares that the Constitution, and the laws of the United States made in pursuance of it, and all treaties made, or which shall be made, under their authority, shall be the *supreme law of the land.* The power which can create the *supreme law of the land* in *any case,* is doubtless *sovereign* as to such case.

· · · · · · ·

The first of these arguments [that is, against the power of the Federal Government to erect corporations] is, that the foundation of the Constitution is laid on this ground: "That all powers not delegated to the United States by the Constitution, nor prohibited to it by the States, are reserved for the States, or to the people." Whence it is meant to be inferred, that Congress can in no case exercise any power not included in those not enumerated in the Constitution. And it is affirmed, that the power of erecting a corporation is not included in any of the enumerated powers.

The main proposition here laid down, in its true signification is not to be questioned. It is nothing more than a consequence of this republican maxim, that all government is a delegation of power. But how much is delegated in each case, is a question of fact, to be made out by fair reasoning and construction, upon the particular provisions of the Constitution, taking as guides the general principles and general ends of governments.

It is not denied that there are *implied* as well as *express powers,* and that the *former* are as effectually delegated as the *latter.* And for the sake of accuracy it shall be mentioned, that there is another class of powers, which may be properly denominated *resulting powers.* It will not be doubted, that if the United States should make a conquest of any of the territories of its neighbors, they would possess sovereign jurisdiction over the conquered territory. This would be rather a result, from the whole mass of the powers of the government, and from the nature of political society, than a consequence of either of the powers specially enumerated.

But be this as it may, it furnishes a striking illustration of the general doctrine contended for; it shows an extensive case, in which a power of erecting corporations is either implied in, or would result from, some or all of the powers vested in the National Government. The jurisdiction acquired over such conquered country would certainly be competent to any species of legislation.

* * * * * * *

To this mode of reasoning respecting the right of employing all the means requisite to the execution of the specified powers of the Government, it is objected, that none but necessary and proper means are to be employed; and the Secretary of State maintains, that no means are to be considered as *necessary* but those without which the grant of the power would be *nugatory*. Nay, so far does he go in his restrictive interpretation of the *word*, as even to make the case of *necessity* which shall warrant the constitutional exercise of the power to depend on *casual* and *temporary* circumstances; an idea which alone refutes the construction. The *expediency* of exercising a particular power, at a particular time, must, indeed, depend on circumstances; but the constitutional right of exercising it must be uniform and invariable, the same to-day as to-morrow.

* * * * * * *

It is essential to the being of the National Government, that so erroneous a conception of the meaning of the word *necessary* should be exploded.

It is certain that neither the grammatical nor popular sense of the term requires that construction. According to both, *necessary* often means no more than *needful, requisite, incidental, useful,* or *conducive to*. It is a common mode of expression to say, that it is necessary for a government or a person to do this or that thing, when nothing more is intended or understood, than that the interests of the government or person require, or will be promoted by, the doing of this or that thing. The imagination can be at no loss for exemplifications of the use of the word in this sense. And it is the true one in which it is to be understood as used in the Constitution. The whole turn of the clause containing it indicates, that it was the intent of the Convention, by that clause, to give a liberal latitude to the exercise of the specified powers. The expressions have peculiar comprehensiveness. They are "to make all *laws* necessary and proper for *carrying into execution* the *foregoing powers,* and *all other powers* vested by the Constitution in the *Government* of the United States, or in any *department* or *officer* thereof."

To understand the word as the Secretary of State does, would be to depart from its obvious and popular sense, and to give it a restrictive operation, an idea never before entertained. It would be to give it the same force as if the word *absolutely* or *indispensably* had been prefixed to it.

Such a construction would beget endless uncertainty and embarrassment. The case must be palpable and extreme, in which it could be pronounced, with certainty, that a measure was absolutely necessary, or one, without which, the exercise of a given power would be nugatory. There are few measures of any government which would stand so severe a test. To insist upon it, would be to make the criterion of the exercise of any implied power, a *case of extreme necessity;* which is rather a rule to justify the overleaping of the bounds of constitutional authority, than to govern the ordinary exercise of it.

. . . .

This restrictive interpretation of the word *necessary* is also contrary to this sound maxim of construction; namely, that the powers contained in a constitution of government, especially those which concern the general administration of the affairs of a country, its finances, trade, defence, etc., ought to be construed liberally in advancement of the public good. This rule does not depend on the particular form of a government, or on the particular demarcation of the boundaries of its powers, but on the nature and object of government itself. The means by which national exigencies are to be provided for, national inconveniences obviated, national prosperity promoted, are of such infinite variety, extent, and complexity, that there must of necessity be great latitude of discretion in the selection and application of those means. Hence, consequently, the necessity and propriety of exercising the authorities intrusted to a government on principles of liberal construction.

. . . .

But while on the one hand the construction of the Secretary of State is deemed inadmissible, it will not be contended, on the other, that the clause in question gives any *new* or *independent* power. But it gives an explicit sanction to the doctrine of *implied powers,* and is equivalent to an admission of the proposition that the Government, as to its *specified powers* and *objects,* has plenary and sovereign authority, in some cases paramount to the States; in others, co-ordinate with it. For such is the plain import of the declaration, that it may pass all *laws* necessary and proper to carry into execution those powers.

It is no valid objection to the doctrine to say, that it is calculated to extend the power of the Government throughout the entire sphere of State legislation. The same thing has been said, and may be said, with regard to every exercise of power by *implication* or *construction.*

The moment the literal meaning is departed from, there is a chance of error and abuse. And yet an adherence to the letter of its powers would at once arrest the motions of government. It is not only agreed, on all hands, that the exercise of constructive powers is indispensable, but every act which has been passed, is more or less an exemplification of it. . . .

The truth is, that the difficulties on this point are inherent in the nature of the Federal Constitution; they result inevitably from a division of the legislative power. The consequence of this division is, that there will be cases clearly within the power of the National Government; others, clearly without its powers; and a third class, which will leave room for controversy and difference of opinion, and concerning which a reasonable latitude of judgment must be allowed.

But the doctrine which is contended for is not chargeable with the consequences imputed to it. It does not affirm that the National Government is sovereign in all respects, but that it is sovereign to a certain extent; that is, to the extent of the objects of its specified powers.

It leaves, therefore, a criterion of what is constitutional, and of what is not so. This criterion is the *end*, to which the measure relates as a *mean*. If the *end* be clearly comprehended within any of the specified powers, and if the measure have an obvious relation to that *end*, and is not forbidden by any particular provision of the Constitution, it may safely be deemed to come within the compass of the national authority. There is also this further criterion, which may materially assist the decision: Does the proposed measure abridge a preexisting right of any State or of any individual? If it does not, there is a strong presumption in favor of its constitutionality, and slighter relations to any declared object of the Constitution may be permitted to turn the scale.

. . . .

It is presumed to have been satisfactorily shown in the course of the preceding observations:

1. That the power of the government, as to the objects intrusted to its management, is, in its nature, sovereign.

2. That the right of erecting corporations is one inherent in, and inseparable from, the idea of sovereign power.

Hamilton's Opinion on National Bank

3. That the position, that the Government of the United States can exercise no power, but such as is delegated to it by its Constitution, does not militate against this principle.

4. That the word *necessary,* in the general clause, can have no *restrictive* operation derogating from the force of this principle; indeed, that the degree in which a measure is or is not *necessary,* cannot be a *test* of *constitutional right,* but of *expediency only.*

5. That the power to erect corporations is not to be considered as an *independent* or *substantive* power, but as an *incidental* and *auxiliary* one, and was therefore more properly left to implication, than expressly granted.

6. That the principle in question does not extend the power of the government beyond the prescribed limits, because it only affirms a power to *incorporate* for purposes *within the sphere* of the *specified powers.*

And lastly, that the right to exercise such a power in certain cases is unequivocally granted in the most *positive* and *comprehensive* terms. To all which it only remains to be added, that such a power has actually been exercised in two very eminent instances; namely, in the erection of two governments; one northwest of the River Ohio, and the other southwest—the last independent of any antecedent compact. And these result in a full and complete demonstration, that the Secretary of State and the Attorney-General are mistaken when they deny generally the power of the National Government to erect corporations.

KENTUCKY RESOLUTIONS OF 1798

The House according to the standing order of the day, resolved itself into a committee of the whole on the state of the commonwealth, Mr. Caldwell in the chair, and after some time spent therein, the Speaker resumed the chair, and Mr. Caldwell reported that the committee had, according to order, had under consideration the Governor's address, and had come to the following resolutions thereupon, which he delivered in at the clerk's table, where they were twice read and agreed to by the House.

1. *Resolved*, That the several States composing the United States of America, are not united on the principle of unlimited submission to their General Government; but that by compact, under the style and title of a Constitution for the United States, and of amendments thereto, they constituted a General Government for special purposes, delegated to that government certain definite powers, reserving, each State to itself, the residuary mass of right to their own self-government; and that whensoever the General Government assumes undelegated powers, its acts are unauthoritative, void, and of no force: That to this compact each State acceded as a State, and is an integral party, its co-States forming, as to itself, the other party: That the government created by this compact was not made the exclusive or final *judge* of the extent of the powers delegated to itself; since that would have made its discretion, and not the

Constitution, the measure of its powers; but that, as in all other cases of compact among parties having no common judge, each party has an equal right to judge for itself, as well of infractions, as of the mode and measure of redress.

2. *Resolved,* That the Constitution of the United States having delegated to Congress a power to punish treason, counterfeiting the securities and current coin of the United States, piracies and felonies committed on the high seas, and offences against the laws of nations, and no other crimes whatever, and it being true as a general principle and one of the amendments to the Constitution having also declared, " that the powers not delegated to the United States by the Constitution, nor prohibited by it to the States, are reserved to the States respectively, or to the people "; therefore, also, the same act of Congress, passed on the 14th day of July, 1798, and entitled, " An act in addition to the act entitled, an act for the punishment of certain crimes against the United States "; as also the act passed by them on the 27th day of June, 1798, entitled, " An act to punish frauds committed on the Bank of the United States " (and all other their acts which assume to create, define, and punish crimes other than those enumerated in the Constitution,) are altogether void, and of no force, and that the power to create, define, and punish such other crimes is reserved, and of right appertains, solely and exclusively, to the respective States, each within its own territory.

. . . .

7. *Resolved,* That the construction applied by the General Government (as is evinced by sundry of their proceedings), to those parts of the Constitution of the United States which delegates to Congress a power to lay and collect taxes, duties, imposts, and excises; to pay the debts, and provide for the common defence and general

welfare of the United States, and to make all laws which shall be necessary and proper for carrying into execution the powers vested by the Constitution in the Government of the United States, or any department thereof, goes to the destruction of all the limits prescribed to their power by the Constitution: that words meant by that instrument to be subsidiary only to the execution of the limited powers, ought not to be so construed as themselves to give unlimited powers, nor a part so to be taken, as to destroy the whole residue of the instrument; that the proceedings of the General Government, under color of these articles, will be a fit and necessary subject for revisal and correction at a time of greater tranquillity, while those specified in the preceding resolutions call for immediate redress.

8. *Resolved,* That the preceding resolutions be transmitted to the Senators and Representatives in Congress from this commonwealth, who are hereby enjoined to present the same to their respective houses, and to use their best endeavors to procure, at the next session of Congress, a repeal of the aforesaid unconstitutional and obnoxious acts.

9. *Resolved lastly,* That the Governor of this commonwealth be, and is hereby authorized and requested to communicate the preceding resolutions to the legislatures of the several States, to assure them that this commonwealth considers union for specified national purposes, and particularly for those specified in their late Federal compact, to be friendly to the peace, happiness, and prosperity of all the States; that, faithful to that compact, according to the plain intent and meaning in which it was understood and acceded to by the several parties, it is sincerely anxious for its preservation; that it does also believe, that to take from the States all the powers of self-government, and transfer them to a general and consolidated government, without regard to the special

obligations and reservations solemnly agreed to in that compact, is not for the peace, happiness, or prosperity of these States; and that, therefore, this commonwealth is determined, as it doubts not its co-States are, tamely to submit to undelegated and consequently unlimited powers in no man or body of men on earth; that if the acts before specified should stand, these conclusions would flow from them: that the General Government may place any act they think proper on the list of crimes, and punish it themselves, whether enumerated or not enumerated by the Constitution, as cognizable by them; that they may transfer its cognizance to the President or to any other person, who may himself be the accuser, counsel, judge, and jury, whose *suspicions* may be the evidence, his order the sentence, his officer the executioner, and his breast the sole record of the transaction; that a very numerous and valuable description of the inhabitants of these States being, by this precedent, reduced as outlaws to the absolute dominion of one man, and the barrier of the Constitution thus swept away from us all, no rampart now remains against the passions and the powers of a majority of Congress, to protect from a like exportation or other more grievous punishment the minority of the same body, the legislatures, judges, governors, and counsellors of the States, nor their other peaceable inhabitants who may venture to reclaim the constitutional rights and liberties of the States and people, or who, for other causes, good or bad, may be obnoxious to the views, or marked by the suspicions of the President, or be thought dangerous to his or their elections, or other interests public or personal; that the friendless alien has indeed been selected as the safest subject of a first experiment; but the citizen will soon follow, or rather has already followed; for, already has a sedition act marked him as its prey: that these and successive acts of the same character, unless arrested on the threshold, may tend to drive these States into revolution and blood, and will furnish new calumnies against republican governments, and new pretexts for those who wish it to be believed that man cannot be governed but by a rod of iron; that it would be a dangerous delusion were a confidence in the men of our choice to silence our fears for the safety of our rights; that confidence is everywhere the parent of despotism; free government is founded in jealousy, and not in confidence; it is jealousy and not confidence which prescribes limited constitutions to bind down those whom we are obliged to trust with power; that our Constitution has accordingly fixed the limits to which and no further our confidence may go; and let the honest advocate of confidence read the alien and sedition acts, and say if the Constitution has not been wise in fixing limits to the government it created, and whether we should be wise in destroying those limits. Let him say what the government is if it be not a tyranny, which the men of our choice have conferred on the President, and the President of our choice has consented to and accepted, over the friendly strangers, to whom the mild spirit of our country and its laws had pledged hospitality and protection; that the men of our choice have more respected the bare suspicions of the President, than the solid rights of innocence, the claims of justification, the sacred force of truth, and the forms and substance of law and justice. In questions of power, then, let no more be heard of confidence in man, but bind him down from mischief, by the chains of the Constitution. That this commonwealth does, therefore, call on its co-States for an expression of their sentiments on the acts concerning aliens, and for the punishment of certain crimes hereinbefore specified, plainly declaring whether these acts are or are not authorized by the Federal compact. And it doubts not that their sense will be so announced, as to prove their attachment unaltered to limited government, whether general or particular, and that the rights and liberties of their co-States will be exposed to no dangers by remaining embarked on a common bottom with their own; that they will concur with this commonwealth in considering the said acts as so palpably against the Constitution, as to amount to an undisguised declaration, that the compact is not meant to be the measure of the powers of the General Government, but that it will proceed in the exercise over these States of all powers whatsoever; that they will view this as seizing the rights of the States, and consolidating them in the hands of the General Government with a power assumed to bind the States (not merely in cases made federal), but in all cases whatsoever, by laws made, not with their consent, but by others against their consent; that this would be to surrender the form of government we have chosen, and to live under one deriving its powers from its own will, and not from our authority; and that the co-States, recurring to their natural right in cases not made federal, will concur in declaring these acts void and of no force, and will each unite with this commonwealth, in requesting their repeal at the next session of Congress.

VIRGINIA RESOLUTIONS OF 1798

1. *Resolved,* That the General Assembly of Virginia doth unequivocally express a firm resolution to maintain and defend the Constitution of the United States, and the Constitution of this State, against every aggression, either foreign or domestic, and that it will support the Government of the United States in all measures warranted by the former.

2. That this Assembly most solemnly declares a warm attachment to the union of the States, to maintain which, it pledges all its powers; and that for this end it is its duty to watch over and oppose every infraction of those principles, which constitute the only basis of that union, because a faithful observance of them can alone secure its existence and the public happiness.

3. That this Assembly doth explicitly and peremptorily declare that it views the powers of the Federal Government as resulting from the compact, to which the States are parties, as limited by the plain sense and intention of the instrument constituting that compact; as no further valid than they are authorized by the grants enumerated in that contract; and that in case of a deliberate, palpable, and dangerous exercise of other powers not granted by the said compact, the States, who are the parties thereto, have the right, and are in duty bound, to interpose for arresting the progress of the evil, and for maintaining, within their respective limits, the authorities, rights, and liberties appertaining to them.

4. That the General Assembly doth also express its deep regret that a spirit has in sundry instances been manifested by the Federal Government, to enlarge its powers by forced constructions of the constitutional charter which defines them; and that indications have appeared of a design to expound certain general phrases (which, having been copied from the very limited grant of powers in the former articles of confederation, were the less liable to be misconstrued), so as to destroy the meaning and effect of the particular enumeration, which necessarily explains and limits the general phrases, and so as to consolidate the States by degrees into one sovereignty, the obvious tendency and inevitable result of which would be to transform the present republican system of the United States into an absolute, or at best, a mixed monarchy.

5. That the General Assembly doth particularly protest against the palpable and alarming infractions of the Constitution, in the two late cases of the "alien and sedition acts," passed at the last session of Congress: the first of which exercises a power nowhere delegated to the Federal Government, and which, by uniting legislative and judicial powers to those of executive, subverts the general principles of free government, as well as the particular organization and positive provisions of the Federal Constitution; and the other of which acts exercises in like manner a power not delegated by the Constitution, but on the contrary expressly and positively forbidden by one of the amendments thereto; a power which more than any other ought to produce universal alarm, because it is levelled against the right of freely examining public characters and measures, and of free communication among the people thereon, which has ever been justly deemed the only effectual guardian of every other right.

6. That this State having by its convention, which

ratified the Federal Constitution, expressly declared, "that among other essential rights, the liberty of conscience and of the press cannot be cancelled, abridged, restrained, or modified by any authority of the United States," and from its extreme anxiety to guard these rights from every possible attack of sophistry or ambition, having with other States recommended an amendment for that purpose, which amendment was in due time annexed to the Constitution, it would mark a reproachful inconsistency and criminal degeneracy, if an indifference were now shown to the most palpable violation of one of the rights thus declared and secured, and to the establishment of a precedent which may be fatal to the other.

7. That the good people of this commonwealth having ever felt, and continuing to feel the most sincere affection to their brethren of the other States, the truest anxiety for establishing and perpetuating the union of all, and the most scrupulous fidelity to that Constitution which is the pledge of mutual friendship, and the instrument of mutual happiness, the General Assembly doth solemnly appeal to the like dispositions of the other States, in confidence that they will concur with this commonwealth in declaring, as it does hereby declare, that the acts aforesaid are unconstitutional, and that the necessary and proper measure will be taken by each, for co-operating with this State in maintaining unimpaired the authorities, rights, and liberties reserved to the States respectively, or to the people.

8. That the Governor be desired to transmit a copy of the aforesaid resolutions to the executive authority of each of the other States, with a request that the same may be communicated to the Legislature thereof. And that a copy be furnished to each of the Senators and Representatives representing this State in the Congress of the United States.

ABSTRACT OF DECISION IN THE CASE OF MARBURY *VS.* MADISON, 1803

THE question whether an act repugnant to the Constitution can become a law of the land, is a question deeply interesting to the United States; but happily not of an intricacy proportionate to its interest. It seems only necessary to recognize certain principles supposed to have been long and well established, to decide it. . . . That the people have an original right to establish for their future government such principles as in their opinion shall most conduce to their own happiness, is the basis on which the whole American fabric has been erected. The original supreme will organizes the government and assigns to the different departments their respective powers. . . . The powers of the Legislature are defined and limited; and that those limits may not be mistaken or forgotten, the Constitution is written. To what purpose are powers limited and to what purpose is that limitation committed to writing, if those limits may at any time be passed by those intended to be restrained? . . . The Constitution is either a superior, paramount law, unchangeable by ordinary means, or it is on a level with ordinary legislative acts, and like any other act is alterable when the Legislature shall please to alter it. If the former part of the alternative be true, then a legislative act contrary to the Constitution is not law. If the latter part be true, then written constitutions are absurd attempts on the part of the people to limit a power in its own nature illimitable. . . . If an act of the Legislature repugnant to the Constitution is void, does it, notwithstanding its invalidity, bind the courts and oblige them to give it effect? Or, in other words, though it be not law, does it constitute a rule as operative as though it was a law? This would be to overthrow in fact what was established in theory; and would seem at first view an absurdity too gross to be insisted upon. It shall, however, receive a more attentive consideration. It is emphatically the province and duty of the judicial department to say what the law is. Those who apply the rule to particular cases must of necessity expound and interpret that rule. If two laws conflict with each other, the courts must decide upon the operation of each. So if a law be in opposition to the Constitution; if both the law and the Constitution apply to a particular case, so that the court must either decide that case conformably to the law, disregarding the Constitution, or conformably to the Constitution, disregarding the law—the court must determine which of these conflicting rules governs the case. This is of the very essence of judicial duty. If, then, the courts are to regard the Constitution, and the Constitution is superior to any ordinary act of the Legislature, the Constitution, and not such ordinary act, must govern the case to which they both apply. Those, then, who controvert the principle that the Constitution is to be considered in court as a paramount law, are reduced to the necessity of maintaining that courts must close their eyes on the Constitution and see only the law.

AMENDMENTS TO THE CONSTITUTION PROPOSED BY THE HARTFORD CONVENTION, 1814

Therefore Resolved—That it be and hereby is recommended to the Legislatures of the several States represented in this Convention, to adopt all such measures as may be necessary effectually to protect the citizens of said States from the operation and effects of all acts which have been or may be passed by the Congress of the United States, which shall contain provisions, subjecting the militia or other citizens to forcible drafts, conscriptions, or impressments, not authorized by the Constitution of the United States.

Resolved—That it be and hereby is recommended to the said Legislatures, to authorize an immediate and earnest application to be made to the Government of the United States, requesting their consent to some arrangement, whereby the said States may, separately or in concert, be empowered to assume upon themselves the defence of their territory against the enemy; and a reasonable portion of the taxes, collected within said States, may be paid into the respective treasuries thereof, and appropriated to the payment of the balance due said States, and to the future defence of the same. The amount so paid into the said treasuries to be credited, and the disbursements made as aforesaid to be charged to the United States.

Resolved—That it be, and it hereby is, recommended

to the Legislatures of the aforesaid States, to pass laws (where it has not already been done) authorizing the Governors or Commanders-in-Chief of their militia to make detachments from the same, or to form voluntary corps, as shall be most convenient and conformable to their Constitutions, and to cause the same to be well armed, equipped, and disciplined, and held in readiness for service; and upon the request of the Governor of either of the other States, to employ the whole of such detachment or corps, as well as the regular forces of the State, or such part thereof as may be required and can be spared consistently with the safety of the State, in assisting the State making such request, to repel any invasion thereof which shall be made or attempted by the public enemy.

Resolved—That the following amendments of the Constitution of the United States be recommended to the States as aforesaid, to be proposed by them for adoption by the State Legislatures, and, in such cases as may be deemed expedient, by a Convention chosen by the people of each State.

And it is further recommended, that the said States shall persevere in their efforts to obtain such amendments, until the same shall be effected.

First—Representatives and direct taxes shall be apportioned among the several States which may be included within this Union, according to their respective numbers of free persons, including those bound to serve for a term of years, and excluding Indians not taxed, and all other persons.

Second—No new State shall be admitted into the Union by Congress in virtue of the power granted by the Constitution, without the concurrence of two thirds of both Houses.

Third—Congress shall not have power to lay any embargo on the ships or vessels of the citizens of the

United States, in the ports or harbors thereof, for more than sixty days.

Fourth—Congress shall not have power, without the concurrence of two thirds of both Houses, to interdict the commercial intercourse between the United States and any foreign nation or the dependencies thereof.

Fifth—Congress shall not make or declare war, or authorize acts of hostility against any foreign nation, without the concurrence of two thirds of both Houses, except such acts of hostility be in defence of the territories of the United States when actually invaded.

Sixth—No person who shall hereafter be naturalized, shall be eligible as a member of the Senate or House of Representatives of the United States, nor capable of holding any civil office under the authority of the United States.

Seventh—The same person shall not be elected President of the United States a second time; nor shall the President be elected from the same State two terms in succession.

Resolved—That if the application of these States to the Government of the United States, recommended in a foregoing Resolution, should be unsuccessful, and peace should not be concluded, and the defence of these States should be neglected, as it has been since the commencement of the war, it will in the opinion of this Convention be expedient for the Legislatures of the several States to appoint Delegates to another Convention, to meet at Boston, in the State of Massachusetts, on the third Thursday of June next, with such powers and instructions as the exigency of a crisis so momentous may require.

SOUTH CAROLINA ORDINANCE OF NULLIFICATION, 1832

AN ordinance to nullify certain acts of the Congress of the United States, purporting to be laws laying duties and imposts on the importation of foreign commodities.

Whereas the Congress of the United States by various acts, purporting to be acts laying duties and imposts on foreign imports, but in reality intended for the protection of domestic manufactures, and the giving of bounties to classes and individuals engaged in particular employments, at the expense and to the injury and oppression of other classes and individuals, and by wholly exempting from taxation certain foreign commodities, such as are not produced or manufactured in the United States, to afford a pretext for imposing higher and excessive duties on articles similar to those intended to be protected, hath exceeded its just powers under the Constitution, which confers on it no authority to afford such protection, and hath violated the true meaning and intent of the Constitution, which provides for equality in imposing the burdens of taxation upon the several States and portions of the confederacy: And whereas the said Congress, exceeding its just power to impose taxes and collect revenue for the purpose of effecting and accomplishing the specific objects and purposes which the Constitution of the United States authorizes it to effect and accomplish, hath raised and collected unnecessary revenue for objects unauthorized by the Constitution.

We, therefore, the people of the State of South Carolina, in convention assembled, do declare and ordain and it is hereby declared and ordained, that the several acts and parts of acts of the Congress of the United States, purporting to be laws for the imposing of duties and imposts on the importation of foreign commodities, and now having actual operation and effect within the United States, and more especially, an act entitled "An act in alteration of the several acts imposing duties on imports," approved on the nineteenth day of May, one thousand eight hundred and twenty-eight, and also an act entitled "An act to alter and amend the several acts imposing duties on imports," approved on the fourteenth day of July, one thousand eight hundred and thirty-two, are unauthorized by the Constitution of the United States, and violate the true meaning and intent thereof and are null, void, and no law, nor binding upon this State, its officers or citizens; and all promises, contracts, and obligations, made or entered into, or to be made or entered into, with purpose to secure the duties imposed by said acts, and all judicial proceedings which shall be hereafter had in affirmance thereof, are and shall be held utterly null and void.

And it is further ordained, that it shall not be lawful for any of the constituted authorities, whether of this State or of the United States, to enforce the payment of duties imposed by the said acts within the limits of this State; but it shall be the duty of the Legislature to adopt such measures and pass such acts as may be necessary to give full effect to this ordinance, and to prevent the enforcement and arrest the operation of the said acts and parts of acts of the Congress of the United States within the limits of this State, from and after the first day of February next, and the duties of all other constituted authorities, and of all persons residing or being within the limits of this State, and they are hereby required and enjoined to obey and give effect to this ordinance, and such acts and measures of the Legislature as may be passed or adopted in obedience thereto.

And it is further ordained, that in no case of law or equity, decided in the courts of this State, wherein shall be drawn in question the authority of this ordinance, or the validity of such act or acts of the Legislature as may be passed for the purpose of giving effect thereto, or the validity of the aforesaid acts of Congress, imposing duties, shall any appeal be taken or allowed to the Supreme Court of the United States, nor shall any copy of the record be permitted or allowed for that purpose; and if any such appeal shall be attempted to be taken, the courts of this State shall proceed to execute and enforce their judgments according to the laws and usages of the State, without reference to such attempted appeal, and the person or persons attempting to take such appeal may be dealt with as for a contempt of the court.

And it is further ordained, that all persons now holding any office of honor, profit, or trust, civil or military, under this State (members of the Legislature excepted), shall, within such time, and in such manner as the Legislature shall prescribe, take an oath well and truly to obey, execute, and enforce this ordinance, and such act or acts of the Legislature as may be passed in pursuance thereof, according to the true intent and meaning of the same; and on the neglect or omission of any such person or persons so to do, his or their office or offices shall be forthwith vacated, and shall be filled up as if such person or persons were dead or had resigned; and no person hereafter elected to any office of honor, profit, or trust, civil or military (members of the Legislature excepted), shall, until the Legislature shall otherwise provide and direct, enter on the execution of his office, or be in any respect competent to discharge the duties thereof until he shall, in like manner, have taken a similar oath; and no juror shall be impanelled in any of the courts of this State, in any cause in which shall be in question this ordinance, or any act of the Legislature passed in pursuance thereof, unless he shall first, in addition to the usual oath, have taken an oath that he will well and truly obey, execute, and enforce this ordinance, and such act or acts of the Legislature as may be passed to carry the same into operation and effect, according to the true intent and meaning thereof.

And we, the people of South Carolina, to the end that it may be fully understood by the Government of the United States, and the people of the co-States, that we are determined to maintain this our ordinance and declaration, at every hazard, do further declare that we will not submit to the application of force on the part of the Federal Government, to reduce this State to obedience; but that we will consider the passage, by Congress, of any act authorizing the employment of a military or naval force against the State of South Carolina, her constitutional authorities or citizens; or any act abolishing or closing the ports of this State, or any of them, or otherwise obstructing the free ingress and egress of vessels to and from the said ports, or any other act on the part of the Federal Government, to coerce the State, shut up her ports, destroy or harass her commerce or to enforce the acts hereby declared to be null and void, otherwise than through the civil tribunals of the country, as inconsistent with the longer continuance of South Carolina in the Union; and that the people of this State will henceforth hold themselves absolved from all further obligation to maintain or preserve their political connection with the people of the other States; and will forthwith proceed to organize a separate government, and do all other acts and things which sovereign and independent States may of right do.

Done in convention at Columbia, the twenty-fourth day of November, in the year of our Lord one thousand eight hundred and thirty-two, and in the fifty-seventh year of the Declaration of the Independence of the United States of America.

PRESIDENT JACKSON'S PROCLAMATION, 1832

WHEREAS a convention, assembled in the State of South Carolina, have passed an ordinance, by which they declare " that the several acts and parts of acts of the Congress of the United States purporting to be laws for the imposing of duties and imposts on the importation of foreign commodities, and now having actual operation and effect within the United States, and more especially ' two acts for the same purposes, passed on the 29th of May, 1828, and on the 14th of July, 1832,' are unauthorized by the Constitution of the United States, and violate the true meaning and intent thereof, and are null and void, and no law," nor binding on the citizens of that State or its officers; and by the said ordinance it is further declared to be unlawful for any of the constituted authorities of the State, or of the United States, to enforce the payment of the duties imposed by the said acts within the same State, and that it is the duty of the Legislature to pass such laws as may be necessary to give full effect to the said ordinance:

And whereas, by the said ordinance it is further ordained, that, in no case of law or equity, decided in the courts of said State, wherein shall be drawn in question the validity of the said ordinance, or of the acts of the Legislature that may be passed to give it effect, or of the said laws of the United States, no appeal shall be allowed to the Supreme Court of the United States, nor shall any copy of the record be permitted or allowed for that purpose; and that any person attempting to take such appeal, shall be punished as for a contempt of court:

And, finally, the said ordinance declares that the people of South Carolina will maintain the said ordinance at every hazard; and that they will consider the passage of any act by Congress abolishing or closing the ports of the said State, or otherwise obstructing the free ingress or egress of vessels to and from the said ports, or any other act of the Federal Government to coerce the State, shut up her ports, destroy or harass her commerce, or to enforce the said acts otherwise than through the civil tribunals of the country, as inconsistent with the longer continuance of South Carolina in the Union; and that the people of the said State will thenceforth hold themselves absolved from all further obligation to maintain or preserve their political connection with the people of the other States, and will forthwith proceed to organize a separate government, and do all other acts and things which sovereign and independent States may of right do:

And whereas the said ordinance prescribes to the people of South Carolina a course of conduct in direct violation of their duty as citizens of the United States, contrary to the laws of their country, subversive of its Constitution, and having for its object the destruction of the Union—that Union, which, coeval with our political existence, led our fathers, without any other ties to unite them than those of patriotism and a common cause, through the sanguinary struggle to a glorious independence—that sacred Union, hitherto inviolate, which, perfected by our happy Constitution, has brought us, by the favor of Heaven, to a state of prosperity at home, and high consideration abroad, rarely, if ever, equalled in the history of nations; to preserve this bond of our political existence from destruction, to maintain inviolate this state of national honor and prosperity, and to justify the confidence my fellow-citizens have reposed in me, I, Andrew Jackson, President of the United States, have thought proper to issue this my PROCLAMATION, stating my views of the Constitution and laws applicable to the measures adopted by the Convention of South Carolina, and to the reasons they have put forth to sustain them, declaring the course which duty will require me to pursue, and, appealing to the understanding and patriotism of the people, warn them of the consequences that must inevitably result from an observance of the dictates of the Convention.

Strict duty would require of me nothing more than the exercise of those powers with which I am now, or may hereafter be, invested, for preserving the Union, and for the execution of the laws. But the imposing aspect which opposition has assumed in this case, by clothing itself with State authority, and the deep interest which the people of the United States must all feel in preventing a resort to stronger measures, while there is a hope that anything will be yielded to reasoning and remonstrances, perhaps demand, and will certainly justify, a full exposition to South Carolina and the nation of the views I entertain of this important question, as well as a distinct enunciation of the course which my sense of duty will require me to pursue.

The ordinance is founded, not on the indefeasible right of resisting acts which are plainly unconstitutional, and too oppressive to be endured, but on the strange position that any one State may not only declare an act of Congress void, but prohibit its execution—that they may do this consistently with the Constitution—that the true construction of that instrument permits a State to retain its place in the Union, and yet be bound by no other of its laws than those it may choose to consider as constitutional. It is true they add, that to justify this abrogation of a law, it must be palpably contrary to the Constitution; but it is evident, that to give the right of resisting laws of that description, coupled with the uncontrolled right to decide what laws deserve that character, is to give the power of resisting all laws. For, as by the theory, there is no appeal, the reasons alleged by the State, good or bad, must prevail. If it should be said that public opinion is a sufficient check against the abuse of this power, it may be asked why it is not deemed a sufficient guard against the passage of an unconstitutional act by Congress. There is, however, a restraint in this last case, which makes the assumed power of a State more indefensible, and which does not exist in the other. There are two appeals from an unconstitutional act passed by Congress—one to the judiciary, the other to the people and the States. There is no appeal from the State decision in theory; and the practical illustration shows that the courts are closed against an application to review it, both judges and jurors being sworn to decide in its favor. But reasoning on this subject is superfluous, when our social compact in express terms declares, that the laws of the United States, its Constitution, and treaties made under it, are the supreme law of the land; and for greater caution adds, "that the judges in every State shall be bound thereby, anything in the Constitution or laws of any State to the contrary notwithstanding." And it may be asserted, without fear of refutation, that no federative government could exist without a similar provision. Look, for a moment, to the consequence. If South Carolina considers the revenue laws unconstitutional, and has a right to prevent their execution in the port of Charleston, there would be a clear constitutional objection to their collection in every other port, and no revenue could be collected anywhere; for all imposts must be equal. It is no answer to repeat that an unconstitutional law is no law, so long as the question of its legality is to be decided by the State itself; for every law operating injuriously upon any local interest will be perhaps thought, and certainly represented, as unconstitutional, and, as has been shown, there is no appeal.

If this doctrine had been established at an earlier day, the Union would have been dissolved in its infancy. The excise law in Pennsylvania, the embargo and non-intercourse law in the Eastern States, the carriage tax in Virginia, were all deemed unconstitutional, and were more unequal in their operation than any of the laws now complained of; but, fortunately, none of those States discovered that they had the right now claimed by South Carolina. The war into which we were forced, to support the dignity of the nation and the rights of our citizens, might have ended in defeat and disgrace, instead of victory and honor, if the States, who supposed it a ruinous and unconstitutional measure, had thought they possessed the right of nullifying the act by which it was declared, and denying supplies for its prosecution. Hardly and unequally as those measures bore upon several members of the Union, to the legislatures of none did this efficient and peaceable remedy, as it is called, suggest itself. The discovery of this important feature in our Constitution was reserved to the present day. To the statesmen of South Carolina belongs the invention, and upon the citizens of that State will, unfortunately, fall the evils of reducing it to practice.

. . . .

I consider, then, the power to annul a law of the United States, assumed by one State, *incompatible with the existence of the Union, contradicted expressly by the letter of the Constitution, unauthorized by its spirit, inconsistent with every principle on which it was founded, and destructive of the great object for which it was formed.*

. . . .

This right to secede is deduced from the nature of the Constitution, which they say is a compact between sovereign States, who have preserved their whole sovereignty, and therefore are subject to no superior; that because they made the compact, they can break it when in their opinion it has been departed from by the other States. Fallacious as this course of reasoning is, it enlists State pride, and finds advocates in the honest prejudices of those who have not studied the nature of our government sufficiently to see the radical error on which it rests.

The people of the United States formed the Constitution, acting through the State legislatures, in making the compact, to meet and discuss its provisions, and acting in separate conventions when they ratified those provisions; but the terms used in its construction show it to be a government in which the people of all the States collectively are represented. We are ONE PEOPLE in the choice of the President and Vice-President. Here the States have no other agency than to direct the mode in which the vote shall be given. The candidates having the majority of all the votes are chosen. The electors of a majority of States may have given their votes for one candidate, and yet another may be chosen. The people, then, and not the States, are represented in the executive branch.

. . . .

The Constitution of the United States, then, forms a *government,* not a league, and whether it be formed by compact between the States, or in any other manner, its character is the same. It is a government in which all the people are represented, which operates directly on the people individually, not upon the States; they retained all the power they did not grant. But each State, having expressly parted with so many powers as to constitute jointly with the other States a single nation, cannot from that period possess any right to secede, because such secession does not break a league, but destroys the unity of a nation, and any injury to that unity is not only a breach which would result from the contravention of a compact, but it is an offence against the whole Union. To say that any State may at pleasure secede from the Union is to say that the United States are not a nation; because it would be a solecism to contend that any part of a nation might dissolve its connection with the other parts, to their injury or ruin, without committing any offence. Secession, like any other revolutionary act, may be morally justified by the extremity of oppression; but to call it a constitutional right is confounding the meaning of terms, and can only be done through gross error, or to deceive those who are willing to assert a right, but would pause before they made a revolution, or incur the penalties consequent upon a failure.

Because the Union was formed by compact, it is said the parties to that compact may, when they feel themselves aggrieved, depart from it; but it is precisely because it is a compact that they cannot. A compact is an agreement or binding obligation. It may by its terms have a sanction or penalty for its breach, or it may not. If it contains no sanction, it may be broken with no other consequence than moral guilt; if it have a sanction, then the breach incurs the designated or implied penalty. A league between independent nations, generally, has no sanction other than a moral one; or if it should contain a penalty, as there is no common superior, it cannot be enforced. A government, on the contrary, always has a sanction, expressed or implied; and, in our case, it is both necessarily implied and expressly given. An attempt by force of arms to destroy a government is an offence, by whatever means the constitutional compact may have been formed; and such government has the right, by the law of self-defence, to pass acts for punishing the offender, unless that right is modified, restrained, or resumed by the constitutional act. In our system, although it is modified in the case of treason, yet authority is expressly given to pass all laws necessary to carry its powers into effect, and under this grant provision has been made for punishing acts which obstruct the due administration of the laws.

It would seem superfluous to add anything to show the nature of that union which connects us; but as erroneous opinions on this subject are the foundation of doctrines the most destructive to our peace, I must give some further development to my views on this subject. No one, fellow-citizens, has a higher reverence for the reserved rights of the States than the magistrate who now addresses you. No one would make greater personal sacrifices, or official exertions, to defend them from violation; but equal care must be taken to prevent, on their part, an improper interference with, or resumption of, the rights they have vested in the nation. The line has been so distinctly drawn as to avoid doubts in some cases of the exercise of power. Men of the best intentions and soundest views may differ in their construction of some parts of the Constitution; but there are others on which dispassionate reflection can leave no doubt. Of this nature appears to be the assumed right of secession. It rests, as we have seen, on the alleged undivided sovereignty of the States, and on their having formed in this sovereign capacity a compact which is called the Constitution, from which, because they made it, they have the right to secede. Both of these positions are erroneous, and some of the arguments to prove them so have been anticipated.

The States severally have not retained their entire sovereignty. It has been shown that in becoming parts of a nation, not members of a league, they surrendered many of their essential parts of sovereignty. The right to make treaties, declare war, levy taxes, exercise exclusive judicial and legislative powers, were all functions of sovereign power. The States, then, for all these important purposes, were no longer sovereign. The allegiance of their citizens was transferred in the first instance to the Government of the United States; they became American citizens, and owed obedience to the Constitution of the United States, and to laws made in conformity with the powers vested in Congress. This last position has not been, and cannot be, denied. How, then, can that State be said to be sovereign and independent whose citizens owe obedience to laws not made by it, and whose magistrates are sworn to disregard those laws, when they come in conflict with those passed by another? What shows conclusively that the States cannot be said to have reserved an undivided sovereignty, is that they expressly ceded the right to punish treason —not treason against their separate power, but treason against the United States. Treason is an offence against *sovereignty,* and sovereignty must reside with the power to punish it. But the reserved rights of the States are not less sacred because they have for their common interest made the general government the depository of these powers. The unity of our political character (as has been shown for another purpose) commenced with its very existence. Under the royal government we had no separate character; our opposition to its oppression began as UNITED COLONIES. We were the UNITED STATES under the Confederation, and the name was perpetuated and the Union rendered more perfect by the Federal Constitution. In none of these stages did we consider ourselves in any other light than as forming one nation. Treaties and alliances were made in the name of all. Troops were raised for the joint defence. How, then, with all these proofs, that under all changes of our position we had, for designated purposes and with defined powers, created national governments—how is it that the most perfect of these several modes of union should now be considered as a mere league that may be dissolved at pleasure? It is from an abuse of terms. Compact is used as synonymous with league, although the true term is not employed, because it would at once show the fallacy of the reasoning. It would not do to say that our Constitution was only a league, but it is labored to prove it a compact (which, in one sense, it is), and then to argue that as a league is a compact, every compact between nations must, of course, be a league, and that from such an engagement every sovereign power has a right to recede. But it has been shown that in this sense the States are not sovereign, and that even if they were, and the national Constitution had been formed by compact, there would be no right in any one State to exonerate itself from the obligation.

So obvious are the reasons which forbid this secession, that it is necessary only to allude to them. The Union was formed for the benefit of all. It was produced by mutual sacrifice of interest and opinions. Can those sacrifices be recalled? Can the States, who magnanimously surrendered their title to the territories of the West, recall the grant? Will the inhabitants of the inland States agree to pay the duties that may be imposed without their assent by those on the Atlantic or the Gulf, for their own benefit? Shall there be a free port in one State, and enormous duties in another? No one believes that any right exists in a single State to involve all the others in these and countless other evils, contrary to engagements solemnly made. Every one must see that the other States, in self-defence, must oppose it at all hazards.

President Jackson's Proclamation

. . . .

Fellow-citizens of my native State! let me not only admonish you, as the first magistrate of our common country, not to incur the penalty of its laws, but use the influence that a father would over his children whom he saw rushing to a certain ruin. In that paternal language, with that paternal feeling, let me tell you, my countrymen, that you are deluded by men who are either deceived themselves or wish to deceive you. Mark under what pretences you have been led on to the brink of insurrection and treason on which you stand! First, a diminution of the value of our staple commodity, lowered by over-production in other quarters, and the consequent diminution in value of your lands were the sole effect of the tariff laws. The effect of those laws was confessedly injurious, but the evil was greatly exaggerated by the unfounded theory you were taught to believe, that its burdens were in proportion to your exports, not to your consumption of imported articles. Your pride was aroused by the assertion that a submission to these laws was a state of vassalage, and that resistance to them was equal, in patriotic merit, to the opposition our fathers offered to the oppressive laws of Great Britain. You were told that this opposition might be peaceably—might be constitutionally made—that you might enjoy all the advantages of the Union and bear none of its burdens. Eloquent appeals to your passions, to your State pride, to your native courage, to your sense of real injury, were used to prepare you for the period when the mask which concealed the hideous features of DISUNION should be taken off. It fell, and you were made to look with complacency on objects which not long since you would have regarded with horror. Look back to the arts which have brought you to this state—look forward to the consequences to which it must inevitably lead! Look back to what was first told you as an inducement to enter into this dangerous course. The great political truth was repeated to you that you had the revolutionary right of resisting all laws that were palpably unconstitutional and intolerably oppressive—it was added that the right to nullify a law rested on the same principle, but that it was a peaceable remedy! This character which was given to it made you receive with too much confidence the assertions that were made of the unconstitutionality of the law and its oppressive effects. Mark, my fellow-citizens, that by the admission of your leaders the unconstitutionality must be *palpable*, or it will not justify either resistance or nullification! What is the meaning of the word *palpable* in the sense in which it is here used? that which is apparent to every one, that which no man of ordinary intellect will fail to perceive. Is the unconstitutionality of these laws of that description? Let those among your leaders who once approved and advocated the principles of protective duties, answer the question; and let them choose whether they will be considered as incapable, then, of perceiving that which must have been apparent to every man of common understanding, or as imposing upon your confidence and endeavoring to mislead you now. In either case, they are unsafe guides in the perilous path they urge you to tread. Ponder well on this circumstance, and you will know how to appreciate the exaggerated language they address to you. They are not champions of liberty emulating the fame of our Revolutionary fathers, nor are you an oppressed people, contending, as they repeat to you, against worse than colonial vassalage. You are free members of a flourishing and happy Union. There is no settled design to oppress you. You have, indeed, felt the unequal operation of laws which may have been unwisely, not unconstitutionally passed; but that inequality must necessarily be removed. At the very moment when

President Jackson's Proclamation 357

you were madly urged on to the unfortunate course you have begun, a change in public opinion has commenced. The nearly approaching payment of the public debt, and the consequent necessity of a diminution of duties, had already caused a considerable reduction, and that, too, on some articles of general consumption in your State. The importance of this change was underrated, and you were authoritatively told that no further alleviation of your burdens was to be expected, at the very time when the condition of the country imperiously demanded such a modification of the duties as should reduce them to a just and equitable scale. But, as apprehensive of the effect of this change in allaying your discontents, you were precipitated into the fearful state in which you now find yourselves.

I have urged you to look back to the means that were used to hurry you on to the position you have now assumed, and forward to the consequences they will produce. Something more is necessary. Contemplate the condition of that country of which you still form an important part; consider its government uniting in one bond of common interest and general protection so many different States—giving to all their inhabitants the proud title of AMERICAN CITIZEN—protecting their commerce—securing their literature and arts—facilitating their intercommunication—defending their frontiers—and making their name respected in the remotest parts of the earth! Consider the extent of its territory, its increasing and happy population, its advance in arts, which render life agreeable, and the sciences which elevate the mind! See education spreading the lights of religion, morality, and general information into every cottage in this wide extent of our Territories and States! Behold it as the asylum where the wretched and oppressed find a refuge and support! Look on this picture of happiness and honor, and say, WE, TOO, ARE CITIZENS

OF AMERICA—Carolina is one of these proud States her arms have defended—her best blood has cemented this happy Union! And then add, if you can, without horror and remorse, this happy Union we will dissolve —this picture of peace and prosperity we will deface— this free intercourse we will interrupt—these fertile fields we will deluge with blood—the protection of that glorious flag we renounce—the very name of Americans we discard. And for what, mistaken men! For what do you throw away these inestimable blessings—for what would you exchange your share in the advantages and honor of the Union? For the dream of a separate independence—a dream interrupted by bloody conflicts with your neighbors, and a vile dependence on a foreign power. If your leaders could succeed in establishing a separation, what would be your situation? Are you united at home—are you free from the apprehension of civil discord, with all its fearful consequences? Do our neighboring republics, every day suffering some new revolution or contending with some new insurrection—do they excite your envy? But the dictates of a high duty oblige me solemnly to announce that you cannot succeed. The laws of the United States must be executed. I have no discretionary power on the subject—my duty is emphatically pronounced in the Constitution. Those who told you that you might peaceably prevent their execution, deceived you—they could not have been deceived themselves. They know that a forcible opposition could alone prevent the execution of the laws, and they know that such opposition must be repelled. Their object is disunion; but be not deceived by names; disunion, by armed force, is TREASON. Are you really ready to incur its guilt? If you are, on the head of the instigators of the act be the dreadful consequences—on their heads be the dishonor, but on yours may fall the punishment—on your unhappy State will inevitably fall all the evils of the conflict you force upon the government of your country. It cannot accede to the mad project of disunion, of which you would be the first victims—its first magistrate cannot, if he would, avoid the performance of his duty—the consequence must be fearful for you, distressing to your fellow-citizens here, and to the friends of good government throughout the world. Its enemies have beheld our prosperity with a vexation they could not conceal—it was a standing refutation of their slavish doctrines, and they will point to our discord with the triumph of malignant joy. It is yet in your power to disappoint them. There is yet time to show that the descendants of the Pinckneys, the Sumpters, the Rutledges, and of the thousand other names which adorn the pages of your Revolutionary history, will not abandon that Union to support which so many of them fought and bled and died. I adjure you, as you honor their memory—as you love the cause of freedom, to which they dedicated their lives—as you prize the peace of your country, the lives of its best citizens, and your own fair fame, to retrace your steps. Snatch from the archives of your State the disorganizing edict of its convention—bid its members to reassemble and promulgate the decided expressions of your will to remain in the path which alone can conduct you to safety, prosperity, and honor—tell them that compared to disunion, all other evils are light, because that brings with it an accumulation of all—declare that you will never take the field unless the star-spangled banner of your country shall float over you—that you will not be stigmatized when dead, and dishonored and scorned while you live, as the authors of the first attack on the Constitution of your country!—its destroyers you cannot be. You may disturb its peace—you may interrupt the course of its prosperity—you may cloud its reputation for stability—but its tranquillity will be restored, its prosperity will return, and the stain upon its national character will be transferred and remain an eternal blot on the memory of those who caused the disorder.

Fellow-citizens of the United States! the threat of unhallowed disunion—the names of those, once respected, by whom it is uttered—the array of military force to support it—denote the approach of a crisis in our affairs on which the continuance of our unexampled prosperity, our political existence, and perhaps that of all free governments, may depend. The conjuncture demanded a free, a full, and explicit enunciation, not only of my intentions, but of my principles of action; and as the claim was asserted of a right by a State to annul the laws of the Union, and even to secede from it at pleasure, a frank exposition of my opinions in relation to the origin and form of our government, and the construction I give to the instrument by which it was created, seemed to be proper. Having the fullest confidence in the justness of the legal and constitutional opinion of my duties which has been expressed, I rely with equal confidence on your undivided support in my determination to execute the laws—to preserve the Union by all constitutional means—to arrest, if possible, by moderate but firm measures, the necessity of a recourse to force; and if it be the will of Heaven that the recurrence of its primeval curse on man for the shedding of a brother's blood should fall upon our land, that it be not called down by any offensive act on the part of the United States.

Fellow-citizens! the momentous case is before you. On your undivided support of your government depends the decision of the great question it involves, whether your sacred Union will be preserved, and the blessing it secures to us as one people shall be perpetuated. No one can doubt that the unanimity with which that decision will be expressed, will be such as to inspire new confidence in republican institutions, and that the prudence, the wisdom, and the courage which it will bring to their defence, will transmit them unimpaired and invigorated to our children.

May the Great Ruler of nations grant that the signal blessings with which He has favored ours may not, by the madness of party, or personal ambition, be disregarded and lost, and may His wise providence bring those who have produced this crisis to see the folly, before they feel the misery, of civil strife, and inspire a returning veneration for that Union, which, if we may dare to penetrate His designs, He has chosen, as the only means of attaining the high destinies to which we may reasonably aspire.

In testimony whereof, I have caused the seal of the United States to be hereunto affixed, having signed the same with my hand.

Done at the City of Washington, this 10th day of December, in the year of our Lord one thousand eight hundred and thirty-two, and of the independence of the United States the fifty-seventh.

ANDREW JACKSON.

By the President,
EDWARD LIVINGSTON, *Secretary of State.*

ABSTRACT OF THE DRED SCOTT DECISION, 1857

. . . .

The question is simply this: Can a negro, whose ancestors were imported into this country, and sold as slaves, become a member of the political community formed and brought into existence by the Constitution of the United States, and as such become entitled to all the rights, and privileges, and immunities, guaranteed by that instrument to the citizens? One of which rights is the privilege of suing in a court of the United States in the cases specified in the Constitution.

It will be observed, that the plea applies to that class of persons only whose ancestors were negroes of the African race, and imported into this country, and sold and held as slaves. The only matter at issue before the court, therefore, is, whether the descendants of such slaves, when they shall be emancipated, or who are born of parents who had become free before their birth, are citizens of a State, in the sense in which the word citizen is used in the Constitution of the United States. And this being the only matter in dispute on the pleadings, the court must be understood as speaking in this opinion of that class only. That is, of those persons who are the descendants of Africans who were imported into this country, and sold as slaves. . . .

The words "people of the United States" and " citizen " are synonymous terms, and mean the same thing. They both describe the political body who, according to our republican institutions, form the sovereignty, and who hold the power and conduct the government through their representatives. They are what we familiarly call the "sovereign people," and every citizen is one of this people, and a constituent member of this sovereignty. The question before us is, whether the class of persons described in the plea in abatement compose a portion of this people, and are constituent members of this sovereignty? We think they are not, and that they are not included, and were not intended to be included, under the word "citizens" in the Constitution, and can therefore claim none of the rights and privileges which that instrument provides for and secures to citizens of the United States. On the contrary, they were at that time considered as a subordinate and inferior class of beings, who had been subjugated by the dominant race, and whether emancipated or not, yet remained subject to their authority, and had no rights or privileges but such as those who held the power and the government might choose to grant them.

It is not the province of the court to decide upon the justice or injustice, the policy or impolicy, of these laws. The decision of that question belonged to the political or law-making power; to those who formed the sovereignty and framed the Constitution. The duty of the court is, to interpret the instrument they have framed, with the best lights we can obtain on the subject, and to administer it as we find it, according to its true intent and meaning when it was adopted.

In discussing this question we must not confound the rights of citizenship which a State may confer within its own limits, and the rights of citizenship as a member of the Union. It does not by any means follow, because he has all the rights and privileges of a citizen of a State, that he must be a citizen of the United States. He may have all the rights and privileges of the citizen of a State, and yet not be entitled to the rights and privileges of a citizen in any other State. For, previous to the adoption of the Constitution of the United States, every State had the undoubted right to confer on whomsoever it pleased the character of citizen, and to endow him with all its rights. But this character of course was confined to the boundaries of the State, and gave him no rights or privileges in other States beyond those secured to him by the laws of nations and the comity of States. Nor have the several States surrendered the power of conferring these rights and privileges by adopting the Constitution of the United States. Each State may still confer them upon an alien, or any one it thinks proper, or upon any class or description of persons; yet he would not be a citizen in the sense in which that word is used in the Constitution of the United States, nor entitled to sue as such in one of its courts, nor to the privileges and immunities of a citizen in the other States. The rights which he would acquire would be restricted to the State which gave them. The Constitution has conferred on Congress the right to establish an uniform rule of naturalization, and this right is evidently exclusive, and has always been held by this court to be so. Consequently, no State, since the adoption of the Constitution, can by naturalizing an alien invest him with the rights and privileges secured to a citizen of a State under the Federal Government, although, so far as the State alone was concerned, he would undoubtedly be entitled to the rights of a citizen, and clothed with all the rights and immunities which the Constitution and laws of the State attached to that character.

It is very clear, therefore, that no State can, by any act or law of its own, passed since the adoption of the Constitution, introduce a new member into the political community created by the Constitution of the United States. It cannot make him a member of this community by making him a member of its own. And for the same reason it cannot introduce any person, or description of persons, who were not intended to be embraced in this new political family, which the Constitution brought into existence, but were intended to be excluded from it.

The question then arises, whether the provisions of the Constitution, in relation to the personal rights and privileges to which the citizen of a State should be entitled, embraced the negro African race, at that time in this country, or who might afterward be imported, who had then or should afterward be made free in any State; and to put it in the power of a single State to make him a citizen of the United States, and endue him with the full rights of citizenship in every other State without their consent? Does the Constitution of the United States act upon him whenever he shall be made free under the laws of the State, and raised there to the rank of a citizen, and immediately clothe him with all the privileges of a citizen in every other State, and in its own courts?

The court think the affirmative of these propositions cannot be maintained. And if it cannot, the plaintiff in error could not be a citizen of the State of Missouri, within the meaning of the Constitution of the United States, and, consequently, was not entitled to sue in its courts.

. . . .

But the power of Congress over the person or property of a citizen can never be a mere discretionary power under our Constitution and form of government. The powers of the government and the rights and privileges of the citizen are regulated and plainly defined by the Constitution itself. And when the territory becomes a part of the United States, the Federal Government enters into possession in the character impressed upon it by those who created it. . . . The territory being a part of the United States, the government and the citizen both enter it under the authority of the Constitution, with their respective rights defined and marked out; and the Federal Government can exercise no power over his person or property, beyond what that instrument confers, nor lawfully deny any right which it has reserved. . . .

These powers, and others, in relation to rights of person, . . . are, in express and positive terms, denied to the general government; and the rights of private property have been guarded with equal care. Thus the rights of property are united with the rights of person, and placed on the same ground by the Fifth Amendment to the Constitution, which provides that no person shall be deprived of life, liberty, and property, without due process of law. And an act of Congress which deprives a citizen of the United States of his liberty or property, merely because he came himself or brought his property into a particular territory of the United States, and who had committed no offence against the laws, could hardly be dignified with the name of due process of law. . . .

The powers over person and property of which we speak are not only not granted to Congress, but are in express terms denied, and they are forbidden to exercise them. And this prohibition is not confined to the States, but the words are general, and extend to the whole territory over which the Constitution gives it power to legislate, including those portions of it remaining under territorial government, as well as that covered by States. It is a total absence of power everywhere within the dominion of the United States, and places the citizens of a territory, so far as these rights are concerned, on the same footing with citizens of the States, and guards them as firmly and plainly against any inroads which

Abstract of Dred Scott Decision

the general government might attempt, under the plea of implied or incidental powers. . . .

And if the Constitution recognizes the right of property of the master in a slave, and makes no distinction between that description of property and other property owned by a citizen, no tribunal, acting under the authority of the United States, whether it be legislative, executive, or judicial, has a right to draw such a distinction, or deny to it the benefit of the provisions and guarantees which have been provided for the protection of private property against the encroachments of the government.

Now . . . the right of property in a slave is distinctly and expressly affirmed in the Constitution.

Upon these considerations, it is the opinion of the court that the act of Congress [Missouri Compromise] which prohibited a citizen from holding and owning property of this kind in the territory of the United States north of the line therein mentioned, is not warranted by the Constitution, and is, therefore, void; and that neither Dred Scott himself, nor any of his family, were made free by being carried into this territory; even if they had been carried there by the owner, with the intention of becoming a permanent resident.

SOUTH CAROLINA ORDINANCE OF SECESSION, 1860

An ordinance to dissolve the Union between the State of South Carolina and other States united with her under the compact entitled "The Constitution of the United States of America."

We, the People of the State of South Carolina, in Convention assembled, do declare and ordain, and it is hereby declared and ordained, that the ordinance adopted by us in Convention, on the twenty-third day of May, in the year of our Lord one thousand seven hundred and eighty-eight, whereby the Constitution of the United States of America was ratified, and also, all Acts and parts of Acts of the General Assembly of this State, ratifying amendments of the said Constitution, are hereby repealed; and the union now subsisting between South Carolina and other States, under the name of "The United States of America," is hereby dissolved.

SOUTH CAROLINA DECLARATION OF INDEPENDENCE, 1860

THE State of South Carolina having resumed her separate and equal place among nations, deems it due to herself, to the remaining United States of America, and to the nations of the world, that she should declare the causes which have led to this act.

In the year 1765, that portion of the British Empire embracing Great Britain, undertook to make laws for the government of that portion composed of the thirteen American Colonies. A struggle for the right of self-government ensued, which resulted, on the 4th July, 1776, in a Declaration by the Colonies, "that they are, and of right ought to be, FREE AND INDEPENDENT STATES, and that, as free and independent States, they have full power to levy war, to conclude peace, contract alliances, establish commerce, and do all other acts and things which independent States may of right do."

They further solemnly declare, that whenever any "form of government becomes destructive of the ends for which it was established, it is the right of that people to alter or abolish it, and to institute a new government." Deeming the Government of Great Britain to have become destructive of these ends, they declared that the Colonies "are absolved from all allegiance to the British Crown, and that all political connection between them and the State of Great Britain is, and ought to be, totally dissolved."

In pursuance of this Declaration of Independence, each of the thirteen States proceeded to exercise its separate sovereignty; adopted for itself a Constitution, and appointed officers for the administration of government in all its departments—Legislative, Executive, and Judicial.

. . . .

Thus were established the two great principles asserted by the Colonies, namely: the right of a State to govern itself; and the right of a people to abolish a Government when it becomes destructive of the ends for which it was instituted. And concurrent with the establishment of these principles, was the fact, that each colony became and was recognized by the mother country as a FREE, SOVEREIGN, and INDEPENDENT STATE.

In 1787, Deputies were appointed by the States to revise the Articles of Confederation, and on 17th September, 1787, these Deputies recommended, for the adoption of the States, the Articles of Union, known as the Constitution of the United States.

The parties to whom the Constitution was submitted were the several sovereign States; they were to agree or disagree, and when nine of them agreed, the compact was to take effect among those concurring; and the General Government, as the common agent, was then to be vested with their authority.

If only nine of the thirteen States had concurred, the other four would have remained as they were—separate, sovereign States, independent of any of the provisions of the Constitution. In fact, two of the States did not accede to the Constitution until long after it had gone into operation among the other eleven; and during that interval, they exercised the functions of an independent nation.

By this Constitution, certain duties were imposed upon the several States, and the exercise of certain of their powers was restrained. . . . To remove all doubt, an amendment was added, which declared that the powers not delegated to the United States by the Constitution, nor prohibited by it to the States, are reserved to the States, respectively, or to the people. On 23d May, 1788, South Carolina, by a Convention of her people, passed an Ordinance assenting to this Constitution, and afterwards altered her own Constitution to conform herself to the obligation she had undertaken.

Thus was established, by compact between the States, a Government, with defined objects and powers, limited to the express words of the grant. This limitation left the whole remaining mass of power subject to the clause reserving it to the States or to the people, and rendered unnecessary any specification of reserved powers.

We hold that the Government thus established is subject to the two great principles asserted in the Declaration of Independence; and we hold further, that the mode of its formation subjects it to the third fundamental principle, namely: the law of compact. We maintain that in every compact between two or more parties, the obligation is mutual; that the failure of one of the contracting parties to perform a material part of the agreement, entirely releases the obligation of the other; and that where no arbiter is provided, each party is remitted to its own judgment to determine the fact of failure with all its consequences.

. . . .

The ends for which this Constitution was framed are declared by itself to be " to form a more perfect union, establish justice, insure domestic tranquillity, provide for the common defence, promote the general welfare, and secure the blessings of liberty to ourselves and posterity."

These ends it endeavored to accomplish by a Federal

Government, in which each State was recognized as an equal, and had separate control over its own institutions. The right of property in slaves was recognized by giving to free persons distinct political rights, by giving them the right to represent, and burthening them with direct taxes for three-fifths of their slaves; by authorizing the importation of slaves for twenty years; and by stipulating for the rendition of fugitives from labor.

We affirm that these ends for which this Government was instituted have been defeated, and the Government itself has been made destructive of them by the action of the non-slaveholding States. These States have assumed the right of deciding upon the propriety of our domestic institutions; and have denied the rights of property established in fifteen of the States and recognized by the Constitution; they have denounced as sinful the institution of Slavery; they have permitted the open establishment among them of societies, whose avowed object is to disturb the peace and to eloign the property of the citizens of other States. They have encouraged and assisted thousands of our slaves to leave their homes; and those who remain, have been incited by emissaries, books and pictures to servile insurrection.

For twenty-five years this agitation has been steadily increasing, until it has now secured to its aid the power of the Common Government. Observing the *forms* of the Constitution, a sectional party has found within that article establishing the Executive Department, the means of subverting the Constitution itself. A geographical line has been drawn across the Union, and all the States north of that line have united in the election of a man to the high office of President of the United States whose opinions and purposes are hostile to slavery. He is to be entrusted with the administration of the Common Government, because he has declared that " Government cannot endure permanently half slave, half free," and that the public mind must rest in the belief that Slavery is in the course of ultimate extinction.

. . . .

On the 4th March next, this party will take possession of the Government. It has announced, that the South shall be excluded from the common Territory; that the Judicial Tribunals shall be made sectional, and that a war must be waged against slavery until it shall cease throughout the United States.

The Guarantees of the Constitution will then no longer exist; the equal rights of the States will be lost. The slaveholding States will no longer have the power of self-government, or self-protection, and the Federal Government will have become their enemy.

Sectional interest and animosity will deepen the irritation, and all hope of remedy is rendered vain, by the fact that public opinion at the north has invested a great political error with the sanctions of a more erroneous religious belief.

We, therefore, the people of South Carolina, by our delegates, in Convention assembled, appealing to the Supreme Judge of the world for the rectitude of our intentions, have solemnly declared that the Union heretofore existing between this State and the other States of North America, is dissolved, and that the State of South Carolina has resumed her position among the nations of the world, as a separate and independent State; with full power to levy war, conclude peace, contract alliances, establish commerce, and to do all other acts and things which independent States may of right do.

PROCLAMATION OF EMANCIPATION

January 1, 1863

WHEREAS, on the twenty-second day of September, in the year of our Lord one thousand eight hundred and sixty-two, a proclamation was issued by the President of the United States, containing, among other things, the following, to wit:

" That on the first day of January, in the year of our Lord one thousand eight hundred and sixty-three, all persons held as slaves within any State or designated part of a State, the people whereof shall then be in rebellion against the United States, shall be then, thenceforward, and forever free; and the Executive Government of the United States, including the military and naval authority thereof, will recognize and maintain the freedom of such persons, and will do no act or acts to repress such persons or any of them, in any efforts they may make for their actual freedom.

" That the Executive will, on the first day of January aforesaid, by proclamation, designate the States and parts of States, if any, in which the people thereof respectively shall then be in rebellion against the United States; and the fact that any State, or the people thereof, shall on that day be in good faith represented in the Congress of the United States, by members chosen thereto at elections wherein a majority of the qualified voters of such State shall have participated, shall, in the absence of strong countervailing testimony, be deemed conclusive

Proclamation of Emancipation

evidence that such State, and the people thereof, are not then in rebellion against the United States."

Now, therefore, I, ABRAHAM LINCOLN, President of the United States, by virtue of the power in me vested as Commander-in-Chief of the army and navy of the United States in time of actual armed rebellion against the authority and government of the United States, and as a fit and necessary war measure for suppressing said rebellion, do, on this first day of January, in the year of our Lord one thousand eight hundred and sixty-three, and in accordance with my purpose so to do, publicly proclaimed for the full period of one hundred days from the day first above mentioned, order and designate, as the States and parts of States wherein the people thereof respectively are this day in rebellion against the United States, the following, to wit:

Arkansas, Texas, Louisiana (except the parishes of St. Bernard, Plaquemine, Jefferson, St. John, St. Charles, St. James, Ascension, Assumption, Terre Bonne, Lafourche, St. Marie, St. Martin, and Orleans, including the city of New Orleans), Mississippi, Alabama, Florida, Georgia, South Carolina, North Carolina, and Virginia (except the forty-eight counties designated as West Virginia, and also the counties of Berkley, Accomac, Northampton, Elizabeth City, York, Princess Anne, and Norfolk, including the cities of Norfolk and Portsmouth), and which excepted parts are for the present left precisely as if this proclamation were not issued.

And, by virtue of the power and for the purpose aforesaid, I do order and declare that all persons held as slaves within said designated States and parts of States are and henceforth shall be free; and that the Executive Government of the United States, including the military and naval authorities thereof, will recognize and maintain the freedom of said persons.

And I hereby enjoin upon the people so declared to be

free, to abstain from all violence, unless in necessary self-defence; and I recommend to them that in all cases, when allowed, they labor faithfully for reasonable wages.

And I further declare and make known that such persons of suitable condition will be received into the armed service of the United States, to garrison forts, positions, stations, and other places, and to man vessels of all sorts in said service.

And upon this act, sincerely believed to be an act of justice, warranted by the Constitution, upon military necessity, I invoke the considerate judgment of mankind and the gracious favor of Almighty God.

In testimony whereof, I have hereunto set my name, and caused the seal of the United States to be affixed. Done at the City of Washington, this first day of January, in the year of our Lord one thousand eight [L. S.] hundred and sixty-three, and of the Independence of the United States the eighty-seventh.

ABRAHAM LINCOLN.

By the President:
WILLIAM H. SEWARD, *Secretary of State.*

BIBLIOGRAPHY

THE following list is intended to serve merely as an introduction to the study of our constitutional history. For general bibliographies, see Channing and Hart, *Guide to the Study of American History*, Boston, 1896, and Hart, *Manual of American History, Diplomacy, and Government*, Cambridge, 1908. Also each volume of *The American Nation* series contains a critical essay on the authorities for the period covered.

GENERAL

American Nation, The, ed. by A. B. Hart. 27 v. N. Y., 1905–1907. Vols. 10–26.
BRYCE, JAMES, *The American Commonwealth*. 2 v. 3 ed. N. Y., 1906.
COOLEY, T. M., and others. *Constitutional History as seen in the Development of American Law*. N. Y., 1889.
COXE, BRINTON, *Judicial Power and Unconstitutional Legislation*. Phila., 1893.
CURTIS, G. T., *Constitutional History of the United States from the Declaration of Independence*. 2 v. N. Y., 1889.
Documentary History of the Constitution of the United States of America, 1786–1870. 3 v. Washington, Department of State, 1894.
FORD, H. J., *The Rise and Growth of American Politics*. N. Y., 1899.
HOLST, H. VON, *The Constitutional History of the United States, 1750–1861*. 8 v. Chicago, 1877–1892.
JOHNSTON, ALEXANDER, *American Political History, 1763–1876*. Ed. by J. A. Woodburn. N. Y., 1905.
KENT, JAMES, *Commentaries on American Law*. 4 v. 14 ed. Boston, 1896.

McKee, T. J., *National Conventions and Platforms.* Baltimore, 1906.

Merriam, C. E., *American Political Theories.* N. Y., 1903.

Messages and Papers of the Presidents. 10 v. Washington, 1899.

Stephens, Alexander H., *Constitutional View of the Late War between the States.* 2 v. Philadelphia, 1868–1870.

Story, Joseph, *Commentaries on the Constitution of the United States.* 2 v. 5 ed. Boston, 1891.

Thorpe, F. N., *The Constitutional History of the American People.* 1776–1850. 2 v. N. Y., 1898.

United States Supreme Court Reports: Dallas, 1790–1800; Cranch, 1801–1815; Wheaton, 1816–1827; Peters, 1828–1842; Howard, 1843–1860; Black, 1861–1862; Wallace, 1863–1874; U. S. Reports, 1875–

The Constitutional Convention

Documentary History of the Constitution of the United States of America. 1786–1870. Vol. iii.

Elliot, *Debates.* 5 vols. New reprint. Philadelphia, 1888.

Farrand, Max, *The Compromises of the Constitution,* in *The American Historical Review,* April, 1904.

——— *The Records of the Federal Convention,* in *Am. Hist. Rev.* Oct., 1907.

Federalist, eds. by Paul Leicester Ford, N. Y., 1898, and H. C. Lodge, N. Y., 1904.

Fiske, John, *The Critical Period of American History.* Boston and N. Y., 1899.

Ford, Paul Leicester, *Pamphlets on the Constitution of the United States,* published during its discussion by the people, 1787–1788. Edited with notes and a bibliography. Brooklyn, 1888.

Hamilton, Alexander, *Notes on the Federal Constitution of 1787,* in *Am. Hist. Rev.* Oct., 1904.

Jameson, J. F., *Studies in the History of the Federal Convention.* Annual Report of the American Historical Association. 1902.

King, Rufus, *Life and Correspondence,* edited by C. R. King, N. Y., 1894–1900. Vol. i., Appendix contains King's Notes of the Constitutional Convention of 1787.

MADISON, JAMES, *Writings*, ed. by Gaillard Hunt. 7 v. N. Y., 1900–1908. Vols. iii. and iv. contain the Journal of the Constitutional Convention.

MCHENRY, JAMES, *Papers on the Federal Convention of 1787*, in *Am. Hist. Rev.* April, 1906.

MCLAUGHLIN, A. C., *The Confederation and the Constitution*. N. Y., 1905. (American Nation Series.)

MARTIN, LUTHER, *Genuine Information*, in *Elliot's Debates*, vol. i.

MEIGS, WM. M., *The Growth of the Constitution in the Federal Convention of 1787*. Phila., 1900.

PATERSON, WILLIAM, *Papers on the Federal Convention of 1787*, in *Am. Hist. Rev.* Jan., 1904.

PIERCE, WILLIAM, *Notes on the Federal Convention of 1787*, in *Am. Hist. Rev.* Jan., 1898.

YATES, ROBERT, *Secret Proceedings and Debates of the Convention Assembled at Philadelphia, 1787, for the Purpose of Forming the Constitution of the United States* in *Elliot's Debates*, vol. i.

HAMILTON

BASSETT, J. S., *The Federalist System, 1789–1801*. N. Y., 1906. (Am. Nat. Ser.)

HAMILTON, ALEXANDER, *Works*, ed. by H. C. Lodge. Constitutional Edition. N. Y., 1904.

HAMILTON, J. C., *History of the Republic . . . as Traced in the Writings of Alexander Hamilton and his Contemporaries*. 7 v. 4 ed. Boston, 1879.

HAMILTON, J. C., *Life of Alexander Hamilton*. 2 v. N. Y., 1840.

LODGE, H. C., *Alexander Hamilton*. Boston and N. Y. 1886. (American Statesmen Ser.)

MORSE, J. T., JR., *Life of Alexander Hamilton*. 2 v. Boston, 1882.

MULFORD, R. J., *The Political Theories of Alexander Hamilton*. (Johns Hopkins University Thesis, 1903.)

OLIVER, FREDERICK SCOTT, *Alexander Hamilton. An Essay on American Union*. New edition. N. Y., 1907.

SUMNER, W. G., *Alexander Hamilton*. N. Y., 1890. (Makers of America Ser.)

WILSON

ALEXANDER, L. H., *James Wilson, Patriot, and the Wilson Doctrine* in *North American Review*, vol. 183, No. 8. Mid-Nov. 1906.

KONKLE, B. A., *James Wilson and the Constitution*. Phil., 1907.

MCLAUGHLIN, A. C., *James Wilson and the Constitution* in *Pol. Sc. Qt.* March, 1897.

MCMASTER and STONE, *Pennsylvania and the Federal Constitution*. Lancaster, Pa., 1888.

SANDERSON, J., *Biography of the Signers of the Declaration of Independence*. Vol. iii., pp. 259–301. Phil., 1828.

WILSON, JAMES, *Works*, ed. by James DeWitt Andrews. 2 v. Chicago, 1896.

JEFFERSON

ADAMS, HENRY, *History of the United States, 1801–1817*. 9 v. N. Y., 1889–91. Vols. i.–iv.

CHANNING, EDWARD, *The Jeffersonian System, 1801–1811*. N. Y., 1906. (Am. Nat. Ser.)

JEFFERSON, THOMAS, *Writings*. Memorial Edition. 20 v. Washington, 1903–1904.

——Also editions by P. L. Ford, 10 v. N. Y., 1892–1899, and by H. A. Washington, 9 v. N. Y., 1861.

MORSE, J. T., Jr., *Thomas Jefferson*. Boston and N. Y., 1895. (Amer. Stat. Ser.)

PARTON, JAMES, *Life of Thomas Jefferson*. 2 v. Boston, 1874.

RANDALL, H. S., *Life of Thomas Jefferson*. 3 v. N. Y., 1858.

SCHOULER, JAMES, *Thomas Jefferson*. N. Y., 1893. (Makers of America Ser.)

TUCKER, GEORGE, *Life of Thomas Jefferson*. 2 v. Philadelphia, 1837.

MADISON

ADAMS, HENRY, *History of the United States*. Vols. v.–ix.

BABCOCK, K. C., *The Rise of American Nationality, 1811–1819*. N. Y., 1906. (Am. Nat. Ser.)

GAY, S. W., *James Madison*. Boston and N. Y., 1899. (Amer. Stat. Ser.)

HUNT, GAILLARD, *Life of James Madison*. N. Y. 1902.

MADISON, JAMES, *Letters and other Writings*. 4 v. Phil., 1865.

——*Writings*. Ed. by Gaillard Hunt. 7 v. N. Y., 1900–1908.

RIVES, W. C., *History of the Life and Times of James Madison.* 3 v. Boston, 1859–1863.

MARSHALL

CARSON, H. L., *The Supreme Court of the United States.* 2 v. Phil., 1891.
Constitutional Decisions of John Marshall. Ed. by Joseph P. Cotton, Jr. N. Y. 1905.
FLANDERS, HENRY, *Life of John Marshall,* in *Lives and Times of the Chief Justices of the United States.* Vol. ii., pp. 279–550.
MAGRUDER, A. B., *John Marshall.* Boston, 1887. (Amer. Stat. Ser.)
PHILLIPS, U. B., *Georgia and State Rights,* in *Annual Report of Am. Hist. Assoc.,* 1901. Vol. ii. Washington, 1902.
VAN SANTVOORD, GEORGE, *Sketches of the Lives of the Chief Justices of the United States.* Vol. iv., pp. 293–456. N. Y., 1854.

JACKSON

BENTON, THOMAS H., *Thirty Years' View; or, a History of the Working of the American Government for Thirty Years, from 1820 to 1850.* 2 v. N. Y., 1854–1856.
BUELL, A. C., *History of Andrew Jackson.* N. Y., 1904.
BURGESS, JOHN W., *The Middle Period.* N. Y., 1905.
JACKSON, ANDREW, *Statesmanship of, as Told in his Writings and Speeches.* Ed. by F. N. Thorpe. N. Y., 1909.
MCDONALD, WILLIAM, *Jacksonian Democracy, 1829–1837.* N. Y., 1906. (Am. Nat. Scr.)
PARTON, JAMES, *Life of Andrew Jackson.* 3 v. N. Y., 1860.
PECK, C. H., *The Jacksonian Epoch.* N. Y. and London, 1899.
POWELL, E. P., *Nullification and Secession in the United States.* N. Y., 1897.
ROYALL, W. S., *Andrew Jackson and the Bank of the United States.* N. Y., 1880.
SUMNER, W. G., *Andrew Jackson as a Public Man.* Boston and N. Y., 1899. (Am. Stat. Ser.)
TURNER, FREDERICK J., *The Rise of the New West, 1819–1829.* N. Y., 1906. (Am. Nat. Ser.)

WEBSTER

BENTON, *Thirty Years' View.*

Burgess, *The Middle Period.*
Hart, A. B., *Slavery and Abolition, 1831-1841.* N. Y., 1906. (Am. Nat. Ser.)
Loring, C. W., *Nullification, Secession, Webster's Argument, and the Kentucky and Virginia Resolutions Considered in Reference to the Constitution and Historically.* N. Y., 1893.
McMaster, J. B., *Daniel Webster.* N. Y., 1902.
Powell, E. P., *Nullification and Secession in the United States.*
Taussig, F. W., *The Tariff History of the United States.* 6th ed. N. Y. and London, 1905.
Writings and Speeches of Daniel Webster. National edition. 18 v. Boston, 1903.

Calhoun

Calhoun, John C., *Correspondence.* Ed. by J. F. Jameson in Annual Report of the American Historical Association for 1899. Vol. 2. Washington, 1901.
—— *Works.* Ed. by R. K. Crallé. 6 v. N. Y., 1861-1874.
Curry, J. L. M., *Civil History of the Government of the Confederate States.* Richmond, 1901.
Davis, Jefferson, *Rise and Fall of the Confederate Government.* 3 v. N. Y., 1881.
Houston, D. F., *A Critical Study of Nullification in South Carolina.* N. Y. and London, 1896. (Harvard Historical Studies.)
Holst, H. von, *John C. Calhoun.* Boston and N. Y., 1899. (Am. Stat. Ser.)
Hunt, Gaillard, *John C. Calhoun.* Philadelphia, 1908. (American Crisis Biographies.)
Powell, *Nullification and Secession.*

Lincoln

Brooks, Noah, *Abraham Lincoln and the Downfall of American Slavery.* N. Y., 1894. (Heroes of the Nations.)
Burgess, John W., *The Civil War and the Constitution, 1859-1865.* 2 v. N. Y., 1901.
Dunning, W. A., *Essays on the Civil War and Reconstruction.* N. Y., 1898.
Lincoln, Abraham, *Complete Works.* Ed. by Nicolay and Hay. 12 v. New ed. N. Y., 1905.
McCarthy, C. H., *Lincoln's Plan of Reconstruction.* N. Y., 1901.

MORSE, J. T., Jr., *Abraham Lincoln.* 2 v. Boston and N. Y., 1903. (Am. Stat. Ser.)
NICOLAY, J. G., *A Short Life of Abraham Lincoln.* N. Y., 1904.
NICOLAY and HAY, *Abraham Lincoln; a History.* 10 v. N. Y., 1890.
RHODES, JAMES FORD, *History of the United States from the Compromise of 1850.* (1850–1877.) 7 v. N. Y., 1893–1906.
SMITH, T. C., *Parties and Slavery, 1850–1859.* N. Y., 1906. (Am. Nat. Ser.)
TARBELL, IDA M., *Life of Abraham Lincoln.* 2 v. N. Y., 1900.

STEVENS

BLAINE, JAMES G., *Twenty Years of Congress; from Lincoln to Garfield.* 2 v. Norwich, Conn., 1884–1886.
BURGESS, JOHN W., *Reconstruction and the Constitution.* N. Y., 1905.
CALLENDER, E., *Thaddeus Stevens; Commoner.* Boston, 1882.
Congressional Globe, 1859–1868, passim for Stevens's speeches.
DUNNING, W. A., *Essays on the Civil War and Reconstruction.* N. Y., 1898.
——*Reconstruction, Political and Economic.* N. Y., 1907. (Am. Nat. Ser.)
MCCALL, SAMUEL W., *Thaddeus Stevens.* Boston and N. Y., 1899. (Am. Stat. Ser.)
RHODES, *History of the United States.*

ROOSEVELT

COOLIDGE, A. C., *The United States as a World Power.* N. Y., 1908.
DEWEY, D. R., *National Problems, 1885–1897.* N. Y., 1907. (Am. Nat. Ser.)
GIDDINGS, FRANKLIN W., *Democracy and Empire.* N. Y., 1900.
HOBSON, J. A., *Imperialism, a Study.* N. Y., 1902.
JORDAN, DAVID STARR, *Imperial Democracy.* N. Y., 1899.
LATANÉ, J. H., *America the World Power, 1897–1907.* N. Y., 1907.
PIERCE, FRANKLIN, *Federal Usurpation.* N. Y., 1908.
RIIS, JACOB A., *Theodore Roosevelt, the Citizen.* N. Y., 1904.
Roosevelt Policy, The; Speeches, Letters and State Papers, Relating to Corporate Wealth and Closely Allied Topics of Theodore Roosevelt. N. Y., 1908.

Roosevelt Doctrine, The; being the Personal Utterances of the President on Various Matters of Vital Interest. Compiled by E. E. Garrison, N. Y., 1904.

SPARKS, E. E., *National Development, 1877–1885.* N. Y., 1907. (Am. Nat. Ser.)

STIMSON, F. J., *The American Constitution.* N. Y., 1908.

INDEX

A

Adams, John, leader in political discussion, 5; not a delegate to Constitutional Convention, 12; member of the committee to draft the Declaration of Independence, 83; appointed to negotiate commercial treaties, 88; malignant assaults upon him, 95; commissioned Marbury Justice of the Peace, 133

Adams, J. Q., elected President by the House of Representatives, 157; had deserted the Federalist party, 160; supports the right of petition, 173

Adams, Samuel, leader in political discussion, 5

Alien and Sedition Acts, 95, 171; surpassed in their infringement upon individual liberty, 100; broke supremacy of Federalist party, 112

American Insurance Co. v. Canter, 144

Annapolis Convention, considered commercial relations, 8; Hamilton drafted address of, 9; recommended a general convention, 9; Madison's part in, 107–108

Articles of Confederation, see Confederation

B

Bank, National, advocated by Hamilton, **37**; established, 46; constitutionality of, 48; second United States Bank attacked by Jackson, 160; Webster's attitude toward, 185; text of Jefferson's opinion on the constitutionality of, 315 *ff*; text of Hamilton's opinion, 318 *ff*

Bedford declares small States will seek foreign ally rather than submit to compulsion of Virginia plan, 16

Benjamin, Senator, accused Douglas of breaking faith with the South, 218

Bibliography, 377 *ff*

Biddle, "Nick," 161

Bill of Rights, *see* **Rights**

Blaine, J. G., 232

Brearly proposed partition of United States into thirteen equal parts, 62

Buchanan, President, attitude toward Secession, 221; believed Congress was powerless to prevent Secession, 235

Burr, defended by Jackson in public harangue, 154

Butler, interests of North and South as different as those of Russia and Turkey, 20; advocates including blacks equally with whites in rule of representation, 20

C

Calhoun, John C., advances idea of indivisibility of sov-

Calhoun, John C.—*Continued*
ereignty, 124; logical successor of Roane, 145; elected Vice-President, 157; opposed by Jackson in 1832, 162 *ff*; course contrasted with that of Webster, 171–172, 191–194; chairman of the Committee on Foreign Affairs and an advocate of the War of 1812, 171, 192; resigned office of Vice-President and elected Senator, 179; argument on Nullification, 179–180; historical argument, 184; chronology, 190; sketch of his life, 190 *ff*; the product of a new era, 192; Secretary of War and Vice-President, 194; change from national views, 195; "South Carolina Exposition," a programme of Nullification, 195; disappointed in hope of relief from Jackson, 196; guiding spirit in South Carolina's action, 196; opposed by President Jackson, 197; secures reduction of the tariff, 198; love for the Union, 198; views as to the nature of the Union, 199 *ff*; the Constitution a compact, 199–200, 205–206; contradiction in his view of democracy, 200; developed the idea of a "concurrent majority," 201; rejects the theory of social contract, 202; origin of society natural, of government, by contract, 203; logical character of his thought, 204; change in meaning of words due to change in philosophical thought, 205–206; sovereignty regarded as indivisible and located in the individual States, 206; attitude toward s l a v e r y, 207; proposed amendment to the Constitution to avoid the dangers of disunion, 207

California, question of admission as a free State, 234

Chase, Justice, 132

Checks and balances, system of, in Federal Government, 25, 128

Cherokee nation *v.* State of Georgia, 164

Chisholm *v.* Georgia, 72, 132

Civil Rights Bill, 245

Civil War, possibility of averting it by vigorous action in 1832, 163; began with firing on Fort Sumter, 237; effect of, upon theory of our government, 261

Clay, Henry, representative of new spirit of the West, 121; favors J. Q. Adams's election in House of Representatives, 157; leader of the opposition to Jackson, 158; leader in forcing on the War of 1812, 171; the "great compromiser," 177; representative of national spirit of the West, 192

Clinton, Governor, view of New York's relation to the Union, 37–38

Cohens *v.* Virginia, 138, 139

Colonies, union of, to throw off oppression, 7; acquisition of, by the United States, 255

Colonists, political theories of the, 5; influenced by Locke and Montesquieu, 6; developed new phase of rights, 6

Commerce, no power in the Confederation to regulate, 8; regulation by Congress, 22–23; "commerce clause" of Constitution b a s i s of large federal powers, 23; power of Congress to regulate, 143; "commerce clause" source of much of recent g r o w t h of Constitution, 269

Compromise, Constitution, the

Index

Compromise—*Continued*
result of, 4; first, between large and small States, 14; "Connecticut," 16–17; second, on slave enumeration in representation, 20–22; third, on regulation of commerce, 22–23; fourth, on character of Executive, 23–25; produced a government "partly national and partly federal," 30; between the Federal Government and South Carolina, 198; compromise of 1850, 211; to reconcile the South, 235

Confederate States of America established, 220, 236

Confederation, weakness of, 7, 109; lack of power to regulate commerce, 8; need of money, 46

Confederation, Articles of, come into existence, 6; amendment of, rejected by Convention, 13; equality of States under, 14; Hamilton believed, must be swept away, 36; appeals of the Annapolis Convention for revision of, 37; text of the, 279 *ff*

Confederation, Congress of, large powers, but no adequate means of enforcing them, 7; no power to regulate commerce, 8; calls Constitutional Convention, 10

Confiscation favored by Stevens, 238

Congress, representation in, 17–18, 21–22; given power to regulate interstate and foreign commerce, 23; leadership passes from the Executive to Congress, 193; power over slavery, 213; Thaddeus Stevens a leader of, 231; regarded by President Buchanan as powerless to prevent Secession, 235; attempts of, at reconciliation with the South, 235; special session of, July 4, 1861, 237; representation in, of the reconstructed States, 243, 249; right of, to regulate the government of national territory, 261

Congressional caucus, 158

Connecticut Compromise adopted, 16–17

Constitution, the story of, 3; not solely the written instrument, 4; the result of compromise, 4; literary finish of, due to Gouverneur Morris, 11; ratification of, by conventions of nine States necessary for its adoption, 13; growth through interpretation, 26; influence of the *Federalist* upon adoption of, 41; Hamilton's view as to the nature of the, 43; "loose" and "strict" construction of, 48–50; not a compact according to Wilson, 70; bounds of "loose" construction of the, passed, 96; "strict" construction of the, and the purchase of Louisiana, 98; regarded by Madison as the social and governmental contract, 115; does not follow the flag, 120, 259; worship of the, 129; "efficiency" of the, demonstrated, 132–135; effect of Jackson upon the, 158 *ff;* whether or not a compact, 177; Webster's argument, 179 *ff;* Calhoun's, 199–200, 205–206; recognition of slavery by the, 213; regarded as indissoluble by Lincoln, 222; proposed amendment to secure slavery, 235; regarded by Stevens as destroyed in the seceding States, 239; development of the, due to territorial and commercial expansion, 255 *ff;* text of the, 292 *ff*

Constitutional Convention, chronology, 2; character of delegates in the, 10; declares that a national government ought to be established, 13; decides to admit new States on terms of equality with the old, 19; main features of the government elaborated by the, 25; withdrawal from the, of Yates and Lansing, 38; of Hamilton, 40; Wilson's part in the, 60 *ff*; Madison's part in the, 107 *ff*; alliance in the, of advocates of State-Rights and of democracy, 200

Constitutionality, *see* Law

Continental Congress, 33

Contract, origin of society and of government in, 5; the social, regarded as basis of society by Wilson, 67; by Madison, 115; the obligation of, not to be impaired by law, 174; as basis of society rejected by Calhoun, 202

Cooper, Dr. Miles, President of King's College, 33

Cooper *v.* Telfair, 132

Cooper Union speech, 219–220

Cornwallis, 106

Corporations, effect of, on constitutional development, 255, 265 *ff*; have menaced safety of society, 266

Cotton, made the "staple product" of the South by the invention of the cotton-gin, 22

Crawford, 157, 158

Critical Period of American History, 7; influence of, missed by Jefferson, 90

Crittenden Resolution opposed by Stevens, 238

D

Dartmouth College case, 144, 174

Davis, Jefferson, elected President of the Confederacy, 236

Declaration of Independence, incorporated the rights of man, 6; text of, 273 *ff*; of South Carolina, 366 *ff*;

Democracy, development of, in colonies, 5; spirit of, embodied in Jefferson, 79; contrast between Jefferson's ideas and modern democracy, 80; distrust of, in Constitutional Convention, 128; contrast between Jeffersonian and Jacksonian democracy, 149–151; triumph of real democracy in Jackson's election, 158–160

Democratic party, Jackson's followers adopt the name of, 157; control of Congress by, feared by the Republicans, 231

Democratic-Republican party, beginning of, as party of "strict" construction, 54–55; organization of, by Jefferson, 94; opposed the Alien and Sedition acts, 95, 112; swallowed up the Federalist party, 99, 129; Jefferson the leader of, 112; modification of principles of, under Jefferson and Madison, 119; success of, in 1800 not complete, 127, 149; unable to overthrow the constructive measures of Federalists, 98, 129; belief in the multitude and local self-government, 149

Dickinson, John, leader in political discussion, 5; delegate to Constitutional Convention, 11

Douglas, Stephen A., author of doctrine of "Squatter Sovereignty," 211, 216; fathered the Kansas–Nebraska Bill and espoused the Dred Scott decision, 216; contradiction between doctrine of "Popular Sovereignty" and the Dred Scott decision, 217

Dred Scott decision, declared Congress and the Territorial Legislatures impotent to prohibit slavery in the national domain, 214; abstract of, 362 ff

Duane, letter to, from Hamilton, on weakness of the Confederation, 36

Dulaney, leader in political discussion, 5

E

"Elastic Clause," of the Constitution, 48

Ellsworth, Oliver, delegate to Constitutional Convention, 10; favors proportional representation in one branch and equality of the States in the other, 17

Emancipation Proclamation, issued by Lincoln, 226; text of, 374 ff

Embargo, 100, 171

Enforcing acts, 100

Entail abolished in Virginia, 85

"Era of Good Feeling," 157

Executive, the, differences of opinion in the Convention regarding, 23-24; kind of, brings aristocratic and democratic elements in Convention into opposition, 24; direct election of, advocated by Wilson, 61; decision of, on political policies, is conclusive, 136; raised to a position of supremacy by Jackson, 156; power of, sinks with Jackson's retirement from the Presidency, 165; power of, increased under Lincoln, 224; recedes after the war, 254; position of, affected by Imperialism, 260

Expansion, key-note of last ten years, 256; as result of Spanish War different from that which had preceded, 258; of recent kind not foreseen by the framers of the Constitution, 259; has increased the centralizing tendencies of the Federal Government, 260; has strengthened the position of the Executive, 260

F

"Fathers, The," 4; distrust of democracy, 128

Federal Government, entrusted with all matters of common interest, 25, 70; regarded as judge of its own powers, 43, 133-136, 138; need of firm financial footing, 46; strengthening effect of Hamilton's policy upon the, 48-49; Wilson's conception of the, 56, 60; no league but a national government, 117; a government of limited powers, 136; power of, to maintain itself against disunion, 162; centralizing tendencies of the, increased by colonial expansion, 260; undertakes new functions, 264

Federal State, idea of a, 56; nature of a, stated by Wilson, 64

Federal Union, nature of, discussed by Wilson, 65, 69; by Madison, 114 ff; nationalizing effect upon, of War of 1812, 120; nature of, in Webster's view, 176 ff; in Calhoun's, 199 ff

Federalist, the, major portion written by Hamilton, 41; Madison and Jay contributors to, 41; influence upon adoption of Constitution, 41; written with a purpose, 66

Federalist party, beginning of, as party of "loose" construction, 54-55; Hamilton the leader of, 94; passed the Alien and Sedition Acts, 95, 112; absorbed by De-

Federalist party—*Continued*
mocratic-Republicans, 99, 129; feared the weakening effects of victory of Democratic-Republicans on Federal Government, 150
Fifteenth Amendment, logical result of reconstruction legislation, 249
Fletcher v. Peck, 174
Foote Resolution, 175
Force Bill, 179
Fort Sumter, firing on, the beginning of war, 237
Fourteenth Amendment, provisions of, 246; rejected by Southern States with exception of Tennessee, 248; adoption by Southern States made a condition of their being entitled to representation in Congress, 249
Franklin, Benjamin, delegate to Constitutional Convention, 11; proposed Convention should open with prayer, 17; member of committee to draft the Declaration of Independence, 83; appointed to negotiate commercial treaties, 88
Free Soilers led by Thaddeus Stevens, 233
Freedman's Bureau Bill, 245
"Freeport heresy," 218
Fugitive Slave Law, influence of, upon Stevens, 233; cause of irritation, 234; revision of, as a concession to the South, 235

G

Genêt, 95
Gerry, Elbridge, delegate to Constitutional Convention, 10; moved to prevent number of representatives in lower house from new States ever exceeding that of the old States, 19; attributes evils to democracy, 39; special envoy to France, 131

Gibbons v. Ogden, 143
Government, questions of, fought out in law courts and public prints, 5; self-, in the colonies, 5; origin of, in contract, 5; strength in, necessary to liberty, 7; difference between federal and national form of, 13; national form of, approved by the Convention, 13; aim of, 20; separation of powers of, in Federal Government, 25; true nature of the Federal Government not determined by the Constitution, 30; Hamilton's views as to the separation of the powers of, 45

H

Hamilton, Alexander, saw need of common commercial regulations, 8; drafted address of Annapolis Convention, 9; delegate to Constitutional Convention, 11; on its authority, 13; disapproves of both the Virginia and the New Jersey plan, 17; chronology, 28; foresaw the possibility of growth in national government, 30; services in forming the Constitution and inaugurating the government, 30; relationship with Washington, 31, 35; sketch of his career, 31 *ff*; first public speech and writings, 34; military career, 34–35; national feeling of, 36; member of Continental Congress, 35; letter to Duane on weakness of the Confederation and plan of national bank, 36–37; in the Annapolis Convention, 37; chosen a delegate to the Constitutional Convention, 38; distrust of democracy, 39; presents his plan of Union, 39; withdrew from Convention, 40; writes major

Hamilton, Alexander—
Continued
portion of *Federalist*, 41; defeats Clinton in New York Convention and secures adoption of Constitution, 42; view as to nature of Constitution and the Federal Government, 43 *ff*; attitude toward a Bill of Rights, 45; appointed Secretary of the Treasury, 46; carries through Congress the Assumption Acts, Excise Bill, and National Bank Act, 46; Tariff Act, 47; attitude toward "implied powers," 48; became the head of the Federalist party, 49; opposed by Jefferson, 49–50; resigned as Secretary of Treasury, 50; idea of government contrasted with that of Wilson and of Jefferson, 80; part in location of national capital, 91; estimate of Jefferson's character, 98; text of opinion as to the constitutionality of the Bank of the United States, 318 *ff*

Hartford Convention, 176, 180; text of the amendments to the Constitution proposed by the, 337 *ff*

Hayes–Tilden election, 253

Hayne, Nullification argument replied to by Webster, 175, 179

Henry, Patrick, leader in political discussion, 5; not a delegate to the Constitutional Convention, 12

House of Representatives, proportional representation in, 17–18; eventual power of electing a President, 25

I

Impeachment rejected as a "political proceeding," 250

Imperialism, ushered in by the Spanish War, 255; effect of, upon the position of the President, 260

"Implied powers," Hamilton's views on the, 48; doctrine of, accepted by the Supreme Court, 138, 142

Industrialism, questions of, linked with Imperialism, 255; individualism and free competition as basis of, have given way to combination, 266

Inherent powers possessed by the Federal Government, 72

Interpretation, peculiar prominence of, in our system of government, 26; Hamilton's view regarding, 37; growth of the Constitution through legal, 127 *ff*

J

Jackson, Andrew, chronology, 148; unconscious embodiment of new conditions, 151; sketch of life, 152 *ff*; public harangue in defence of Burr, 154; conception of democracy, 154 *ff*; introduced "spoils system" into the national administration, 156; raised the Executive to position of supremacy, 156; victory at New Orleans, 156; Seminole War, 156; defeated for the presidency, 157; followers of, take name of Democrats, 157; effects of Jackson's election, 158 *ff*; Executive regarded as direct representative of the people, 158, 164; works third revolution in our history, 160; elected on anti-Hamilton platform, 160; fight with the Bank, 160 *ff*; second administration almost a fight between classes, 161; influence upon national development, 161; proclamation against Nullification, 162, 179; asserts equal right of

Jackson, Andrew—*Continued*
President to pass on constitutionality of laws, 164; condemned for assumption of unconstitutionality of the Bank, 164, and for refusal to carry out the judgment of the Supreme Court, 165; hatred of, for Marshall and Calhoun, 197; text of proclamation, 345 *ff*

Jay contributes to *Federalist*, 41

Jefferson, Thomas, not a delegate to Constitutional Convention, 12; opposed a national bank, 49; opposition to Hamilton, 49-50; retired from the Cabinet, 50; chronology, 78; embodiment of spirit of democracy, 79; cardinal political principles, 79; idea of government contrasted with that of Hamilton and of Wilson, 80; sketch of his life, 81 *ff*; author of Declaration of Independence, 83; work in the Virginia House of Delegates, 84-87; entail and primogeniture, 85; religious freedom, 85-86; education, 86; drew up civil and criminal code, 86; attitude toward slavery, 86; governor of Virginia, 87-88; member of Congress, 88; signed treaty of peace with Great Britain, 88; minister to France, 88; relation to French Revolution, 89; attitude toward proposed Constitution, 90-91; appointed Secretary of State, 91; part in location of national capital, 91; opposition to Hamilton, 92-93; regarded Hamilton's financial measures as a puzzle, 92; professed to fear the destruction by Hamilton of republican government, 93; organizes a political party, 94-95; triumph due largely to influence of foreign affairs, 95, and to Alien and Sedition Acts, 95; believed bounds of "loose" construction had been passed, 96; wrote the original draft of the Kentucky Resolutions, 97, 112; triumph did not lessen strength of Federal Government, 98; purchase of Louisiana, 98, regarded as unconstitutional, 99; retirement to Monticello, 100; text of opinion on the constitutionality of a national bank, 315 *ff*

Johnson, Andrew, attitude toward Lincoln's plan of Reconstruction, 231; early attitude of hostility to the South soon changed, 231; plan of Reconstruction proposed, 243; but discredited with Congress, 244, 245; "swinging around the circle," 247; impeachment of, 249

Johnson, Dr., proposed that in one branch the people, and in the other, the States, ought to be represented, 17

K

Kansas-Nebraska Bill, 211; threw open the Territories to slavery, 214; fathered by Douglas, 216

Kentucky Resolutions, 50, 95, 96, 133, 139, 171, 176, 180; Jefferson's draft of, 97, 112; advocate right of revolution, Madison said, 98; views of, advanced in Richmond *Enquirer*, 139; claimed as lawful source of Nullification, 195; text, 326 *ff*

King, Rufus, delegate to Constitutional Convention, 10; would prohibit number of representatives in lower house from new States ever exceeding that of the old States, 19

Index

L

Labor unions, a controlling factor in modern industrial world, 265; have menaced safety of society, 266
Lansing, supports Paterson's plan, 15; delegate from New York to the Constitutional Convention, 38; discusses the Virginia and the New Jersey plans, 63
Law, power to determine constitutionality of, 113; located in Supreme Court, 113; asserted by Marshall, 133
Legal tender, issue of, advocated by Stevens, 240
Lewis, William B., Jackson's political manager, 157
Lincoln, Abraham, chronology, 210; sketch of his life, 212 *ff*; attitude toward slavery, 213; opposition to the Dred Scott decision, 215; fear of extension of slavery to the free States, 216; joins Republican party, 216; rivalry with Douglas and the senatorial contest of 1858, 216 *ff*; not an abolitionist, 217; debates with Douglas, 217 *ff*; position on the slavery question when a presidential candidate, 219; Cooper Union speech, 220; Secession changes issue from extension of slavery to preservation of the Union, 221; view as to the indissoluble character of the Union, 222; Secession ordinances regarded as having no legal effect, 223; use of the war-power to preserve the Union, 224; led to temporary dictatorship, 224; development of the "war-powers," 225; Emancipation Proclamation, 226; the Union regarded as more precious than the liberty of the slaves, 226–227; views on Reconstruction, 227, 242; plan of Reconstruction approved by Johnson and rejected by Congress, 231
Locke, theory of, followed by colonists, 6; idea of delegated authority followed by Hamilton, 43
Louisiana, purchase of and "strict" construction, 98; purchase of, regarded as unconstitutional by Jefferson, 99; and by Madison, 119; importance of a closer union of, realized by Jackson, 154

M

Madison, James, saw need of common commercial regulations, 8; delegate to Constitutional Convention, 12; shows coercion of State under the Confederation would be war, 15; argues against evils of New Jersey plan, 16; defended admission of new States on terms of equality with the older States, 19; antithesis of States not due to size, but to climate and to presence or absence of slaves, 20; contributes to *Federalist*, 41; aided Jefferson in Virginia legislature, 87; drafted the Virginia Resolutions, 96; regards Nullification not as a "constitutional" but as a "natural" right, 98; chronology, 102; the "Father of the Constitution," 103; leader of opposition in Congress to Hamilton's policy, 103–104; antagonism due to economic difference between the States, 104; unconscious agent of centralizing forces, 105; sketch of his life, 105 *ff*; early national tendencies, 106; part in the Constitutional Convention, 107 *ff*;

Madison, James—*Continued*
  need of fundamental change in Articles of Confederation, 109; the Federal Government a compound form, 110, 121; reaction against centralizing tendencies, 111; drafted Virginia Resolutions, 113; interpretation of the Resolutions, 114–115; regarded State as founded upon a contract, 115; rejects right of Nullification and Secession, except as revolutionary, 115–117; Union not regarded as a mere league, 117; appointed Secretary of State, 118; faults as an executive officer, 118; opposed purchase of Louisiana, 119; nationalizing effects of his career, 119–121; War of 1812 forced upon him, 120; retired from the Presidency, 121; retirement spent largely in expounding the Constitution, 121–122; untenable position of "Madisonian Federalism," 122; attitude toward sovereignty, 123; refused to issue Marbury his commission, 133; protests against the use of Jefferson's name in support of Nullification, 195
Madisonian Federalism, 122
Marbury v. Madison, 71, 113, 133, 137, 139; abstract of decision in the case of, 335 *ff*
Marshall, seized possibilities of "commerce clause" of Constitution, 23; anticipated by Wilson, 71; asserts power of Supreme Court to declare a law unconstitutional, 113; chronology, 126; interprets Constitution in national sense, 127–129; "expounder of the Constitution," 130; sketch of his life, 130 *ff*; demonstrates the "efficiency" of the Constitution, 132–135; and the "extent" of the judicial power of Supreme Court, 137–143; contests with the Virginia courts, 137–143; approves doctrine of "implied powers," 141–143; lays down fundamental principles of "commerce clause," 143; Dartmouth College case, 144; establishes right of the Union to acquire territory, 144; in conflict with Jackson, 164
Martin, Luther, delegate to Constitutional Convention, 11; supporter of the rights of the small States, 11; opposes Virginia plan, 16
Martin v. Hunter's lessee, 138
Mason, George, delegate to Constitutional Convention, 11; defended admission of new States on terms of equality with the older States, 19
McCulloch v. Maryland, 138
Mexican War, Lincoln's attitude toward, 212; brought question of the extension of slavery to the front, 234
Mississippi, dispute concerning free navigation of, 9; cession of Mississippi valley to Spain opposed by Madison, 106; importance of, appreciated by Jackson, 154
Missouri Compromise, passed, 172; repealed, 211
Monroe, 157
Monroe doctrine reformulated by Roosevelt, 263
Montesquieu, influenced American thought, 6; separation of powers of government based upon a misconception, 44
Monticello, Sage of, 100
Morocco, United States participates in conference on, 264
Morris, Gouverneur, delegate to Constitutional Convention, 11; stated difference between federal and national government, 13; feared control of

Index

Morris, Gouverneur—*Continued*
the Atlantic States by the West, 19; moved that representatives and direct taxes should be apportioned according to numbers, 21

Morris, Robert, delegate to Constitutional Convention, 11; loss of his fortune affected his reputation, 58

N

National Anti-Slavery Society established, 186

National Bank, *see* Bank

National Government, vote of the Constitutional Convention to establish a, 13; growth of the power of the, 25

Nature, state of, eighteenth-century view of, 5; according to Wilson, not a state of war, 67

Navigation Act, passage of a, by Congress desired by the Eastern and Middle States, 22

Negro suffrage, adoption of, forced on the Southern States, 249

New England opposed the War of 1812, 192

New Jersey plan, equality of States retained in, 15; centre of the struggle between the large and the small States, 15, 39; presented by Paterson, 15, 63; discussed, and rejected, 63

North, the, difference between, and the South, 20; felt the force of national sentiment, 170; rejects Nullification and Secession as destructive of the Union, 185; attitude of, toward the Fugitive Slave Law, 234

Nullification, by a single State not intended by Jefferson, 98; support sought for in Virginia Resolutions, 114; rejected by Madison, 115-117; secession its logical successor, 130, 177; attacked by Jackson, 162; defended by Hayne, 175; who asserted right of each State to judge as to the constitutionality of laws, 182; asserted to be a constitutional right, 184; declared revolutionary by Webster, 184; programme of, set forth by Calhoun, 195; text of South Carolina ordinance of, 340 *ff*

O

Ordinance of Secession of South Carolina, text, 368

Otis, James, leader in political discussion, 5

P

Pacific Blockade of Venezuelan port regretted by Roosevelt, 263

Paine, Thomas, champion of democracy, 5; *Common Sense*, 83

Pakenham, 156

Panama Canal, building of, made possible by Roosevelt, 264

Paterson, William, delegate to Constitutional Convention, 11; presented New Jersey plan, 15, 63; contests right of Convention to vary idea of equal sovereignty, 15, 62; discusses the two plans, 63

Pinckney, Charles, delegate to Constitutional Convention, 12; difference between North and South due to divergent economic interests, 20

Pinckney, C. C., delegate to Constitutional Convention, 12; advocates including blacks equally with whites in rule of representation, 20; abolition of slave trade an invitation to South Caro-

Pinckney, C. C.—*Continued*
lina to withdraw from the
Union, 22; special envoy to
France, 131
Primogeniture abolished in
Virginia, 85

R

Randolph, Edmund, delegate
to Constitutional Convention, 12; on the authority of
the Convention to go beyond
mere amendment of the
Articles of Confederation,
13; presented Virginia plan,
15; defines national plan
as a resort to national legislation over individuals,
16
Reconstruction, Lincoln's views
of, 227; Lincoln's theory of,
227, 242; period of, begun,
231; Stevens, the dictator of
the early period of, 237;
Stevens's "conquered province," theory of, 243; effects of Johnson's plan of,
244; by Executive opposed
by Stevens, 245; by Congress, 247–249; dependent
upon adoption of Fourteenth
Amendment, 249; military
governments during, 249
Religious freedom secured in
Virginia, 85–86
Representation, equal under
Articles of Confederation,
14; under Constitution, proportional in lower house,
equal in Senate, 18; direct
taxes in proportion to representation, 21; slaves counted
at three-fifths ratio in, 22;
Wilson's views on, in the
Convention, 62
Republican party, Lincoln
early a member of, 216;
fears the Lincoln–Johnson
plan of Reconstruction, 231;
firm against the extension of
slavery, 235–236

Revolution, the, preceded by
political discussion, 5; no
new ideas of government developed during, 6; with close
of, national feeling weakened, 7; assured the right
to life, liberty, and the
pursuit of happiness, 12
Rights, Bills of, 6; opposed by
Hamilton, 45; lack of in the
Constitution, a cause of
Jefferson's opposition, 90;
Rights of man developed by
the colonists, 6
Roane, Judge, 138
"Roosevelt Policies," guides of
government action, 256
Roosevelt, Theodore, chronology, 252; identified with
the changes of the last ten
years, 256; sketch of his
life, 257; relation to changes,
258; influence upon the position of the Executive, 261;
leader in bringing realization of position of United
States as a world-power,
263; reformulates the Monroe Doctrine, 263; action in
San Domingo, 263; makes
Panama Canal possible, 264;
secures participation of
United States in conference
on Morocco, 264; secures admission of South and Central American States to
second Hague Conference,
264; typical of constitutional changes resulting
from modern industrial conditions, 264; influence used
to settle coal strike, 266;
perceived the dangers from
combinations of labor and of
capital, 267; theory of government, 267–268; contrasted with Jefferson and
Jackson, 268; belief in government as an organ for
the advancement of the interests of society, 268; resemblance of theory of, to
that of Wilson, 268

Rutledge, John, delegate to the Constitutional Convention, 12

S

Schuyler, Miss Elizabeth, married to Alexander Hamilton, 35
Scott, see Dred Scott
Secession, logical successor to Nullification, 130; declared revolutionary by Webster, 184; ordinance of, passed, 220, 235; regarded by Lincoln as rebellion, 221–223
Second Hague Conference, admission of South and Central American States, 264
Sedition, see Alien and Sedition Acts
Seminole, War, 156
Senate, equal representation in, proposed, 17; agreed to, 18; vote per capita, not by States, 19; equal representation in, opposed by Wilson, 62–63
Separation of the powers of government, see Government
Shays's Rebellion, in full swing, 8; alarm caused by, 9, 24
Sherman, Roger, delegate to Constitutional Convention, 10; proposes proportional representation in first branch and equality in Senate, 17; distrust of the people, 39
Slavery, belief that it would die out, 22; demands extension, 173; the great issue from days of Nullification, 185; National Anti-Slavery Society established, 186; attitude toward, of Webster, 186; of Calhoun, 196, 207; of Lincoln, 213; in the Territories, 214; existence of, the cause of difference between North and South, 225; regarded as a "positive good" by the South, 234
Slaves, counted at three-fifths ratio in enumeration for representation in lower house, 21–22; importation not to be forbidden before 1808, 23; emancipated, 226
South, the, difference between the North and, 20; slaves a special kind of property in, 20; not yet set apart in thought and feeling, 163; felt the force of national sentiment, 170; eager for the War of 1812, 192; favor of the, courted by Johnson, 231; attitude of, toward the Fugitive Slave Law, 234; acceptance by, of Johnson's plan of Reconstruction, 244
Sovereignty, Hamilton's conception of, 44; resides in the people according to Wilson 68; regarded as divisible by Madison and as indivisible by Calhoun, 123–124; meant to Calhoun the final and ultimate power of judgment, 206; of the nation, 254
Spain, dispute with, over the free navigation of the Mississippi, 8
Spanish War ushered in Imperialism, 255
Spoils System introduced into the national administration by Jackson, 156
Squatter Sovereignty, 211
State-Rights, Calhoun, the champion of, in the Senate, 196; conflict between, and democracy, 200; a new kind of, 262
States, experience of, in making constitutions, 6; attitude of the, toward the Confederation, 7; opposition between the large and the small, 14, 43–44, 62–64; real difference was between Northern and Southern, 20; Hamilton's idea of the re-

States—*Continued*
  lation of the, to the Federal Government, 44; Wilson's, 64, 69–70, 72–73, 110; Jefferson's, 96; Madison's, 109–110, 115; Marshall's, 132; Jackson's, 162; Webster's, 179; Calhoun's, 199–200; Lincoln's, 222; Stevens's, 236; Roosevelt's, 261–262
States, Northern, desired closure of the Mississippi in return for commercial treaty, 9; opposition of, to the Southern States, 20–22; desired regulation of commerce by Congress, 22; slavery disappeared in the, 22
States, Southern, opposition of, to closure of the Mississippi by Spain, 9; opposition of, to Eastern States, 20–22
Stevens, Thaddeus, chronology, 230; leader in Congress in fight against Johnson, 232; chairman of the Committee on Ways and Means, 232; sketch of his life, 232 *ff*; views on slavery, 233; leader of the Free Soilers in Congress, 233; opposed to compromise with the South, 236; influence of, became dominant with Lincoln's death, 237; dictator during early Reconstruction, 237; theory regarding Secession, 237 *ff*; opposed the "Crittenden Resolution," 238; advocated confiscation, 238; not scrupulous about the constitutionality of means employed to uphold the Constitution, 239; advocated the issue of legal tender notes, 240; attitude toward the admission of West Virginia, 240–241; regarded proclamation of blockade as recognition of Confederate States, 241; in conflict with theory of Reconstruction of Lincoln and Johnson, 242; "conquered province" theory, 243; leader of the radical reaction in North against Johnson's plan of Reconstruction, 244; House Chairman of Committee on Reconstruction, 245; opposed Reconstruction by Executive action alone, 245; secures passage of the Freedman's Bureau Bill and Civil Rights Bill, 245; introduced Fourteenth Amendment in the House, 246; makes Reconstruction the result of Congressional action, 247; refutation of argument that the seceding States had never been out of the Union, 247–248; attempted impeachment of President Johnson, 249
Story, Judge, opinion of Hamilton's argument on the National Bank, 48
Sumter, Fort, fired upon, 237
Supreme Court, part played by James Wilson in establishing, 57, 71; first constitutional case presented to, 72; question of jurisdiction of, 72–73; right to declare a law unconstitutional asserted, 113; doctrine established by, that Constitution does not follow the flag, 120; under Marshall as chief justice, develops national tendencies, 128; right to declare a law unconstitutional, 133–135; political policies not subject of decision by, 136; "extent" of judicial power of, 137; attempt of, in Dred Scott decision, to settle the slavery question, 215

T

Tariff, of 1832 reasserts principle of protection, 178; Webster's opposition to a protective, 171; change in Webster's attitude toward the, 172

Index

Territories, power of Congress over slavery in the, 213; thrown open to slavery, 214
Texas, annexation of, 173
Thirteenth Amendment, abolished slavery, 226, 246
Trust, a controlling factor in modern industrial world, 265

U

Union, sought by colonists to throw off oppression, 7; revision of the government of the, recommended by the Annapolis convention, 9; effect upon, of New York's adoption of the Constitution, 42; Hamilton's view of the nature of the, 42 *ff*; supremacy of, settled by the Civil War, 74; Wilson's view of the nature of the, 56, 64, 69, 73; Jefferson's view of, 96; Madison's view of, 114 *ff*; not a mere league, 117; Jackson's proclamation in defence of, 162; liberty and, inseparable, 176; preservation of the, sought by Calhoun through Nullification, 199; preservation of the, became chief concern of Lincoln, 220; seceding States never out of the, 242
United States *v.* Fisher, 141

V

Venezuela, Pacific blockade of ports of, 263
Virginia plan, centre of the struggle between the large and the small States, 15, 39; presented to the Constitutional Convention by Randolph, 15; equality of States abolished by, 15; reported by Committee of the Whole and adopted by the Convention, 63
Virginia Resolutions, 50, 95, 96, 133, 139, 171, 176, 180; Madison said they advocated natural right of revolution, 98; drafted by Madison, 113; views of, advanced in Richmond *Enquirer*, 139; claimed as lawful source of Nullification, 195; text, 332 *ff*

W

War of 1812, forced upon Madison, 120; nationalizing effects, 120–121, 129, 171; opposition to, secured Webster's election to Thirteenth Congress, 171
Washington, saw need of common commercial regulations, 8; chosen presiding officer of the Constitutional Convention, 11; attended first of Wilson's lectures, 66; appointed commander-in-chief, 83; desired neutrality, 95
Webster, Daniel, advocate in Dartmouth College Case, 144; wished to test the strength of Federal Government against South Carolina, 163; chronology, 168; attitude of his generation toward the Constitution, 169; voiced the growing national sentiment, 170, 177; sketch of his life, 171; opposition to protective tariff and to the War of 1812, 171; career contrasted with Calhoun's, 171; opposed "Tariff of 1824" and supported the "Tariff of Abominations" in 1828, 172; grew up in a Federalist atmosphere, 173; part in Dartmouth College Case, 174–175; reply to Hayne, 175 *ff*; seeks chief argument in provisions of Constitution itself, 178; reply to Calhoun, 179 *ff*; strength and weakness of his argument, 180; denies right of Nullification, 183; regards Federal Government

Webster, Daniel—*Continued*
as final and conclusive judge of its own powers, 183; defends the Bank, 195; joins in passing the Resolution of Censure upon Jackson, 185; condemned slavery but was not an abolitionist, 186; opposed compromise in 1832, but favored it in 1850, 186; desired always to preserve the Union, 186

West, need of expansion toward, foreseen in the Constitutional Convention, 19; political ideas of the, triumph over the East, 160; attitude of the, toward the Union, 184; eager for the War of 1812, 192

West Virginia, admission of, 240–241

Whigs, led by Clay, 158; led by Thaddeus Stevens, 233

Whitney, influence of cotton-gin on slavery, 22

Wilkinson, General, 154

Wilson, James, delegate to Constitutional Convention, 11; favors the Virginia plan, 15, 16; defended admission of new States on terms of equality with the older States, 19; opposes admission of blacks at three-fifths ratio, 21; chronology, 54; conception of a federal State, 56, 69; part in establishing position of Supreme Court, 57; reasons why he is not better known, 57–58; sketch of his life, 58 *ff*; service in Continental Congress, 59; in Constitutional Convention, 59, 60; on Supreme Court Bench, 59; professor of law, 59; conception of law, 60; believer in democracy, 61; advocated direct election of Executive and both branches of Congress, 61–62; opposed equality of representation in Senate, 62–63; advocates the Virginia plan, 63; tenacious of idea of preserving the States, 64; perceived true nature of Federal State, 64; opposed election of members of second branch of the legislative body by the State legislatures, 64; twofold relation of citizens under the proposed form of Union, 64; stood for strong national state, 65; lectures on law and the Constitution, 65 *ff*; conception of society, 66–67; distinguishes between society and government, 68; idea of sovereignty, 68; regards United States as forming one nation, 69, 73; constitution not founded upon compact, but upon the power of the people, 70; anticipates Marshall, 71; believed in inherent powers of United States as a sovereign nation, 72; decision in Chisholm *v.* Georgia, 73; signer of Declaration of Independence, 74; guide for Roosevelt's political actions, 75; idea of government contrasted with that of Hamilton and Jefferson, 80

Wythe, George, delegate to Constitutional Convention, 11; Jefferson studied law under, 81

X

X Y Z letters, 131

Y

Yates, delegate from New York to Constitutional Convention, 38; left the Convention, 38